D1203477

INTEGRATION AT OLE MISS

INTEGRATION AT OLE MISS

by RUSSELL H. BARRETT

FOREWORD BY JAMES W. SILVER

CHICAGO
QUADRANGLE BOOKS
1965

 For information, address: Quadrangle Books, Inc., 180 North Wacker Drive, Chicago 60606. Manufactured in the United States of America. Library of Congress Catalog Card Number: 65-12777.

First Printing

TO FOUR COURAGEOUS WOMEN

Mada, Valerie, and Pamela Barrett

and

Mrs. Mildred S. Topp (1897-1963)

FOREWORD

Between the Vicksburg surrender in 1863 and the adoption of Mississippi's present constitution in 1890, the promise of meaningful emancipation was shamefully warped into the neo-slavery of the caste system. In the twentieth century white supremacy in Mississippi has been fiercely guarded by a faithful bureaucracy, by ceaseless, high-powered, and skillful indoctrination employing both persuasion and fear, and by the elimination, without regard for law or ethics, of those who would not go along with the system. Those of us at the University of Mississippi who were oppressed with melancholy by the state's successful nullification of the federal constitution should not have been surprised that Mississippi intransigence would be breached only by a powerful outside force.

We were caught napping, even the ones who welcomed and were helping prepare the doom of second-class citizenship in the state. I am sure that Russell Barrett, despite his intimate and professional knowledge of the government of Mississippi, his association with the United States Department of Justice, and his activity in civil rights matters, was shocked by the incredible violence of the Mississippi insurrection and the subsequent involvement of more federal troops than General Washington had ever commanded at one time. All because of the desire and determination of one Negro to spend his last undergraduate college year at Ole Miss.

From his ringside seat Professor Barrett had watched each maneuver of the guardians of a sick society, each desperate and forlorn strategem to maintain a system which the country as a whole was in the final stages of repudiating. The embattled Mississippi leadership apparently hypnotized itself into believing it could outsmart not only the United States Supreme Court but the entire civilized world. Ole Miss faculty members who thought otherwise were for the most part silent if entranced observers of the farce being played out before them. A very few, and one of these was Barrett, became increasingly involved as the forces of law and order systematically eliminated each barrier so painstakingly erected to thwart the stated purpose of James Howard Meredith.

From the beginning of his tenure at the University, Professor Barrett had "almost complete academic freedom in the classroom," which he exercised on the side of liberalism and the destruction of much of the Mississippi mythology. But from the moment Mr. Meredith arrived on the campus, the gentle academician was transformed into a veritable crusader in matters pertaining to University discipline and civil rights in general. A quiet but stubborn man with a wry sense of humor, he has been the stalwart champion of each of the four Negro students on the Oxford campus. During these years he has maintained the confidence of most of the University faculty and administration, of the Department of Justice, the civil rights groups, and in fact of almost everyone mixed up in the continuing crisis except the more rabid of the white supremacists. Just as essential for the book he later conceived, Barrett has from the start been an indefatigable collector of documents. So it is fair to say that because of his participation in many of the events, because of his training and knowledge of the state and its people, and because of his unsurpassed access to primary evidence, he has been in a better position to tell the story of integration at Ole Miss than anyone else in the country. For no outsider could hope in a few weeks or months to comprehend the complexities of the Mississippi society and few insiders had the ability or desire to see the national point of view.

In this book Professor Barrett displays neither vindictiveness nor anger. Not one to short-change the reader in the matter of chasing down elusive details, nor a jumper-to-conclusions, he has come up with a remarkably accurate and moving account of a significant episode in state-federal relations. He calls the shots as he sees them and is not reticent about criticizing the state and federal courts, including the court of last appeal, or in pointing out the shortcomings of his friends in the University or even of himself. His book is far from inflammatory, yet he writes of fraud, hypocrisy, and outright lying, of a "fantastic ruling," a "devious piece of nonsense," of a "transparent dodge" of University officials, and of the "irresponsible legislature." When the Board of Trustees changes the rules solely to keep Negroes out of the University, Professor Barrett says just that. With a high degree of realism he reserves his sharpest condemnation for Governor Barnett and his political and Citizens' Council henchmen (whom the governor betrayed when the chips were down). After all, it was the failure of a miserable Mississippi leadership which brought on the Ole Miss riot, just as a more enlightened Mississippi leadership brought off peacefully the inevitable integration of the Jackson and Biloxi schools two years later.

This volume is important for all the country. It illuminates many dark corners of a major domestic crisis which have too long been blackened with ignorance and prejudice and propaganda. My suggestion to the concerned American is that he purchase a copy, read it, and then send it to a friend in Mississippi.

JAMES W. SILVER

University of Notre Dame

INTRODUCTION

The American problem of racial integration cannot be understood without examining the Mississippi case, including its culmination in the enrollment of James Howard Meredith at the University of Mississippi in September, 1962. The resistance, riot, and insurrection at Ole Miss cannot be understood without looking at the University in the context of Mississippi, and at Mississippi as the most hard-nosed of the Southern states. Before 1954 neither the state nor the University seemed much more resistant than the rest of the South, although Mississippi's support of the Dixiecrat ticket in 1948 indicated the potentiality, as it did in Alabama, Louisiana, and South Carolina. This potentiality was strengthened by the weakness of the Supreme Court's 1955 follow-up decision on the Brown Case, by President Eisenhower's weakness in pressing integration, and by the NAACP's reluctance to tackle Mississippi in the courts—notably in the failure of Medgar Evers to seek legal help in his attempt to enter the Ole Miss School of Law in 1954. In spite of his concessions to moderation, Evers was murdered in 1963.

Because it was apparent that protracted delay of integration would be possible, the Citizens' Council organizers saw their chance. A small band of zealots was able to take over the leadership of Mississippi and to put under its control the really substantial leaders of the state—business, newspaper, political, religious, and educational. This was attempted in other Southern states, but success there never matched that in Mississippi. This conquest by the Citizens' Council, unchallenged by most of its victims in the state and unconsciously assisted by the slow pace of integration elsewhere, was the most important single cause of Mississippi's legal resistance and physical insurrection. For ten years the Citizens'

Council has been the dominant factor in Mississippi.

Once the Citizens' Council had assumed power, the rest of the story was bound to unfold as a battle against the United States. The central difficulty was that the rest of the country did not see this. The nature of our system, which assumes reasonable national loyalty and good faith on critical issues, made national awareness of the situation impossible. The nation was blinded by its own rationale. Mississippi was deceived by its willing acceptance of Citizens' Council dominance. The University of Mississippi drifted into increasingly more rationalized acceptance of the state position, yet assumed that somehow the American pattern of lawfulness would save it. In the long run it would, but people also must live in the short run.

The importance of the whole story lies partly in the willingness of the United States to spend millions of dollars and untold hours of official time to protect the rights of one Negro and thereby to vindicate the American conscience. On the matter of race that conscience has been none too clear. Its importance lies also in the demonstration and warning to other states and to the nation of what can happen when resistance goes beyond the law before being checked by self-control or by national force. Finally, its importance is that individuals do not always face difficult problems sensibly, morally, or legally. Some learn from experience, and some do not. Whatever else may be said about Mississippi in 1962 and after, it did not prevent the passage of the Civil Rights Act of 1964. Perhaps most Americans do learn from experience.

The story has been partly told in the newspapers, in magazines, and in some books. But important parts of the story have not been revealed at all, while others are incomplete or simply wrong. It is not strange that such a complex series of developments has been reported incompletely, and necessary secrecy explains some of the important gaps. I have tried to be complete in detail, but never to sensationalize at the expense of truth. Some individuals will be unhappy with my treatment of them, but no one has been needlessly subjected to derogatory description. All whose actions were of any importance should realize that they will be judged on the basis of their actions, and the judgment may be by the courts, by their administrative superiors, by the newspapers, by the writers of books, or by almost anyone. They can expect fairness, but they cannot escape responsibility for what they have done.

This book has both the advantages and disadvantages of being written by a participant. As such, I witnessed many events and took part in some of them, and I have access to documentary sources not available to others. I also took sides in the controversial aspects of the story, for I was on the side of James Meredith, the United States, the University of Mississippi, and nondiscriminatory education. Most segregationists will find the fact impossible to accept, but I was also attempting to salvage some honor for Mississippi, whose recent past has dishonored the contributions of earlier Mississippians. When I went into the U.S. District Court with an affidavit in support of Negro Cleveland Donald in 1964, I took a public position against the unwritten code of Mississippi. This position gives me little possibility of securing the cooperation of the Citizens' Council or the segregationist political leaders of Mississippi, but they and their supporters have unintentionally supplied some of the material for this book in the form of telephone calls and other communications. But participants tend to overemphasize their own importance, and I have tried to guard against this as I have tried to tell the story of those on "the other side" by using their own words.

There are many who have helped me in writing this book and others who have helped by urging me to write it. Much of this assistance is documented, but in some cases names must be omitted to protect individuals from harassment or because their help was unofficial.

Numerous officials of the U.S. Department of Justice and of the University of Mississippi have given me assistance on matters of fact. I do not list them because doing so might lead some critics to hold them responsible for some of my conclusions. All were faithful to their official responsibilities in providing information, sometimes more so than I would have liked. They had to consider that some aspects of the case are still in the courts, and they bear no responsibility for my statements. Part of the research was made possible by a grant-in-aid from the Social Science Research Council. The NAACP Legal Defense and Educational Fund provided important assistance from its documentary files.

The following faculty members of the University of Mississippi, some of whom have moved to other universities, gave varying amounts of assistance: Carl Alette, Joseph O. Baylen, Lewis C. Bell, T. A. Bickerstaff, Theodore I. Bieber, Marvin M. Black (deceased), Samuel F. Clark, Roscoe Cross, William F. Crowder, Hector Currie, Arthur B. Custy, Paul A. D. de Maine, Joseph D. Elmore, Robert J. Farley, C. N. Fortenberry, Frederick H. Gareau, W. Parks Grant, A. Wigfall Green, Paul G. Hahn, Evans B. Harrington, John Sykes Hartin, Charles F. Haywood, William C. Herndon, Edward H. Hobbs, Franklin P. Howard, Huey B. Howerton, Richard Joslin, G. Ray Kerciu, William J. Knightley, Lutz Leopold, Russell W. Maatman, Clare L. Marquette, Barton Milligan, John H. Moore, Karl Morrison, William P. Murphy, Lawrence E. Noble, Albert W. Oldham, Robert L. Rands, Katharine Rea, Donald G. Rhodes, Robert K. Rushing, James W. Silver, Thomas W. Stallworth, Richard S. Stewart, William E. Strickland, Whitney D. Stuart, Julien R. Tatum, Pedro C. Teichert, Mildred S. Topp (deceased), Richard G. Touart, Tom J. Truss, Jr., Lucy C. Turnbull, Dwight Van de Vate, Jr., Donald S. Vaughan, Wendell N. Vest, Gerald Walton, William H. Willis, and John B. Wolfe.

Ole Miss students who gave the most assistance, although I talked with many others, include Herman Carl Abelein, Sidna Brower, Jeremy J. Eskridge, Edward R. Gaines, Judith L. Gardner, Richard O. Greene, Leonard H. Higginbotham, Walter Charles Larry, M. Bradley Lawrence, Frank C. Leeming, Prentiss C. McLaurin, Thomas B. May, James H. Meredith, Gerald C. Mertens, Theodore E. Newark, Nancy R. Preston, and Donald J. Proehl.

Ministers of the Oxford churches who gave major help include Donald H. Anderson, Duncan M. Gray, Jr., Clifford A. McKay, Jr., Wofford K. Smith, and Murphey C. Wilds.

Outside of the Oxford area, those who were particularly helpful include Derrick A. Bell, Jr., Henry T. Gallagher, Aaron E. Henry,

Everett C. Hughes, Constance Baker Motley, Frank E. Smith, Hazel Brannon Smith, Rhoten A. Smith, Peter H. Odegard, and David Riesman.

Part of this book could have been written a year or more ago, but I have waited so that the book itself will not have disturbing effects on the progress of integration at Ole Miss. Even more important is that much of the material could not have been made public earlier, including some which I did not yet have. No doubt an earlier book would have had greater popular appeal nationally, but one who lives in Mississippi—and intends to continue living there—must weigh factors other than popular appeal.

R.H.B.

January, 1965

CONTENTS

INTEGRATION AT OLE MISS

1 BUILDING THE WALL

Before the application of James Meredith in 1961, most of the thinking people in Mississippi believed that the state would accept school integration after a show of token resistance, as had other deep South states. I had said many times that it would be the last such state to integrate and that it would do so with less pain if it were the last to yield. Even those who thought that Mississippi would be the toughest of the Southern states did not expect the degree of violent insurrection which developed in September, 1962. Nor did they expect a self-righteous defense of the insurrection, including the equating of the forces of resistance with the authors and proponents of the Declaration of Independence. As ludicrous as it may seem, Mississippi was portrayed by the insurrectionists as a sovereign state fighting for independence against an oppressive, colonialist foreign power—the United States.[1]

On September 30, 1962, after eighteen months of procedural complexity, James H. Meredith was at the University of Mississippi under the orders of all three levels of the national court system and with the protection of federal marshals and troops. Although the nationwide shock at the events produced simple judgments—such as a proposal for the establishment of Mississippi as a "national wilderness"—the problem could not be solved so easily. It included much more than the education of one human being at a state university. It was more than this to all of the participants: the nation, the state, the University, and the student. The characteristics of these participants—right or wrong as they may have been—produced a setting in which violence and injury to all was inevitable, because there was no common ground for settling the problem by other methods. None of them was willing to go beyond the standard pattern of behavior to cut through the complexity of the situation. The unrecognized contradictions in the roles of all the forces required that they play out those roles to the end. The end was violence and conflict, but beyond was another conclusion: the painful but eventually successful adjustment of Mississippi to the inevitable. The process was made more difficult because two other Southern states had not yet surmounted the problem of school integration, and because the whole of America was a long way from squaring its preachings and practices in the field of race.

But other states before and after 1962 accomplished token integration without substantial violence. Some turmoil had accompanied Autherine Lucy's brief stay at the University of Alabama and the integration of high schools in Little Rock, but it was little more than a sample of what occurred at Ole Miss. Since events elsewhere demonstrate that major violence was not inevitable, what factors made it seem so in Mississippi?

Although details of the story as it began in 1961 provide most of the answers, critical developments had already occurred as the state built its defense against the Supreme Court's desegregation decisions of 1954 and 1955. Other Southern states also set up barriers, but nowhere else were they so rigid and virulent as in Mississippi. After the 1955 decision Senator James O. Eastland proclaimed, "I know Southern people will not surrender their dual school system and their racial heritage at the command of this crowd of racial politicians in judicial robes." He urged noncompliance by arguing, "Southern people will not be violating the Constitution when they defy this monstrous decision. They will be defying those who would destroy our system of government." Some Mississippians saw the possibilities of delay in the decision. The relatively moderate Governor Hugh White commented, "It was more than we expected, because we thought the court would set a deadline on integration." Even Robert B. Patterson of the Citizens' Council acknowledged that the Supreme Court justices "showed the best reasoning they have shown yet."[2] To the segregationist leaders of Mississippi the 1955 decision meant they could try tactics of delay first and then fall back on massive resistance.

The University of Mississippi, since its beginning in 1848 with eighty students, had two major encounters with political crisis and worse before 1962. The Civil War ended the chancellorship of Frederick A. P. Barnard, and the events of the war included the use of both the Lyceum and "Y" buildings as hospitals by forces of both North and South. (The same buildings became focal points in the riot a hundred years later.) In the 1930's Governor Theodore Bilbo committed political aggression against the University and other state schools to provide jobs for his friends and punish his enemies. He discharged administrators and faculty in such numbers that Ole Miss lost its accreditation. Among other difficulties of the depression period, the state paid University salaries partly with "IOU's" of dubious value, delayed payment for more than two years, and never made full payment to faculty members even at the low rates provided by their contracts. It was a long road back from Bilboism and depression to accreditation and academic acceptability.

A necessary consequence of Bilbo's damage was the adoption in 1944 of an amendment to the Constitution of Mississippi intended to remove the University and other state institutions of higher learning from the area of political domination. This provided for a twelve-member Board of Trustees serving for twelve-year terms, one-third of whom would be appointed every four years by the governor, who cannot succeed himself in office. These trustees were to be "of the highest order of intelligence, character, learning, and fitness for the performance of such duties, to the end that such Board shall perform the high and honorable duties thereof to the greatest advantage of the people of the State of such educational institutions, uninfluenced by any political considerations." This intended insulation from political interference by an incumbent governor was reinforced by giving the board complete authority over "the management and control" of the institutions of higher learning, including power to appoint administrative heads, deans, professors, and administrative employees and to terminate contracts "for malfeasance, inefficiency or contumacious conduct, but never for political reasons."[3] This placed the University in a protected legal position and gave the politicians an excuse for being "unable" to respond to the inevitable pressures for political interference. Even though the law made the University a "privileged sanctuary" for the propagation of ideas contrary to those of many Mississippians, it did not eliminate all attempts at interference. It did prevent most of the bald attempts at political control, and political pressure had to be exerted by indirect methods. But it did not prevent willing cooperation between the Board of Trustees and the politicians, and that is what occurred after 1954.

As in most other state university systems, the political vulnerability of the board helps produce a defect in educational organization which is not apparent in the formal structure. This is the tendency of the board to keep a string on its grant of power to the chancellor of the University and heads of other institutions, and to pull it back in critical situations. The argument that this serves to protect the chancellor and the University may be genuine or a pretext, but it still restricts the University's independence. The chancellor knows that he really does not run the University, and this weakness constantly endangers its prestige in the academic world. Regardless of the constitutional protections, the common public attitude in Mississippi is that the University should be responsive to political pressure, and most politicians talk and act as though there were no constitutional safeguards. This situation is one of the main factors which brought the University to September, 1962, in such a position of weakness.

In 1858 Chancellor Frederick Barnard, later president of Columbia, stated that the destiny of the University was "to do more than any other single cause to stamp upon the intellectual character of Mississippi the impress it is to wear, to determine the respectability of the State in the eyes of mankind, to stimulate her industry, to multiply the sources of her material wealth, to elevate and purify the tastes of her people, to enlarge their capacities for happiness, and to enable them to fill up those capacities by supplying them with continually growing means of rational enjoyment." This was a large and probably impossible order, but many administrators, faculty, and citizens have worked hard during the 106 years since his statement to give it meaning. Others outside the University have worked equally hard to frustrate it, and where segregation was the issue they usually succeeded.

Although James Meredith was the first really determined Negro applicant for admission to Ole Miss, there had been four earlier attempts important enough to deserve mention. Just after World War II the first of these applied on the basis of an undergraduate degree from a non-accredited Negro college in Ohio. He was rejected because the Association of American Law Schools had adopted a requirement that accredited law schools, such as that of the University of Mississippi, could not admit students with less than two years of undergraduate work at an accredited school. The other three cases were handled in accordance with a policy of the Board of Trustees that all Negro applications should be submitted to the board. There was also an informal understanding that after the Supreme Court decision in *Sweatt v. Painter* in 1950, no Negro would be rejected on the ground of race.

In 1953 Charles Dubra applied for admission to the School of Law. His undergraduate degree was from Claflin College, Orangeburg, South Carolina, in 1928, and the college was not accredited until 1947. He had also received a master of arts degree from Boston University in 1946, but that was not considered as meeting the requirement and he made no attempt to challenge the decision against admission. Dean Robert J. Farley of the School of Law considered Dubra to be an ideal applicant because of age and maturity, and he might have been able to get a favorable court decision on the basis of the graduate degree. By this time there were signs that the board members would have welcomed a strong applicant, but they probably would not have surrendered without a court decision.

Medgar Evers applied next after the 1954 Supreme Court decision, but there were deficiencies in one of his two letters of recommendation. Such letters had been required for law school admission for some years, since a law diploma from Ole Miss carries automatic admission to the bar and that requires proof of good moral character. Dean Farley advised Evers to consult the board concerning the status of his application. He visited the board office with an attorney and was given an extension of time to submit another letter. Since there were no other deficiencies in his application, Evers might even have been admitted without a court order. But he never submitted the letter and instead became field secretary for the NAACP. Admission of either Dubra or Evers would have avoided any challenging of accreditation, would have permitted the University—and the state—to begin adjusting to the inevitable, and would have been a tribute to the integrity of both the University and the state. But even at this point the wall could be penetrated only by determined effort, and neither applicant was willing to press his case.

Politicians and others were busy in Mississippi after Medgar Evers' application and the Supreme Court decision in *Brown v. Board of Education* on May 17, 1954. In enacting a pupil assignment law, approved on March 10, the state legislature had produced a weapon against integration which anticipated the Brown decision. In September the legislature, at a special session, approved an amendment to the state constitution which would authorize it "to abolish the public schools." In December, with about one-third of the qualified voters participating, the state voted approval of the amendment by more than a two-to-one margin.[4] When the legislature belatedly produced a detailed statute for school abolition in 1958, it authorized the governor to abolish any or all schools, including the institutions of higher learning.[5] During the campaign for adoption of the school abolition amendment, its legislative proponents stated as one of their supporting arguments, "It will be a warning to alien organizations that we intend to preserve our way of life." One of the very few newspapers opposing the amendment, the *Tupelo Daily Journal*, editorialized that a vote against would help the state "climb out of the hole in which our state politicians have held us so long."[6] Mississippi voted to stay in the hole.

Also in September, 1954, the Board of Trustees helped dig the hole a little deeper by adopting unanimously a requirement that applicants for admission to any institution supply five letters from alumni in their county certifying to their "good moral character." Non-residents could comply by providing letters from "reputable sources" in their communities of residence. There were, of course, no Negro alumni of white institutions in Mississippi. In November one more possible loophole was supposedly closed by a board decision that non-residents could be denied admission "without a stated reason."

These legislative and administrative moves coincided with increased activity by private citizens. In the summer of 1954 a small band of fanatics began a drive to gain control over the political and economic leadership of the state. In organizing the Citizens' Council their approach was to secure as members "the so-called best people—bankers, lawyers, politicians, planters, merchants, and some businessmen."[7] By 1955 the Council claimed a membership of sixty thousand, a tenth of it in the state capital of Jackson. Many were brought in by the judicious application of pressure—if you're not for us, you're not for segregation—yet the leadership of the Council did not include top politicians or businessmen. A "blueprint for victory" adopted by Citizens' Councils of America in 1956 outlined the overt part of their program:

1. Sharp counter-attack, already well under way, against the NAACP and other radical race-mixing groups.
2. Encourage the people to organize to protect and preserve their separate schools, other social institutions, and their personal rights and liberties.
3. Assert the invocation of Interposition by the States to guard and recover their sovereign rights from unconstitutional federal invasions.
4. Present forcefully and accurately at the national level through all modern methods the cause of constitutional government and freedom of personal association.[8]

The methods of accomplishing these ambitious goals were to include the gaining of political power, the use of economic and other pressures, and the promotion of propaganda through the press, radio, television, and schools.

In their early years the Councils worked hard to reduce the number of Negro voters, and within one year in four key counties in Mississippi the total fell by 75 percent. In the most successful effort, in Sunflower County, Negro voters dropped to zero, and the Circuit Clerk replied when asked, "No Negro voters. This is the home of the Citizens' Councils."[9] In Humphreys County one Negro active in voter registration was killed and another badly wounded, with no convictions for either crime.[10] If this was the fate of Negroes who worked for the vote, what could they expect from attempts to enroll in white schools? By 1955 the Councils were on their way toward dominion over the substantial political and economic leadership of Mississippi. They failed to elect their candidate as governor in 1955, but they succeeded in the election of Ross Barnett in 1959.

Meanwhile, they worked on the schools, and among other approaches a high school essay contest encouraged students to read and get their ideas from the "C.C." gospel in books such as *Black Monday* (referring to the Monday of the Brown decision) by Judge Tom P. Brady. A contest winner, who did not become a student at Ole Miss in 1962, wrote the following: "We do not intend to obey men, however exalted their seats or black their robes and hearts. We intend to obey the laws of God and the laws of this country which are made in accordance with the Constitution. As long as we live, so long shall we be segregated."[11]

Citizens' Council activities paid off when the legislature enacted two laws in 1956 calculated to preserve segregation. One created a Sovereignty Commission to "perform any and all acts and things deemed necessary and proper to protect the sovereignty of the State of Mississippi, and her sister states from encroachment thereon by the Federal Government. . . ."[12] Its public activities were to consist of information programs in support of segregation and of investigations of activities threatening segregation, although it has never conducted a public and non-secret investigation since its inception. It has been active in sending pro-segregation speakers to other states and in giving financial support to radio and television programs produced by the Citizens' Council. Its secret investigations have consisted mainly of clumsy efforts to track down enemies of segregation, including the Negro who attempted to enter the University of Southern Mississippi; newspaper editors such as Hazel Brannon Smith; college professors, and other such dangerous adversaries. The commission, along with the governor and the Citizens' Council, receives reports from student spies at Ole Miss, who dutifully relate their versions of the facts about professors and other students. In some of my classes I have occasionally suggested that the "spies" sit near the front so they will have the maximum opportunity to produce accurate reports.

The joint efforts of the Sovereignty Commission, the governor (ex officio chairman of the commission), and the Citizens' Council culminated in an effort in 1960 to defeat a candidate for the editorship of the Ole Miss student newspaper on the ground that he was an integrationist. Information supplied by the Sovereignty Commission's equivalent in Georgia was turned over to the incumbent editor, on the assumption that he would use it against the "traitor." But he turned it over to the victim of the attack, and the opposing candidate refused to make any use of it. Oddly enough, Governor Barnett's "candidate," James Robertson, turned out to be as "anti-Mississippian" by the governor's warped standards as the candidate he defeated. All of this would be funny were it not being carried on by the leaders of a state.

The second action of the legislature in 1956 was a "Resolution of Interposition," implemented by a statute which directed all state and local officials to "comply fully with the Constitution of the State of Mississippi, the Statutes of the State of Mississippi, and said Resolution of Interposition," and to "prohibit, by any lawful, peaceful, and constitutional means, the implementation of or the compliance with the Integration Decisions of the United States Supreme Court. . . ."[13] The legislature did not specify how this contradictory set of instructions was to be followed, since it required lawful methods of violating the law. But the actions already taken by the legislature, the Board of Trustees, and others demonstrated that the meaning was clear enough. The whole approach was to erect a series of hurdles in the form of laws and regulations. These were intended to exhaust the legal, financial, and physical resources of any organizations or individuals attempting to break through the wall of segregation. They would be supported by a monolithic pattern of support for segregation and its defenses by all groups and individuals in the state, and this meant that internal opposition could not be tolerated.

There were some who spoke out in opposition, but they had

little support and their main reward was vilification or worse. They included newspaper editors in Lexington, Greenville, McComb, Tupelo, Canton, and, in a limited way, Jackson. None of these were active integrationists, but their calls for caution and reason indirectly supported integration. Conservative Oliver Emmerich of McComb for a few years edited the *Jackson State Times,* a daily financed by Jackson businessmen. Emmerich warned editorially of "violence, heated tempers, night marches, aroused passions, stimulated hatred," and he committed the sin of moderation by writing, "The South must decide what in 'the status quo' we can preserve with wisdom—and what we must yield."[14] Soon after the election of Ross Barnett as governor in 1959, the *State Times* went out of business.

The major voice of moderation in Mississippi was an out-of-state newspaper, the *Memphis Commercial Appeal.* With a daily and Sunday circulation in Mississippi larger than any in-state daily, it subjected the state's political leadership and the Citizens' Council to constant critical analysis. Newspapers in New Orleans and Birmingham played a similar but less extensive role.

The dominant Citizens' Council viewpoint was expressed by the two main Jackson papers, the *Daily News* and the *Clarion Ledger.* The Council-newspaper coordination was demonstrated clearly in the 1954 campaign for adoption of a constitutional amendment to restrict Negro voting. On October 31 the *Daily News* published a statement by Council leader Robert Patterson, stating that the amendment was needed because "the Negroes have been voting in large numbers." On November 1 the paper printed the same statement as its own editorial advice to voters. With less than one-fifth of those qualified bothering to vote, the amendment passed by a five-to-one margin.

Although a few individual ministers and one denomination did speak out, the churches either supported the dominant viewpoint or said nothing. The Mississippi Diocese of the Episcopal Church in 1954 issued an unequivocal call for Mississippians to comply with the Supreme Court decision. Distributed in the form of a small pamphlet, the statement concluded, "Thus, from the standpoint of Christian principle, we cannot believe that the Supreme Court's decision was anything but just and right. In our Christian faith, as well as in our political creed, we are committed to the principle of the equality of all men before God and before the law." I made a pro-integration speech before a Presbyterian women's group in 1957; although at least half of those present agreed with me, some said it was wrong to talk about the problem and others that I "didn't understand the problem." A determined enunciation of Christianity by the churches could have saved Mississippi from years of self-injury, but not enough leaders or followers saw the relevance of Christianity.

William Faulkner thought it was important to speak, and he did speak in the form of letters to newspapers and in a speech at the Southern Historical Association in Memphis in 1955. This man, to whom few Mississippians paid any attention, said, "To live in the world of A.D. 1955 and be against equality of race or color is like living in Alaska and being against the snow. . . . I think what he [the Negro] wants is equality, and I believe that he knows there is no such thing as equality per se, but only equality TO—equal right and opportunity to make the best one can of one's life within one's capacity and capability, without a fear of injustice or oppression or threat of violence."[15] Even William Faulkner could not have made that speech in Mississippi, and the arrangements for making it in Memphis were made by Professor James W. Silver of the University. Most Mississippians are morally and psychologically incapable of listening to such ideas, and their attitudes were given expression by William's brother John in a letter to the *Memphis Commercial Appeal*. Commenting on President Eisenhower's use of troops at Little Rock, he said he agreed with "Lincoln's view" that "the Negro was so constituted that he would never be able to live in the same community with white men on terms of equality—that one or the other would be on top and he, as much as any man, wished to see the white man in that top position."[16] These would hardly be the views of Lincoln today, but they certainly were those of most Mississippians.

While the cauldron boiled, another policy decision by the Board of Trustees produced difficulties related to integration at Ole Miss. Following criticism of a "religious emphasis" speaker at Mississippi Southern College in 1955, the board bowed to political pressure and adopted what is commonly known as the "speaker screening" resolution. This requires the heads of institutions to investigate and approve every speaker invited to the campus and to file a statement of approval with the board. Although there was no intimation that the board would disapprove speakers, it is clear that the politicians whose pressure produced the board policy knew that the screening procedure would reinforce the university and college administrators' normal sensitivity to public and political criticism. The screening policy was protested in resolutions by the Ole Miss chapter of the American Association of University Professors, by the State Council of the A.A.U.P., and by the Campus Senate of Ole Miss. In spite of this and critical editorials in the student newspapers at the three principal state schools, the policy remained in effect.

The first proposed speaker to produce controversy at Ole Miss was another speaker for religious emphasis week, the Reverend Alvin Kershaw, who was invited in 1955 to speak at a convocation on "Jazz Music and Religion." After State Representative J.A. Morrow publicly criticized Kershaw's views on segregation, the editor of the student newspaper asked him for a statement. He candidly wrote that he would express his support of integration and the NAACP, particularly since the question had already been raised by others. After considerable controversy the invitation to Kershaw was postponed or withdrawn by Chancellor J. D. Williams, who used one of his less fortunate choices of rhetoric in saying, "This is not the ditch I choose to die in." There is no doubt that he had consulted with several leading faculty members before making his decision and that a majority of the faculty supported him—and a minority which included me disagreed. But the fact is that without the advance publicity Kershaw would have appeared and given his views on segregation with little difficulty; other supporters of the NAACP and of integration appeared on the campus before and after this incident. The result was that all out-of-state speakers for that year's religious emphasis week refused to appear, and the local ministers refused to serve as substitutes. The chairman of the Department of Sociology and Anthropology, Morton King, resigned in protest against the cancellation of Kershaw's appearance. Religious emphasis week was abolished permanently, and the promoters of censorship might well have wondered just what they had accomplished—but they didn't. Many side issues complicated the "Kershaw affair," but the empty victory of the censors was also a defeat for educational acceptance of freedom even to talk about integration.

In the summer of 1958, Clennon King, an instructor at Alcorn Agricultural and Mechanical College (Negro), attempted to enroll at Ole Miss for graduate study in history and thus became the fourth Negro to test segregation at the University. King had written a series of newspaper articles defending segregation, had cooperated with the Sovereignty Commission, and had precipitated a strike directed against him by students at Alcorn A & M. The students had demonstrated against his segregationist opinions, and the controversy resulted in the replacement of the president of the college, who partially sided with the students. Clennon King, who probably thought that he had made himself acceptable to the "white folks," arrived at the University on a hot summer day with no lawyer and without having prepared much of a case for admission, legally or academically. Governor J. P. Coleman, the Highway Patrol, and numerous plainclothesmen were there to get the situation in hand. King's admission was denied on the ground that he was applying for study beyond the Master of Arts degree level in history and that the University had no such program. Just to be on the safe side, the state authorities hauled him off to the state mental hospital for a psychiatric examination, but the doctors demonstrated their lack of understanding by ruling him sane. Someone commented that any Negro who attempted to enter a white college in Mississippi must be insane. Sane or not, King had demonstrated his impracticality in assuming that even a "white man's nigger" could gain admission without going to court. He later attempted to organize a Negro political party in California, and failing in that started a "back to Africa" movement. King's unsuccessful and poorly planned attempt to enter Ole Miss was a major defeat for the cause of equal educational rights for the Negro.

All of these early attempts at integration failed because the Negroes involved ignored the central fact—that Mississippi was prepared to erect a line of procedural and legal defenses which could be breached only by a determined legal assault. It soon became apparent that these defenses were mainly to be improvised as the problem developed, and this was their basic weakness. While no legal and procedural hurdles could forever hold the line, a strict set of admission requirements might have kept out practically all Negroes. Improvised requirements were doomed because it could be shown that they were produced to keep out specific Negroes, and only fools could have believed otherwise. Yet the Board of Trustees and its legal advisers played a game of "hide and seek" in drafting ever more ridiculous requirements, and their deviousness later led them to feign innocence when asked if they had ever "discussed" their policies regarding the admission of Negroes. They also weakened their position by applying some of the requirements only to Ole Miss and not to other institutions under state control, since Negroes did not consider the other white institutions worth attending. The difficulty with establishing a strict set of requirements for all institutions, as they purported to do for the University, was that too many white students would have been excluded. As one segregationist professor at Ole Miss said after a new set of requirements had been added to deal with James Meredith, "They'll fix it to keep all the white folks out and let the niggers in." The professor overstated the situation somewhat, but he knew what was going on. The drafters of admission requirements may find some excuse for failure in the fact that they were attempting the impossible, but they worked hard at it.

From a practical point of view it was fear rather than technical requirements which kept Negroes from attempting to gain admission to the white schools of Mississippi, even though the requirements reinforced this fear by demanding that applicants go to court. The requirement that five alumni recommend admission extended the fear of reprisal to any who would violate "the code" by recommending admission of a Negro. Even so, it was clear that inevitably a Negro would apply regardless of the consequences for himself and his family, and no one seemed to believe the requirement of five recommendations would hold up in court. The academic people involved in administering the maze of admission requirements —all of them University administrators with considerable knowledge of requirements in other institutions—knew they were helping to fabricate a series of dodges, and there was much "unofficial" but cynical conversation about this over coffee.

The political pressure which motivated these requirements was not direct and obvious, but it was there. Part of the naiveté of the politicians who really seemed to believe the dodges would work was their belief that everything would be "legally" acceptable if the rules were made by the Board of Trustees and the University rather than by the legislature. The board undercut the politicians in its failure to apply the requirements uniformly to all institutions. Only the requirement of five recommendations was so applied, and that because it was the board's pathetic reply to the Supreme Court's 1954 decision in the Brown case. The catalogs of the various state institutions include a bewildering variety of requirements, but there is almost no uniformity. To cite but two examples, the deadline for applications varies, and some institutions accept transfer students only from accredited schools while others have no such requirement. One important result of the restrictive requirements for Ole Miss is that they put the University in an unfavorable position in competing with other institutions for student enrollment. This is vital because state funds are distributed on the basis of enrollment, and the Board of Trustees has not been willing to compensate Ole Miss for the financial losses resulting from the board's admission requirements. But then the purpose of the scheme was to apply state policy rather than to help the University.

Before 1954, Ole Miss admission requirements were not difficult, and as explained in the 1953-1954 Bulletin, "A fundamental philosophy of the University is that any student who can profit from the University experience should have the opportunity to attend."[17] After the Supreme Court's 1954 decision, that philosophy turned out to be not so fundamental after all, because the statement was omitted and the requirement of recommendations regarding moral character was inserted.[18] The specific requirement was that the applicant file "five letters from responsible citizens who have known him for at least two years, certifying to the applicant's good moral character and recommending his admission to the University." This was in accordance with an order adopted by the Board of Trustees on September 16, 1954, stating that the "welfare" of the institutions "would be better served" by such a requirement. There was no requirement or implication of any other methods of establishing moral character, and the board order made it clear that the letters would be *the* method to be used.

There had been no specific cases of alleged low moral character of students during the months just preceding the board action, and only the naive would believe that the requirement would produce students of good moral character or that such was the board's intention. Among students and others at the University, the letters were regarded either as a joke or as one of the bureaucratic details associated with admission and registration. It was common knowledge that the only purpose of the requirement was to exclude Negro students. It is an odd but not surprising detail that, for reasons of administrative efficiency, the applicant was not required to "file" the letters with the University, but simply to list six names so that the University might send form letters to them for signature. It might be argued technically but pointlessly that every student admitted to the University since 1954 has been admitted in violation of the rules. This would be even truer of those students allowed to register and attend classes before the University received the letters of recommendation, since the board rule stated, "No application shall be considered by the institution until and unless" the letters have been filed.

When James Meredith applied for admission under the provisions of the 1960 catalog, the other requirements, effective for many years, were that he should have fifteen units of high school credit, could transfer from any "approved" institution, and could be admitted as a resident if his "legal residence" had been in Mississippi for twelve months preceding his application.[19] The lengthy and confusing regulations on residence, frequently evaded by white students, stated that the residence of an adult was "the place where he is domiciled; that is, the place where he is generally understood to reside with the intention of remaining there indefinitely or of returning there when absent." Although the status of an adult returning from military service was not specified, parents in the military forces stationed outside of Mississippi "but who are understood to be primarily residents or citizens of Mississippi" could enroll their children as residents. At that time—and now—the University regarded as a resident any Mississippian who returned after his discharge from the military service. If the usual procedures had been followed, this interpretation would have been applied to Meredith without difficulty. The various entrance requirements were more confusing than demanding, but James Meredith's attempt to gain admission would have been simpler had not the authorities begun drafting new requirements on the basis of information in his application. Of course they did not know his race until he submitted his application.

Although the state and University authorities did not realize it, the combination of an atmosphere of fear plus the proliferation of requirements made it inevitable that the first Negro to seek admission with determination would be a man like James Meredith. They may not have wanted "a man with a mission and a nervous stomach," but they consciously designed standards which guaranteed just that.

2 IN THE EERIE ATMOSPHERE OF NEVER-NEVER LAND

Much legal procedure in the courts is concerned with laboring the obvious or attempting to prove the ridiculous. This is particularly true of *Meredith v. Fair, et al*, in which the original trial record ran to 1,241 pages and the time dragged from May 31, 1961, to September 25, 1962, not including the contempt trials of Governor Ross Barnett and Lieutenant Governor Paul Johnson.[1] The length of this case may be a tribute to the thoroughness with which both relevant and meaningless issues are considered, but it is also a standing indictment of the failure of our legal system to protect an individual's rights with reasonable speed. For James Meredith "all deliberate speed" meant all deliberate delay; the courts bear some of the responsibility for that delay by contributing to the assumption that resistance would be successful, an attitude which helped produce the riot at the University of Mississippi. When the U.S. Supreme Court in its 1955 follow-up decision in the Brown case seemed to invite delay, it played into the hands of those in Mississippi to whom "all deliberate speed" really meant NEVER.

James Meredith's first exchange of correspondence with the Ole Miss registrar was friendly enough. He sent an undated letter, received on January 25, 1961, in which he requested an application blank, a catalog, and "any other information that might be helpful."[2] On January 27 Registrar Robert B. Ellis mailed a form letter reply with the appropriate forms and instructions and the statement, "If we can be of further help to you in making your enrollment plans, please let us know." On January 31 Meredith sent his application, by registered mail and with return receipt requested, and wrote the following lettter:

> I am very pleased with your letter that accompanied the application forms you recently sent to me. I sincerely hope that your attitude toward me as a potential member of your student body reflects the attitude of the school and that it will not change upon learning that I am not a White applicant.
>
> I am an American-Mississippi-Negro citizen. With all of the occurring events regarding changes in our old educational system taking place in our country in this new age, I feel certain that this application does not come as a surprise to you. I certainly hope that this matter will be handled in a manner that will be complimentary to the University and to the State of Mississippi. Of course, I am the one that will, no doubt, suffer the greatest consequences of this event, therefore, I am very hopeful that the complications will be as few as possible.
>
> I will not be able to furnish you with the names of six University Alumni because I am a Negro and all graduates of the school are White. Further, I do not know any graduate personally. However, as a substitute for this requirement, I am submitting certificates regarding my moral character from Negro citizens of my State.
>
> Except for the requirement mentioned above, my application is complete. All colleges previously attended have been contacted and my transcripts should already be in your office or on the way. I am requesting that immediate action be taken on my application and that I be notified of its status, as registration begins on February 6th, 1961, and I am hoping to enroll at this time.
>
> Thank you very much.
>
> Very hopefully yours,
>
> J. H. Meredith
> Applicant

Except for the points mentioned in his letter, Meredith's application was not unusual. His transcripts of transfer credit showed a grade-point average of better than "B," including thirty-four hours from the Far East Division of the University of Maryland, six from the University of Kansas, three from Washburn University (Topeka, Kansas), and eighteen quarters from Jackson State

College. Jackson State had also accepted fifty-seven quarter-hours of credit on the basis of tests given by the Armed Forces Institute in 1954 and 1956. Meredith's grades were better than those of many Ole Miss transfer students; and if the photograph and racial designation on his application had been white there would have been nothing special about the handling of it.

According to his application James Howard Meredith was born on June 25, 1933, the sixth of ten children born to Moses A. and Roxie M. Meredith. His sixty-nine-year-old father was described as a "retired farmer" by 1961, but white residents of Kosciusko, Mississippi, have told me that the Meredith family was hard-working, independent, and proud. After attending the Attala County Training School from 1940 to 1950, James Meredith moved to St. Petersburg, Florida, lived with an uncle, and was graduated from Gibbs High School in June, 1951. In July he enlisted in the Air Force and served a four-year hitch until July 27, 1955. After attending Wayne State University for two weeks he re-enlisted, reaching the rank of staff sergeant before his discharge on July 21, 1960. He earned college credits from three different universities during his military service, mostly from the University of Maryland branch at Tachikawa Air Force Base in Japan. His wife accompanied him during different military assignments, working as a civilian employee, and they concentrated on saving money. After his discharge Meredith moved to Jackson and enrolled at Jackson State College in September. He had completed the fall quarter with a "B" average and was enrolled in the winter quarter when he applied for admission to the University of Mississippi.

The reaction to Meredith's application was immediate. On February 4 the registrar telegraphed Meredith, IT HAS BEEN FOUND NECESSARY TO DISCONTINUE CONSIDERATION OF ALL APPLICATIONS FOR ADMISSION OR REGISTRATION FOR THE SECOND SEMESTER WHICH WERE RECEIVED AFTER JANUARY 25, 1961. YOUR APPLICATION WAS RECEIVED SUBSEQUENT TO SUCH DATE AND THUS WE MUST ADVISE YOU NOT TO APPEAR FOR REGISTRATION. This transparent move to keep Meredith out of the University might have been credible had the telegram been dispatched before receipt of his application. Dean of Students L. L. Love later testified that he ordered the registrar to send the telegrams "a few days" before January 25 even though they were not sent until *two weeks* later. It is clear that the sending of the telegrams marked the real beginning of the policy of changing the rules as abruptly as necessary in order to keep Negroes out of Ole Miss. Even if the decisions were not made by University officials, it was a shabby approach for what purported to be an educational institution. In fairness to some of the administrators, it must be noted that there was some dissension over the decision to send the telegrams.

James Meredith's next move was to confer with Medgar Evers, state field secretary for the NAACP, and on his advice he telephoned Mrs. Constance Baker Motley, attorney for the NAACP Legal Defense and Educational Fund, on February 6. Although he decided to comply with the telegram and not go to the University for registration, state and University officials did not know what his next move would be. As in the earlier case of Clennon King, state officials came to the campus to handle the situation. I have been told there were plans to have Meredith killed.[3] The state officers had been supplied with photographs so they could identify Meredith, and two of them spotted a dark-skinned individual with a thin mustache and started to carry him away. A dean informed them that their victim was an Indian who was already a student, to which they replied, "He's black, isn't he?" After further explanation they released the Indian and one of the pair remarked, "Let's get the hell out of here. This place is already integrated."

On February 7 the Board of Trustees adopted two new admission requirements, both of which happened to apply to James Meredith's application. One provided that state institutions could accept transfer students "only when the previous program of the transferring college is acceptable to the receiving institution, and the program of studies completed by the student, and the quality of the student's work in said transferring college is acceptable to the receiving institution and to the Board of Trustees." This verbiage meant that the University could refuse to accept transfers from Jackson State College even though it was on the accredited list of the Mississippi

College Accrediting Commission and the Council on Study and Accreditation of Institutions of Higher Learning in Mississippi. The University had previously accepted transfers on the basis of that list—from white institutions, that is—and the hypocrisy of the change was obvious. The other change stated, "No student will be allowed to transfer during the midst of a quarter, semester, or trimester except that the student be an exceptional student and when and where the best interest of the student can be shown and the receiving institution and the Board of Trustees consents to the acceptance." This devious piece of nonsense applied to James Meredith because Jackson State College was on a quarter system while Ole Miss was on a semester system. The regulation was made to order for discriminatory application because it authorized exceptions on purely subjective grounds. Even if Meredith had attempted to enroll on February 7, the board had supplied the University with custom-tailored means for rejecting him. It is important that February 7, the first Tuesday of the month, was not the regularly scheduled meeting day for the Board of Trustees, and they were obviously preparing a special welcome for Meredith in case he decided to come with a court order rejecting the requirement of letters of recommendation.

Meredith and his attorneys realized the significance of the telegram, that their fight had just begun, and decided there was no time for legal action to gain admission in February. Instead, Meredith wrote a polite and mild letter on February 20 in which he expressed his disappointment that consideration of applications had been halted but noted his "gratitude for the respectable and humane manner" in which his application was being handled and his hope that such an attitude would continue. He requested that this application be considered as a continuing one for the summer session and asked whether the registrar had received his transcripts from the other schools he had attended. On February 21 the registrar returned his $10 deposit for a dormitory room, and on February 23 Meredith sent it in again, referring to his request for admission to the summer session.

After a month passed with no reply from the registrar, Meredith wrote a letter of inquiry on March 18 and specifically requested acknowledgment of receipt of the letter. After his attorney discovered that the five letters accompanying his original application had only certified to his moral character and had not recommended his admission, he sent additional letters to correct the deficiency on March 26. He also asked for an evaluation of his credits by the registrar and by Dean Arthur B. Lewis of the College of Liberal Arts, and expressed his hope "that the entire matter will be handled in a manner complimentary to the University of Mississippi" and that he would hear from the registrar "soon." After another sixteen days of waiting—and seven weeks since his last letter from the University—Meredith wrote to Dean Lewis, stating his conclusion that "Mr. Ellis has failed to act upon my application solely because of my race and color." He pointed out that in spite of inquiries he had not been advised of any deficiencies in his application and asked the Dean to review his case with the registrar and advise of any deficiencies. Almost another month later, on May 9, the registrar wrote, "Of course, your application has been received and will receive the proper attention." He stated, without giving specific reasons, that only forty-eight of Meredith's ninety hours of transfer credits could be accepted and went on to inquire whether in view of this discouraging news Meredith still desired his application to be treated as "pending."

On May 15 the University Committee on Admissions adopted a new rule which would permit the transfer of credits "only from institutions which are members of a regional accrediting association or a recognized professional accrediting association."[4] The registrar pointed out at the committee meeting that there were nine applicants for the summer session and the fall semester of 1961 who had submitted such credits. This rule added another barrier for Meredith, who was one of the nine. Also on May 15 Meredith wrote that he did want his application to be considered as one for the June summer session and asked to know of its status "at the earliest possible date." He added, "It certainly would be a grand accomplishment if we could devise a system of education whereby all capable and desirous prospective recipients could receive the desired training without having to suffer the consequencies [sic] of undesirable concomitant elements." He also enclosed an application for a student apartment for his family—a wife and year-old son—and a deposit of $25. Since summer session registration was to be June 8 and he had received no reply, he wrote again on May 21 and requested notification of admission. Finally, on May 25, the registrar wrote the following letter:

> I regret to inform you, in answer to your recent letters, that your application for admission must be denied.
>
> The University cannot recognize the transfer of credits from the institution which you are now attending since it is not a member of the Southern Association of Colleges and Secondary Schools. Our policy permits the transfer of credits only from member institutions of regional associations. Furthermore, students may not be accepted by the University from those institutions whose programs are not recognized.
>
> As I am sure you realize, your application does not meet other requirements for admission. Your letters of recommendation are not sufficient for either a resident or a nonresident applicant. I see no need for mentioning any other deficiencies.
>
> Your application file has been closed, and I am enclosing with this letter your money orders for $10.00 and $25.00 which you submitted to me earlier.

As the Court of Appeals stated later, "The axe fell." Four months after his first letter James Meredith finally had a decision on his application. If Ole Miss cared for all applications with such speed, it would have no students. Of course it had handled this application with deliberate delay, particularly so that Meredith would be virtually unable to go to court in time to gain admission to the summer session. The registrar later testified that he and Hugh Clegg, Director of Development for the University, agreed—in a conversation that probably took place before February 4—that Meredith was going to "face the University with a lawsuit."[5] Up to this point delay at the University level had been eminently successful, since Meredith could not go to court until the University definitely and finally rejected his application.

On May 31, five days after receipt of the registrar's letter, James Meredith's NAACP attorneys, Mrs. Motley, Derrick A. Bell, Jr., and R. Jess Brown, filed his complaint in the U.S. District Court of Judge Sidney C. Mize. Named as defendants were the thirteen members of the Board of Trustees, Chancellor John D. Williams, Dean A. B. Lewis, and Registrar Robert B. Ellis. In his complaint

Meredith alleged that the University admission requirement of alumni recommendations was unconstitutional as applied to Negroes, placing a special burden on them because all alumni were white. He also stated that "the policy of the State of Mississippi as clearly understood and interpreted by its officials and residents is that Negroes and whites are educated in separate institutions of higher learning." He asked for a "speedy hearing" so that he might enter the summer session and requested that the court issue a temporary restraining order without notice, to be followed by preliminary and then permanent injunctions. The complaint emphasized that this was a class action for an order which would prevent discrimination against any Negro at any of Mississippi's white institutions.

Meredith and his attorneys did not know of the new rules (regarding transferring during a school term and the acceptance of credits only from schools which belonged to accrediting associations) which provided an important part of the basis for rejecting his application. The registrar did not inform Meredith of the changes in the rules, and both the University and the Board of Trustees carefully avoided any public announcement of the changes adopted on February 7 and May 15. Such knowledge would have strengthened Meredith's allegations of discrimination, particularly as an argument for immediate court action.

As the Court of Appeals was later to point out, Judge Mize did anything but expedite the case. He set the hearing for June 12, four days after the start of summer session classes and the last day for late enrollment, but on the same day he postponed it until July 10. On June 8 he denied the request of Meredith's attorneys to take a deposition from the registrar, but granted the request of the attorneys for the board and the University to take a deposition from James Meredith. During the taking of Meredith's deposition, Judge Mize permitted extremely broad questioning by Assistant Attorney General Dugas Shands and overruled all objections by Mrs. Motley. The long-term effects of this unfairness were minor, but in relation to any possibility of a speedy hearing it was important that Shands had already questioned Meredith at length while Meredith's attorneys had not been permitted to ask pre-trial questions of the registrar.

In effect Judge Mize's delay of the hearing until June 12 meant that he was—without a hearing—denying Meredith even the possibility of gaining admission for the summer session. He did the same thing again on July 10 and would not even admit that he was in effect refusing to grant the preliminary injunction for admission to the second summer session. After the hearing on the preliminary injunction was finally concluded on August 16, he delayed his decision until December 12 and thus prevented Meredith's admission to the term beginning in September, 1961. Even after the trial on the merits began on January 16, Judge Mize granted a seven-day postponement to the board and University attorneys which prevented an appeal in time for Meredith to enter the term beginning in February, 1962. The simple fact is that the Meredith case was carried on from start to finish—and the end is yet to come—in a legal "Never-Never Land."* Judge Mize's delays were only the worst of many delays.

The first major step in producing a record in the case was the taking of James Meredith's deposition, which lasted from 11 A.M. until 4:30 P.M. on June 8. Assistant Attorney General Shands engaged in a rambling, confusing line of questioning, presumably intended either to trap Meredith into contradicting himself or to turn up facts which might be used in the actual trial. During this "fishing expedition," Shands always addressed Meredith as "James," thus indicating that he would follow the standard Mississippi practice of never referring to an adult Negro as "Mr." Although everything of consequence from the deposition was covered in the trial, one exchange is worth noting:

SHANDS: What do want to go to the University to do? What do you want to do there?

MEREDITH: I want to get an education.

SHANDS: An education? You are getting an education at Jackson College, aren't you?

MEREDITH: It is a substandard education.

SHANDS: Oh, a substandard? You mean Jackson College is not

* See the chronology of the case in Appendix A.

an accredited institution?

MEREDITH: That is what the—(interrupted by Shands)

SHANDS: I am asking you, as a matter of fact, isn't Jackson College a fully accredited institution? You say it is a substandard spot.

MEREDITH: I have never seen the accredited rating.

SHANDS: I am not asking you that. Jackson College, you said was a substandard institution, is that right, or did you—

MEREDITH: I said it was a substandard institution.

SHANDS: That is what you believe?

MEREDITH: That is what I believe.

This exchange points up what later became a major issue in the case, that Meredith, whose military record indicated a strong interest in getting an education, was interested in transferring to Ole Miss on the ground that it was the "best" institution in the state. Those trying to prove Mississippi's case found themselves arguing at one time that Jackson State College was "fully accredited," then shifting to the argument that the University could not accept its credits because it was not fully accredited. Their position was particularly untenable because the Board of Trustees was responsible for the quality of education at both schools and was presumably attempting to apply the state policy of "separate but equal."

When Mrs. Motley announced at the beginning of the hearing on June 12 that she had subpoenaed several witnesses, Judge Mize replied as though surprised, "I had just assumed you were going to hear it on affidavits and argument. But you prefer to hear it on oral testimony, do you?"[7] By refusing to allow the taking of the registrar's deposition, he had made it virtually impossible for Meredith's attorneys to make their case without questioning the registrar in court. They had seen no University records, and the University and board defendants had not yet filed their answers to Meredith's complaint. It seems incredible, but the hearing on the *preliminary* injunction did not end until nearly two months later. Most of the testimony was by Meredith and the registrar, and only two other witnesses testified very briefly. The time dragged on because Judge Mize permitted the Mississippi attorneys to take numerous recesses, to argue and reargue repetitious objections, to produce testimony with no regard for relevancy, and to take long delays because of the illness of Dugas Shands, the chief defense attorney. Judge Mize seemed willing and eager to assist in Mississippi's strategy of delay, and his lack of sympathy for those seeking legal support of their civil rights has been demonstrated in many cases. During the course of the hearing Shands told a University official that he had enough legal devices for delay to prevent a Negro from ever gaining admission to the University. As I told the University official at the time, Shands was wrong, although he worked diligently and energetically at his mission. Mississippi segregationists should honor him with a statue, even though his legal prediction was faulty and his optimistic enthusiasm aggravated his recurrent heart disease.

These were the major issues of the case: (1) the general policy of Mississippi regarding segregated education, (2) the requirement of letters of recommendation, (3) the acceptability of transfer students and credits from Jackson State College, (4) the residence requirement, and (5) the question of Meredith's motive. Although our system of trying cases by putting two adversaries into a courtroom rarely produces such rational organization of the issues, all of the points raised in the case can be so classified.

The most legal nonsense and even outright lying was produced by the attempt of the attorneys for the Board of Trustees and the University to deny that the state followed a policy of segregated education. Of course this was possible only because the state had formulated a set of restrictive requirements which were not discriminatory on their face. But the proponents could not quite bring themselves to appear to be integrationist legally while being segregationist practically. As a result the legislature had passed a series of laws which made it clear that segregation was the policy, all of which implemented Section 207 of the Constitution: "Separate schools shall be maintained for children of the white and colored races." A 1955 law made it a crime for a Caucasian to attend the same school as a Negro.[8] Although the statutes clearly provide that the other state institutions are to be segregated, it is odd but was of some legal consequence that there was no such provision regarding Ole Miss.[9] In 1956 the legislature adopted a "Resolution of Interposition" and implemented it with a statute which directed all state and local executive officials

> . . . to comply fully with the Constitution of the State of Mississippi, the Statutes of the State of Mississippi, and said Resolution of Interposition, and are further directed and required to prohibit, by any lawful, peaceful and constitutional means, the implementation of or the compliance with the Integration Decisions of the United States Supreme Court of May 17, 1954 and of May 31, 1955 and to prohibit by any lawful, peaceful, and constitutional means, the causing of a mixing or integration of the white and Negro races in public schools, public parks, public waiting rooms, public places of amusement, recreation or assembly in this state, by any branch of the federal government, any person employed by the federal government, any commission, board or agency of the federal government, or any subdivision of the federal government, and to prohibit, by any lawful, peaceful and constitutional means, the implementation of any orders, rules or regulations of any board, commission or agency of the federal government, based on the supposed authority of said Integration Decisions, to cause a mixing or integration of the white and Negro races in public schools, public parks, public waiting rooms, public places of amusement, recreation or assembly in this state.[10]

Considering that this section was titled, "Compliance with the Principles of Segregation," and it was but one of many laws establishing segregation as state policy, there should have been no difficulty in reaching the conclusion that Mississippi's policy was segregated education. But there was a game to be played, and its "Alice in Wonderland" rules required state attorneys and educational officials to argue the reverse.

The brief submitted by Meredith's attorneys alleged what almost every Mississippian knew to be a fact, that "the University of Mississippi, as a matter of policy, custom and usage, has been limited by defendants to white persons only." When Mrs. Motley attempted to ask the registrar whether this was the policy, Judge Mize sustained Shands's objection on the ground that all such questions were "foreign to the issues here." He added—rather incredibly for one who permitted so much delay—that answering such questions would "unduly prolong" the trial.[11] He had already upheld objections to seven previous questions regarding the registrar's knowledge of Mississippi customs, although the registrar testified that he had lived in the state since 1940. Registrar Ellis testified that he had never been given specific authorization regarding the admission of Negro or white applicants, and that he did not consider race in acting on applications.[12] When asked to state the purpose of the racial designation on the application form, he answered, "Well, the university is made of—its student body is made up of many diverse kinds of students, and we feel that we need as much information about all of our students for statistical purposes, for counseling purposes, and any number of reasons." When pressed by Mrs. Motley, he could not recall any use of racial information for statistics or counseling.[13]

The delays in processing Meredith's application were a major instrument of the policy of racial discrimination. They had worked to keep Medgar Evers out, so why not James Meredith? The cut-off telegram of February 4 was the first of these. The registrar testified that the division heads of the University decided to stop considering applications to relieve "the crowded housing and academic environment."[14] Yet the Admissions Committee had recommended a deadline for applications for the fall semester rather than for the spring. Even though all subsequent deadline dates have been announced in official notices from the registrar, there was no written notice of this one. This was a hurried decision, as indicated by the curt and almost impolite wording of the telegrams. It might have been offset by sending to Meredith and the "thirteen or fourteen" white applicants affected a follow-up letter with a tactful explanation of the situation, but there was no such letter. Mrs. Motley did not ask very penetrating questions about the telegram, and it may have been impossible to establish what was common knowledge at the University, that the purpose of the cut-off date was to keep out a Negro applicant. She did question the registrar pointedly about his delay in giving Meredith specific answers on the acceptability of his application. With the elimination of objections and other verbiage, Mrs. Motley's questioning on Meredith's failure to submit recommendations from alumni went this way:

MOTLEY: Why didn't you write him and tell him that at that point? Why didn't you say, "Mr. Meredith, since you can't meet this requirement, I can't consider your application"?

ELLIS: I thought I answered the reason for not answering all this volume of correspondence from Meredith. I—

MOTLEY: I'm talking about February 20th now. I'm talking about February 20th. I want to know why at that time—you only had a couple of letters at that point from him—you didn't have the voluminous file at that point, so let's don't go into that.

ELLIS: As I recall it from the file, on the very same day that this letter was received in my office, we had already mailed a letter dated February 21st to Meredith, returning his room deposit. Then on February 23rd he returned that deposit, and then we get into March, with other letters. And my answer to the question is exactly the same answer I gave you a while ago. I do have other responsibilities. I simply didn't get around to writing all of the answers that I had to write to all of the applicants at this particular period of time.[15]

In other answers the registrar stated that Meredith's application posed "peculiar problems" that required his personal attention.[16] It is clear that Meredith had not met the admission requirement of letters of recommendation, and it would have been a simple matter to inform him that his admission had been denied on that ground. But that denial would have permitted him to go to court immediately, and the strategy was to avoid a clear rejection for as long as possible. This is why the registrar never did answer Mrs. Motley's question, but instead attempted to shift to the generalities of "voluminous correspondence" with Meredith and mail "a foot high" on his desk. The facts are that the registrar received the last of Meredith's transcripts on March 3, but sent only an incomplete evaluation of the application more than two months later. Delay was at the heart of the policy of discrimination, and because of legal astigmatism it turned out to be the most effective and also the most dangerous of the devices used.

Meredith pointed out in his brief that the requirement of letters of recommendation from alumni was "clearly invalid," citing court decisions in Georgia and Louisiana.[17] The registrar and other defendants denied that the requirement placed any burden on Negroes and argued, "In operation and effect it admits the better and higher type of student. . . ." Having stated what would be taken as a joke by both students and faculty at Ole Miss, they also questioned the "truthfulness or authenticity of the said five purported letters." Such questions had never been raised before, simply because too many of the letters for white students would be found neither "truthful" nor "authentic." Mrs. Motley pointed out the unfairness in the administration of the requirement: "In the case of whites this is all facilitated for them. In the case of Negroes this was not done at all."[18] She referred to the University practice of having students choose names from a list of alumni provided by the registrar, with the University actually securing letters from those named. Over repeated objections by Shands the registrar testified that students could attend classes before receipt of the letters even though they had not actually been admitted to the University.[19]

Although neither the Board of Trustees nor the University rules required anything other than the letters to prove moral character, the defense attempted to challenge Meredith's morality on several grounds. Shands attempted to get Meredith to say that he stole from the Air Force the paper on which his letters were written. Consciously or not, Shands demonstrated his ignorance of the military facts of life by asking, "You mean to charge the government with throwing away perfectly good paper? Where in the world did they throw it and where did you get it?" Meredith explained that his organization was being disbanded and was discarding expendable supplies: "It wasn't much, just a little brown folder. I remember I put it in a little brown folder out of trash disposal and carried it home with me."[20]

On the basis of an examination of Meredith's military medical record, secured with his consent, the defense attempted to prove that he lied in stating on his University application that he was not troubled by "nervous trouble" and "depression or excessive worry." He had indeed checked different squares on the military and University reports, but he said the military doctor told him, "I had not had any trouble, any that would be considered as nervous trouble." It developed that the military psychiatrist had suggested that Meredith take tablets "to relieve his nerves," that Meredith declined, and the doctor noted on the report, "No treatment recommended."[21] Mrs. Motley called as a witness Charles Clark, the attorney who had secured the Air Force records, and Clark admitted that he had not even secured all of the medical records and didn't know much about what he had secured.[22] Since no medical experts were called by either side, the testimony was a confusing exhibition of "the blind leading the blind." This was one of numerous side roads along which Judge Mize permitted the case to wander, since Meredith's military record was secured more than six months after his application by an attorney not connected with the University, which had shown little interest in such records of white applicants. Other glancing blows at Meredith's morality included questioning his failure to submit a transcript from Wayne State University (he attended two weeks) and alleged fraudulent voter registration. The latter will be considered in relation to the question of residence, but the whole line of argument against James Meredith demonstrated a concern with moral standards which were never applied to white students.

Meredith's brief referred to the registrar's rejection of his application on the ground that Jackson State College was not a member of the regional accrediting association and pointed out that there was "no mention of this policy in the University's General Information Bulletin." Since the registrar knew the facts by February 1, asked Meredith's attorneys, why did he wait four months to tell Meredith he was ineligible for transfer? The simple answer, never really clarified in the hearing, was that the rule did not exist when Meredith applied and was made especially to keep him out. The registrar testified regarding the adoption of the new policy on May 15, 1961, by the Committee on Admissions: "I do know this: that there were no applications considered by the Committee in adopting this policy, and I know for a fact that there were not more than two men on this eight-person committee who had any awareness of the application of the plaintiff. I also know that there was no discussion which included the names of particular institutions."[23] Yet the Jackson newspapers in February had reported that there was an applicant to Ole Miss from Jackson State, partly on the basis of a speech by a University official, and there was widespread knowledge of it on the campus.[24] Presumably the registrar meant that only two persons knew of the applicant by name, but those were not his words. Many faculty and staff members knew of the application long before they knew the identity of the applicant; the secrecy was part of a design which would permit officials to testify later that they never discussed the application of a Negro, and certainly not one named Meredith. But they knew what the policy was concerned with. It was no great tribute to either the literacy or awareness of the committee members to claim that only two "had any awareness of the application."

There was a long series of exchanges on the accreditation status of Jackson State, consisting mainly of argument over objections. Only in a foggy way did it get at the facts, which were that Jackson State was accredited by the Mississippi College Accreditation Commission but was not a member of the Southern Association of Colleges and Secondary Schools.[25] The registrar pointed out that apart from course work at Jackson State, Meredith would not be able to transfer the equivalent of thirty-eight semester hours (approximately one academic year) of credits allowed by Jackson State on the basis of military tests. In his answer to Meredith's complaint the registrar stated that he was "amazed and shocked" that Meredith would risk losing so much credit along with "all of his GI benefits." Mrs. Motley pointed out that he would lose many credits if he transferred to any other college, although Judge Mize prohibited testimony on that point.[26] She stated her general argument in the brief, that the University policy "clearly prevents Negro college students presently attending unaccredited state schools from ever obtaining the advantages of an accredited education offered to white students at the University of Mississippi."

The question of James Meredith's residence was complicated enough to allow argument, although a reasonable application of University policies would have classified him as a resident of Mississippi. In attempting to prove otherwise the defense rambled through his Air Force record, voter registration, driver's licenses, and previous academic records. Meredith made the most sensible statement of the whole trial about residence: "I have been to my legal officer while I was in service to discover residence and I still didn't come up with any concrete answer to determine residence in different cases."[27] At various times in the trial, and for different purposes, Shands seemed to be trying to prove that Meredith was a resident of Gary, Indiana; Detroit; Jackson; and Kosciusko, Mississippi. A bewildering collection of terms was used to refer to residence, including "home of record," "home address," "mailing address," "permanent address," "domicile," and "permanent home address." Meredith testified that his "home of record" for both Air Force enlistments was Detroit, Michigan, but that his "residence" was Kosciusko, Mississippi.[28] After his discharge in 1960 the Air Force paid his travel to Detroit but also paid for shipment of his furniture, at a cost of "several thousand dollars," to Kosciusko.[29] Meredith testified that he had secured driver's licenses in at least four states at various times during the preceding ten years. When Shands asked, "And when you get a Michigan driver's license, you have to state you're a resident of Michigan, do you not?" Meredith replied, "No, sir, not as I know of."[30] As Shands probably knew, Meredith was right, since states require driver's licenses with little regard for residence in any strict sense.

During Shands's badgering questions on Meredith's application for voter registration in Jackson and Hinds County, Meredith described his conversation with the clerk: "I just told him I had been in the service, and he told me that in this court—he told me to fill out the paper and then he told me to go out and tell all the niggers they can register and vote in this court; all they got to do is pass the test. And I didn't have much to say."[31] Meredith said that he signed the papers he was told to sign. Shands tried to establish that he lied in swearing to a year's residence in Hinds County, and that he could not be a resident of Hinds County for voting purposes and of Attala County (Kosciusko) as an applicant for admission to Ole Miss. On the matter of voting the registration clerk admitted he could not remember his conversation with Meredith and finally testified, "Yes, he was qualified to vote in Hinds County."[32] For purposes of admission to the University, Meredith stated he had been a resident of Attala County "all the time" and "only people in Kosciusko knew me and had known me for two years."[33]

Yet the registrar testified he was "convinced that this man in terms of the University regulations is a non-resident." He justified his conviction with the facts that Meredith had listed Detroit as his home address when he attended Washburn and Wayne State Universities, and that his wife's home address on the University medical form was listed as Gary, Indiana.[34] In giving his answer to one of Shands' major questions, the registrar neglected to mention that Meredith had shown Kosciusko as his home address on his records at the University of Maryland and Jackson State College, and that even the Washburn record showed Kosciusko as his parents' address. Of course he had lived there until going to Florida for his senior year of high school, had bought property there while in the Air Force, and had visited there on many military leaves. The fact was that James Meredith was a Mississippian who had many "residences" during a long period of military service, but that his "permanent residence" was Kosciusko.

In challenging Meredith's motives in seeking admission to Ole Miss, the defense attempted unsuccessfully to prove that the NAACP paid him to make the attempt, but mainly tried to establish that he was obsessed with race. The registrar stated, "This man was looking for a lawsuit. He was trying to get into the University because he was a Negro and not because he wanted an education." Regarding Meredith's charge that he was denied admission because of race, the registrar said it was "insulting" and that "a man who is ready to go off in all directions making charges of this serious nature is certainly not one who would be willing to abide by the regulations of the University and be an acceptable student."[35] In his answer to Meredith's complaint the registrar said he was "shocked and amazed" that Meredith would make such an "unjustified" charge of discrimination.

James Meredith gave candid answers to questions about his racial views. When Shands asked, "Are you sensitive on the subject of race?" he replied, "Very much so." He added, "And sometimes when these racial incidents would come up throughout the years, when at the peak of them I would become a little tense in the stomach."[36] The military psychiatrist had reported, "This is a 26 year old negro S Sgt who complains of tension, nervousness, and occasional nervous stomach. Patient is extremely concerned with the 'racial problem' and his symptoms are intensified whenever there is a heightened tempo in the racial problems in the US and Africa."[37] There was no doubt about James Meredith's consciousness of and concern with race problems. The question was whether this gave him an unjustified motive for seeking admission to Ole Miss. The relevance of motive is one matter totally ignored by the admission requirements.

After final arguments by the opposing attorneys on August 16, Judge Mize indicated that he would be in no hurry to decide the case, even though it was only for a preliminary injunction. In giving the defense twenty days in which to file an answer to Meredith's brief and ten days for Mrs. Motley's reply, Mize explained, "I want to give counsel an opportunity to reply, but anything she says will not change my mind as to what I'm doing, because I have listened to it all the way through and it is an important case and is going to take some time." He again intimated delay when he said, "If the petitioner is entitled to be admitted, he should be admitted if not for the first semester of the regular term, then it should be for the second semester [spring]. I take it that this case is of sufficient importance that regardless of how I may decide it, it will go on to a higher court; and it will probably be the second semester before he could be admitted if he should be ordered to be admitted by this court. So I want some time to study this record and study the authorities."[38] Of course Mize had already eliminated any real possibility of admission for the first semester in delaying the deadline for the filing of briefs and answers until September 15, only a week before the first day of classes.

On December 12, 1961, Judge Mize finally got around to deciding the case and to writing a remarkable opinion.[39] He accepted all admission requirements at Ole Miss at face value, including those adopted after Meredith applied for admission. Although he made no ruling on the general state policy of segregation, Mize concluded, "The testimony shows, and I find as a fact, that there was no discrimination against any student, and particularly the plaintiff, solely because of his race or color. . . ." In justifying this conclusion Mize made two strange statements. In upholding the validity of the cut-off of applications after January 25 he said, "The facts show that this was due to an overcrowded condition existing in the University classrooms and dormitories . . . ." The only piece of evidence on this was the registrar's statement on crowding, supported only by figures to show that the *women's* dormitories were crowded, and the judge had specifically limited testimony to *males*. Mize also ruled that the registrar's testimony "shows conclusively that he gave no consideration whatsoever to the race or the color of the plaintiff" and that this was "corroborated by other circumstances *and witnesses*." Since the only other witness to testify in any way on this point was James Meredith, the judge must have heard witnesses who did not appear on the stand.

Mize did not rule on the validity of the requirement of letters of recommendation, but he noted that Meredith's letters did not meet the requirement. He ruled that the action of the Committee on Admissions in refusing credits from schools not included in the membership of the Southern Association was "not taken in any attempt direct or indirect, to discriminate against anyone solely on the ground of race and color." Although the registrar testified that only two members of the committee knew of Meredith's application, I know of at least two others who knew that there was an applicant from Jackson State College and that the committee policy would exclude transfer of credits from Jackson State. If the other members—all deans—did not know the situation, they could only be described as abysmally ignorant of matters critically important to the University.

Mize did settle the question of residence by stating that Meredith "was and is now a citizen of Attala County, Mississippi." He also concluded that Meredith knew he swore falsely in registering to vote in Hinds County. He drew no conclusion from that or any other testimony regarding Meredith's moral character or his motive on racial grounds in seeking admission to Ole Miss. Mize concluded that Meredith had "failed to meet the burden" of proving that his admission was refused on racial grounds. He denied the motion for a preliminary injunction and set the date for trial of the case on its merits for January 15, 1962. Two days later, on December 14, Meredith's attorneys appealed to the Court of Appeals for the Fifth Circuit.

On December 29 former General Edwin A. Walker delivered a significant speech before what the Citizens' Council called "a cheering crowd of 5,000 packed" into Jackson's City Auditorium.[40] After commending Mississippians for having voted against both major political parties in the 1960 presidential election, he proclaimed, "I stand firm in the Gospel of Christ. . . . The Potomac Pretenders do not believe in the sovereignty and independence of the United States! . . . Let everyone face the fact that the resolute determination with which the State of Mississippi has defended its sovereignty is related to the fact that few states have as high a percentage of men, and women, who know how to use firearms! This, too, is a constitutional right, and an historic American tradition. . . . 'Super-Patriots' have led many squads and platoons. They have died in the assault. Fear and moderation have made followers and not leaders." This prophetic message may have been clouded somewhat by double-talk, but it was clear to the ignorant. This was not to be Walker's last visit to Mississippi, and the content of his message was disseminated to Mississippians repeatedly by Citizens' Council and other leaders. Legal proceedings seemed irrelevant to the approach, but they continued with meticulous slowness.

Circuit Judges Elbert Tuttle, Richard T. Rives, and John Minor Wisdom heard Meredith's appeal and on January 12 ruled against his request for a preliminary injunction for admission to the term beginning February 8, 1962.[41] But in unusually sharp language for a federal court they overruled Judge Mize on several points, reprimanded him for his conduct of the trial, and "suggested" that he expedite hearing of the case. In the opinion Judge Wisdom stated, "This case was tried below and argued here in the eerie atmosphere of never-never land." He took "judicial notice" that Mississippi "maintains a policy of segregation" and termed it a "plain fact known to everyone." He pointed out that the policy of segregation "is an important factor in determining the purposes and effects of statutes and actions superficially innocuous," a point which Mize had ignored completely. The judges ruled that the requirement of moral recommendations by alumni "is a denial of equal protection of the laws, in its application to Negro candidates," since it is a burden on them but not on white applicants. Regarding Meredith's motives in seeking to transfer from Jackson State College, Judge Wisdom commented, "Throughout his years of seeking to improve himself, he elected to study demanding and challenging subjects indicative of a determined effort to obtain a solid education."

But, wrote Judge Wisdom, Meredith must prove that he was discriminated against because of his race, and "the state of the record is such that it is impossible to determine whether there were valid, non-discriminatory grounds for the University's refusing Meredith's admission." He then proceeded to outline several "observations" for the "guidance" of Judge Mize in trying the case. First, the record produced "a welter of irrelevancies" and "a conspicuous omission of evidence" because Meredith's attorney was "severely circumscribed" in presenting her case while the defense was allowed too much latitude. Second, the limiting of evidence on admissions to the summer session of 1961 was "erroneous since the policy and practice of the University were at issue." As later developments demonstrated, the Court of Appeals should have ordered admission of evidence for at least one semester prior to Meredith's application. It should have ordered also that Mize permit testimony on the admission policy for all schools and colleges of the University, since limiting evidence to undergraduate transfers to the College of Liberal Arts prevented full examination of University records. Third, the court pointed out that Jackson State College had been admitted to the regional accrediting association since Mize's decision and this had "a material bearing" on the case. Fourth, the record was not clear as to which of Meredith's transfer credits the University would accept. Fifth, the record was also unclear as to whether Meredith could transfer at all from Jackson State or whether only certain of his credits would be rejected. It would appear that the appeals judges failed to read the record carefully on this point, because it was perfectly clear that both his transfer and all of his credits from Jackson State were rejected.

It is hard to blame the judges for having gotten lost in this part of the testimony, even though it was clear to anyone familiar with the problem of transfers. Although the point was never really brought out because of Mrs. Motley's unfamiliarity with University procedures and the registrar's unwillingness to volunteer information, James Meredith had simply not received an evaluation of his credits. As might be expected, there is a standard printed form for this, and it was never sent because Meredith's application never got that far. The registrar really indicated this when he testified, "There was no consideration on the merits of his application."[42] The policies adopted by the Board of Trustees on February 7 and by the Committee on Admissions on May 15 ruled out acceptance of credits or transfers from Jackson State and made it unnecessary for the registrar to make a specific evaluation of Meredith's credits. The appeals judges simply missed the significance of these policies.

With unjustified optimism the Court of Appeals suggested that Judge Mize "proceed promptly with a full trial on the merits and that judgment be rendered promptly, especially in view of the fact that a new term of the University of Mississippi begins February 6, 1962." Judge Wisdom must not have realized how much delay was ahead when he wrote, "A full trial on the merits is needed in order to clarify the muddy record now before us. *Within proper legal bounds,* the plaintiff should be afforded a fair, unfettered, and unharassed opportunity to prove his case. A man should be able to find an education by taking the broad highway. He should not have to take by-roads through the woods and follow winding trails through sharp thickets, in constant tension because of pitfalls and traps, and, after years of effort, perhaps attain the threshold of his goal when he is past caring about it." James Meredith, nearly a year after applying for admission to Ole Miss, might have thought this decision would get him off the by-roads and onto the broad highway, but it led instead to still more detours.

3 NONE SO BLIND

Judge Mize began the trial one day late, on January 16, and Shands began the defense by questioning the subpoena of the registrar's records on admissions.[1] He argued that Meredith had not submitted a new application for admission and that the records were not relevant because they "deal with the past." Mrs. Motley stated that the records sought covered all semesters beginning with February, 1961, because the Court of Appeals had ruled they were relevant. Shands replied that the court's statement was not a ruling but only an "observation" which did not entitle Meredith to examine the records! The judge placed a restricted meaning on a phrase which was italicized in the opinion of the Court of Appeals, that *within proper legal bounds* Meredith was entitled to a fair trial, and ruled that only records for the summer, fall, and spring sessions of 1961-1962 need be produced. He also ruled that only the registrar was qualified to remove the records from the files and announced he would recess the case for five days until January 23 to permit collection and examination of the records. Mrs. Motley complained that it had cost $700 for the travel of numerous witnesses and announced that she would withdraw the subpoena for the records so the hearing could proceed. But Judge Mize, unwilling to expedite the case in any way, pointed out that under a procedure of waiting to subpoena the records the hearing "might have to be set for a later date." Shands's next move was to ask for a full day's delay so he could "confer with the witnesses." Mrs. Motley pointed out that he had had eight months to confer with his witnesses and that there were no new issues in the present trial. Mize, who had criticized Mrs. Motley for not having subpoenaed the records earlier, had no words of criticism for Shands and allowed a twenty-five-hour recess.

When court reconvened on January 17, the next detour appeared. The defense asked for a continuance or postponement of the trial because of a resumption of Shands's heart illness and the inability of the replacement attorneys "to go forward at this moment."[2] Principal substitute Charles Clark stated that he was "not ready," although he had worked "seventy-five to one hundred days" on the Meredith case, had worked fifteen days on the brief, and had delivered the opening argument before the Court of Appeals. After he testified "as a positive fact under oath" that he had not even conferred with all of the defendants, Mrs. Motley remarked, "I guess the State is in a bad state." Clark replied, "I can't dispute that," and said that he didn't know how long it would take him to get ready. A medical doctor testified regarding Shands's condition, "In my opinion it would be dangerous for him to continue any significant activity at the present time." Mrs. Motley pointed out that he was ill the preceding July and the judge had "made it quite clear to the lawyers for the State they would have to hire somebody to take his place. . . . Mr. Clark was hired for the purpose of taking over and he now suggests he didn't take over." Judge Mize gave his standard ruling in favor of the defense. Shands had taken "the entire brunt of the battle," and "justice requires that the attorneys upon whose shoulders the brunt of the battle will now fall should be entitled to a reasonable length of time in which to prepare." He then postponed the case a full week until January 24. By this action he effectively decided without hearing any further evidence that Meredith could not enter Ole Miss for the semester beginning in February.

Mrs. Motley made two other attempts to expedite the case on January 17 and was overruled on both. In view of the postponement she requested that the admission records be produced on January 19, but Mize ruled they would not have to be produced until the resumption of the hearing on January 24. She also requested that the registrar and members of the Board of Trustees appear for the taking of depositions on January 18, but Mize ruled the request was too late, particularly because of Clark's "unfamiliarity with the present progress of the case." The "observations" of the Court of Appeals had not yet dented Judge Mize's handling of the trial.

Judge Mize reconvened the trial at 2 P.M. on January 24, and it concluded with final arguments on the morning of January 27. The most remarkable aspect of this "trial on the merits," supposedly the really important presentation of evidence, was the scarcity of new evidence or amplification of the old.

One after another of the members of the Board of Trustees testified that they had never discussed the general question of admission of Negroes or the specific application of James Meredith. Tally D. Riddell stated that the board "never had the question of any distinction between whites and nigras at any time."[3] With but one exception the board members who were asked testified they "did not know" whether there were any Negro students or alumni of Ole Miss. Dr. Verner S. Holmes said he did not know of any Negro students since 1954.[4] Chancellor Williams stated that he "never" had discussed "the admission of Negroes generally" with the board, did not know of "any" action of the board since 1954 regarding admission of Negroes, had instructed Dean Love to handle Meredith's application "as all others," but never told Love "that Negroes were admitted the same as anybody else."[5] After several officials testified that they did not know whether they had seen Negro students because they did not know their genealogy —an irrelevant qualification according to the Court of Appeals— two deans did manage to remember something about this obvious fact. Dean of Women Katharine Rea testified that she had never seen Negro students at the University or any graduates at alumni meetings.[6] Dean Farley of the School of Law stated that he never knew of any Negroes being admitted to the University. He was not permitted to testify regarding the failure to admit Charles Dubra, because his application was before 1954 and was for the School of Law rather than the College of Liberal Arts.[7] Judge Mize had made a curious ruling to that effect, stating that the Court of Appeals took judicial notice that Mississippi policies "up until the Brown case in 1954 were for the separation of races."[8]

The fact is that the Court of Appeals was very explicit in stating precisely the opposite; it ruled, "The state of Mississippi maintains a policy of segregation" and cited a court decision, statutes, and a constitutional amendment all dated *after* 1954. Apparently Mize was unusually accurate when he stated at the *conclusion* of the trial, "Frankly, I haven't had an opportunity to really study the opinion of the Court of Appeals."[9]

Dean Farley later wondered why Mrs. Motley had not asked him about the application of Medgar Evers in 1954 after the Brown decision, but the judge's ruling would have prevented it. The gentle hint of the Court of Appeals to Judge Mize regarding latitude for introduction of evidence did not go far enough. Since the only serious applications for Negro admission had been in the School of Law, evidence regarding them would have been the only way to get at the record of the past. The defense knew it; Mrs. Motley knew it; and Judge Mize probably knew it. Apparently the Court of Appeals did not.

The only other substantial aspect of the segregation policy on which there was new evidence related to the registrar's telegram of February 4, 1961. Dean Love testified that neither resident nor non-resident students were "turned away" in February, 1961 (when Meredith first applied), because of a shortage of housing. Yet he stated only a few minutes later that the telegrams which rejected at least two hundred applications were sent because "we had problems, terrific administration problems, with late acceptancy, housing, scheduling their classes, and everything else." The dean testified that he told the registrar to send the telegrams "a few days" before January 25, but also that he knew Meredith would be affected by them even though Meredith's application was not received until February 1. Mrs. Motley did not ask about this discrepancy or about the apparent delay of *two weeks* in sending the telegrams. Dean Love did not remember the enrollment figures very accurately. Although he testified that male enrollment was about 2,500 for both semesters of the 1961-1962 academic year, the fact is that it dropped from about 2,800 in the fall to 2,600 in the spring. With all of this confusion, the cutoff of applications still appeared as it had in the initial hearing: a transparent dodge to avoid consideration of Meredith's application. The record did show that the University was willing to exclude up to two hundred white applicants in order to keep Meredith out. That fact damaged the University's reputation, but it hardly proved lack of discrimination.[10]

Since the Court of Appeals had already rejected the recommendations of moral character as applied to Negroes, testimony regarding them seemed pointless. But on January 15 two defense attorneys had gone to Kosciusko to secure affidavits from the five Negroes who had signed recommendations for James Meredith. Four of them signed affidavits, secured with the help of State Senator John Clark Love, stating that Meredith had not told them of the purpose of the original affidavit, or that he had said it was to help him get a job.[11] Attorney General Patterson then mailed the affidavits to the registrar, who argued they were further evidence of Meredith's moral unacceptability. The registrar testified, "I'm convinced that the Board's requirement requires that we investigate applicants' moral character to attempt to select students of good moral character, and from what I have learned in the trial, in the deposition that has been taken of the plaintiff, even from what I have read in the newspaper, this fellow is a troublemaker." He also testified that any applicant with Meredith's "background," regardless of race, would be rejected.

There is nothing in the board's statement of policy to imply even remotely such an approach, yet the registrar seemed to be saying that every student's moral character should be tested by a deposition, a trial, and a check of the newspapers. The registrar has since told me that he always regarded the moral recommendations requirement as a transparent device which would not hold up in court. The board statement of 1954 required the recommendations as *the method* of establishing good moral character and pointedly avoided requiring anything else. More demanding procedures would have been impossible to administer, and the purpose of the recommendations was not to guarantee students of high morality but to keep Negroes out. The registrar admitted that the University did not check the authenticity or truthfulness of the moral recommendations of even a small minority of students other than Meredith. He conceded, "Offhand, I don't know of any that we have checked into recently." Although he could not remember the name or the year, he cited a case in which a student's admission was canceled because he had failed to list on his application all the colleges he had attended.[12] Since the defense surely knew questions would be asked on the policy, it is clear that the University had no proof that other students had been subjected to the same tests as were applied to Meredith. Many students of dubious morality have been admitted to Ole Miss. One such case involved a student who had been convicted of committing manslaughter while intoxicated; he was admitted and was awarded a degree in 1961.

Although the Court of Appeals had said the first hearing record was unclear on the matter of transfer credits, the main trial did little to clarify the situation. Meredith took the position that his application had been unlawfully denied and did not submit a new one. The registrar argued that his application had been rejected and was inactive. Therefore his credits would not be evaluated unless he submitted a new application, and the "muddy record" could not be cleared. Since Jackson State College had become a member of the regional accrediting association on December 7, 1961, the registrar stated, "We recognize the accreditation of Jackson State College, and if we had a proper application we would admit such students."[13] The registrar's preliminary evaluation of Meredith's credits did go into the record, but in no clearer fashion than in the first trial.[14] It simply meant that if Meredith submitted another application, the University would accept thirty-three hours from the schools he had attended in the service plus actual course work completed at Jackson State College. Since neither the Court of Appeals nor Judge Mize had ruled that his application was a pending one, there was no way that either the first or second trial record could show more. Mrs. Motley did establish that numerous students were permitted to attend the University before being actually admitted, pending the receipt of transcripts and other material, and also that many admission certificates were not even dated. The examination of records did not show much worthwhile information for or against Meredith, mainly because no records were provided for the semester of February, 1961, or any previous terms. They did show that six white students were denied admission *partly* because they had attended non-accredited colleges, but unlike Meredith their work at accredited colleges had been of poor quality. This was presumably the best evidence the University could produce to try to prove fair application of the rule, but it didn't amount to much—and Jackson State was now accredited.[15] Mrs. Motley established one point not brought out clearly in the first hearing—that at the time of Meredith's original application the University did not limit transfers to students from colleges belonging to regional accrediting associations but accepted transfers from "approved" institutions, of which Jackson State College was one.[16]

Although even Judge Mize had ruled that Meredith was a resident of Mississippi, Registrar Ellis continued to say, "As far as the regulations of the University of Mississippi, he is a non-resident." He substantiated his attitude only with one listing of Detroit on a transcript, Meredith's registration with a Michigan draft board, and "my suspicions from his activities in the Air Force." At one point Ellis argued that residence was important because Ole Miss is a tax-supported institution requiring higher fees from non-residents, while he later acknowledged that Meredith was a property owner (three farms and three automobiles) and therefore a taxpayer. He also stated that residence had nothing to do with admission except for tuition, but neglected to add that the board policy of November 18, 1954, permitted rejection of applications from non-residents without a stated reason.[17] After having said, "I certainly accept this Court's ruling that he is a legal resident," the registrar still claimed Meredith was not a resident under University rules. He was laboring a worthless point.

There was more testimony on a point the Court of Appeals had not considered worth questioning: Meredith's motives in seeking to attend Ole Miss. The registrar continued his earlier argument, "He is a man who is trying to make trouble simply because he is a Negro. . . . The man does have psychological problems in connection with his race. . . . He is a man that is not trying to be a student for the sake of learning a profession or getting an education, but a man who has got a mission in life to correct all the ills of the world; . . . He would be a very bad influence at my institution." Mrs. Motley asked, "Would you name all the white students to whom you have applied these tests you have just enumerated as to Meredith before you admitted them to the University?" The registrar could cite only two marginal cases in which there was any consideration of moral or psychological problems. He admitted Meredith was "the only case that I have dealt with that was obsessed with race," and said, "I have never known very many white people that were worried about their race." There have certainly been white students obsessed with their race both before and after 1962—in many cases much more so than Meredith—and some were well known on the campus before 1962. They were to become much better known later that year.

Judge Mize provided the next road block for Meredith one week later. On February 3 he denied Meredith's request for admission to the University.[18] Contrary to what everyone in Mississippi knew, Mize ruled with a judicially straight face "that the University is not a racially segregated institution." He disposed of the fact that the Court of Appeals had taken "judicial notice" of the existence of a policy of segregation by saying, "Judicial notice of facts is not conclusive on factual matters." Mize defended his decision on the grounds that "every witness" called by Meredith "testified that the race of the Plaintiff was not discussed or considered at all" and that the board members testified that "the question of race was not at any time discussed . . . concerning the admission of applicants to the University of Mississippi." He neglected to point out that he had prohibited testimony on the officials' "understanding" of the policy and would not accept testimony on the situation before 1954 or after the filing of the suit in 1961. He also ignored the testimony of two deans and one board member that there had never been Negro students at Ole Miss. His fantastic ruling was that the University was not segregated even though it had no Negro students.

His curious handling of the 1954 decision was that there might have been segregation before 1954, but that the Brown decision had ended it in Mississippi. Judge Mize ignored all but one of the legal bulwarks against integration, the interposition law of 1956. He tried to explain it away by pointing out that it did not require officials to "disobey" decisions of the U.S. Supreme Court. Actually, apart from the fact that interposition itself was unlawful, the act indicated to officials that they should engage in exactly the type of "lawful" violation of the Brown decision which was keeping James Meredith out of Ole Miss.

The second basis for Judge Mize's decision was that the registrar would be justified in denying admission on non-racial grounds because

> credible evidence had been furnished to him since Plaintiff's applications had been presented and rejected that Plaintiff was a rather unstable person; was depressed at times and of a highly nervous temperament; that the Plaintiff had sworn falsely before the Circuit Clerk of Hinds County in making application to register as a voter . . .; that Plaintiff had filed five certificates by citizens of Attala County, certifying that he was of good moral character and recommending him for admission to the University, but that subsequent investigation showed that in procuring these certificates Plaintiff made false representations to the signers as to the purpose for which he intended to use them . . .

On this Judge Mize stated, "Some of this evidence was objected to, . . . and since these facts were not known to the Registrar at the time the application was rejected, I have concluded that this testimony should not be considered and have not considered it in reaching my conclusions." Although the judge's statement is one of hopeless confusion, he seems to be saying that he considered none of the registrar's stated reasons for rejecting Meredith, since all of the above information was secured after the rejection of his application. If so, his only basis for upholding the registrar was his unsupported assertion that "the race of the Plaintiff did not enter into his judgment." Even though Mize's opinion was considerably more "muddy" than the first hearing record, he did appear to say that Meredith was acceptable on grounds of residence, transfer credits, and the requirements of letters of recommendation.

At least it was clear that Judge Mize denied the order for admission requested by James Meredith. On February 5 Meredith asked the Court of Appeals in New Orleans for an immediate injunction pending formal appeal. On February 10 the Board of Trustees secretly ordered the University not to admit Meredith.

On the Ole Miss campus the belief was strong that the court would order Meredith's admission. After hearing from the wife of a University official that a high-level state leader had said, "Meredith will never get to the campus alive," I telephoned a warning to U.S. Assistant Attorney General Burke Marshall that the Department of Justice might wish to do some planning. Several faculty members inquired into the University plans for Meredith's arrival, and we reported to the Department of Justice that there seemed to be a serious and honest effort to handle matters so that he could safely attend the University. We also warned that there was always the possibility that someone other than University officials—state political and Citizens' Council leaders— might try to control the situation.

Among the students a bitter argument developed between the moderate editor of the student *Mississippian,* James Robertson, and an anonymous and undated broadside called the *Rebel Underground.* In addition to criticizing such policies as the state "right-to-work" law, Robertson editorialized that the "unwritten law" which prohibited athletic competition with integrated teams should be changed. The *Underground,* mimeographed in an almost illegible fashion, proposed that Robertson should "quit harassing and antagonizing the state government and alumni." It called for passage of a resolution in the Campus Senate to reprimand Robertson for his "extreme left-wing" editorials, claiming that the *Mississippian* had been "spieling the same liberal tripe as emanates from such magazines as EBONY, NEW REPUBLIC (the voice of socialism), USSR—cultural exchange magazine, and the newsletters of CORE and the NAACP." In a long section headed "Meredith—The Darkie. Is He A Liar?" the *Underground* charged that Meredith lied about his income and his registration to vote and stated that he had mental problems and an antagonistic attitude. The *Rebel*

Underground proclaimed, "If you value your racial heritage, if you have even the smallest regard for the future of this South of ours—you will be for segregation one hundred per cent. We must lock shields. We must fight for our race and for the South to the last bitter ditch. We must never lose heart. WE CAN TRIUMPH. WE WILL TRIUMPH. WE MUST TRIUMPH! ! ! ! ! ! !" This material was being distributed on the campus during the same month the registrar testified he did not know of many white people who were "worried about their race."

With a news story which implied that the Court of Appeals would order Meredith's admission, the *Mississippian* editor on February 9 published a front-page "special report" titled "Meredith—the Man." This article was completely sympathetic to Meredith, totally contradicting the critical trial testimony and the claims of the *Rebel Underground*. The report gave a factual description of his military and academic background and quoted Jackson State College officials as saying Meredith was "a quiet student with few outside interests" and that his wife was an "honor student and a brilliant girl." The editor of the Kosciusko newspaper was quoted as saying, "The Merediths are all good, solid, substantial citizens." The report concluded, "Meredith insists he would like to enroll at Ole Miss because Jackson State is an 'inferior school' and his educational opportunities would be greatly advanced at the state university." The *Rebel Undergound* replied to the student newspaper's sympathetic treatment by charging that it was "an obvious attempt to plant into the mind of the student that Meredith is just a quiet timid young Negro, similar to our janitors." If the Court of Appeals ordered Meredith's admission, it was clear that he would find both sympathizers and enemies at Ole Miss.

On February 12 the Court of Appeals, in a two-to-one decision, missed its chance to prevent violence by refusing Meredith's request for an immediate injunction. It had asked Judge Mize to expedite the case to permit a firm decision on whether Meredith was qualified before the beginning of the February term, and he had produced just enough delay to prevent that. Now this was but the first of three delays produced by a court which had asked

Mize for speed. Meredith's attorneys had argued that he would graduate from Jackson State in June and that his case would become moot, that is, legally pointless. The defense replied that he could simply stop going to school to avoid graduation, and the Court of Appeals outdid Judge Mize in accepting that argument. It "directed" the parties to the case and its own clerk to "expedite" the hearing of the appeal.

Chief Judge Tuttle dissented from the decision by stating what was clearly the case, that "the record already submitted, without the benefit of the record in the trial on the merits, calls for our granting the injunction." He argued that every one of the "stated grounds" on which the University had based its denial of admission had already been disposed of by the January 12 decision of the Court of Appeals. Tuttle pointed out that Meredith would jeopardize his G.I. benefits if he dropped out of school and argued against forcing him to do so. Referring to the majority opinion of Judges Rives and Wisdom that Meredith might suffer "irreparable damages" if he were temporarily admitted and later excluded after the hearing of the formal appeal, Judge Tuttle commented, "He does not need for us to help him decide whether he really wants what he is here fighting so hard to get." Anyway, he said, "this court may well ultimately decide he is entitled to" enter the University.

At Ole Miss the decision produced uncertain relief among those who opposed Meredith's admission. Among those who favored it, disillusion was summed up in the question, "Don't those judges know what's going on?" Over coffee the combination of cynical and joking remarks directed at those who had testified amounted to, "You've won so far, but do you really believe you told the truth?" Dean Farley was disappointed that Mrs. Motley had treated him as a hostile witness and wished he could have talked about the obvious discrimination in law school admissions. He had even taken with him to the trial a letter which would have proven discrimination, but a combination of Mrs. Motley's limited questioning and Judge Mize's restrictions on questions prevented him from submitting it. The widespread conclusion among faculty members and administrators was that the judges thought it would be better to delay Meredith's admission until the summer session.

Within the student body the Senate did its bit to prepare for riot by voting to reprimand editor James Robertson for his editorial policies, and in what was apparently its fourth edition of the year the *Rebel Underground* congratulated the Senators. One Senator accused those who voted for the reprimand of doing so "to appease" the legislature, but the *Rebel Underground* told Robertson, "If you are truly for segregation and the preservation of our way of life, as you stated, then you will realize that there is no middle of the road—either you have segregation or you do not have it." There was a steady flow of outspoken letters to the editor in the *Mississippian*. One writer who signed his letter "True Southerner" wrote, "You can see that the Communists are pushing integration and the Jews are behind all of this trouble."[19] A woman student commended Robertson and criticized the anonymous *Underground*, arguing, "It's time that Ole Miss finished growing up, along with some of the people in it."[20] In the same issue the intrepid Robertson ran a cartoon showing figures in white hoods mimeographing the *Rebel Underground* and printed beneath it another editorial supporting integrated athletic competition. It is interesting that in the student elections for the next year the "moderates" won, including Sidna Brower as new editor of the *Mississippian*.

When the 1962 University catalog was published in February, there was no mention of race but there were changes in which the intention was clear enough. For the first time there was a statement that admissions were controlled by regulations of the Board of Trustees, with the understatement that "revisions are sometimes made without prior notice in order to cope with changing conditions." An application deadline twenty days before each term was provided, and a new provision stated, "An application containing false, contradictory, questionable, or uncertain data, or which fails to comply with the requirements will be rejected." Applicants from outside the state would have to score at least 19 on the American College Test (slightly below the national mean), and there was an intimation that the University was about to set a minimum score for residents. Oddly enough, the explanation was not racial but simply that there was as yet no solution to the problem of eliminating the lowest rank of resident applicants without going too far.[21] Three main changes were made in the regulations regarding non-resident students, and all rules on residence were written into state law by the legislature in 1962.[22] The changes provided that anyone reaching the age of twenty-one while residing in another state would be a non-resident, eliminated a provision under which the children of Mississippians stationed outside of the state in the military service would be considered residents, and gave the registrar complete authority to determine residence.[23] Although almost all of the changes were devised to deal with James Meredith, faculty members and some administrators held to their previous belief that the admissions "merry-go-round" provided by the Board of Trustees would keep out far more whites than Negroes.

As the summer approached the prevalent belief at Ole Miss was that Meredith would have his court order for admission to the session which began on June 8. There was also some anticipation of what did happen, and it was an unsurprising example of the standard Mississippi approach to "uppity niggers." In a story headlined MEREDITH IS JAILED IN JACKSON, the *Mississippian* of June 8 reported that Meredith had been arrested the day before on a charge of false registration to vote, carrying a penalty of up to $100 fine and one year in the county jail. A disgusted faculty member promptly wrote the following letter, marked "confidential," to the U.S. Department of Justice:

> It has come to my attention that Mississippi authorities have arrested Mr. Meredith on charges of perjury in connection with his application for admission to the University.
>
> It might be possible that you would want to consider the possibility of perjury charges against several officials of the University of Mississippi, including Registrar Robert B. Ellis and Chancellor John D. Williams. There is a good possibility that you could find several faculty members who would be willing to testify that they had heard Chancellor Williams state at Faculty Meetings in 1960 and previous years that the state policy in education was one of segregated schools. He made no such statement at the opening meeting of 1961; neither did he make any statement that the policy had in any way been changed. It is worth noting that

> such testimony might be gotten from faculty members who have left the institution, notably Dr. George Carbone, Department of History, Portland State College, Portland, Oregon, and Dr. William Doherty, Kansas State University, Manhattan, Kansas.
>
> There had been rumors here for some months that the perjury arrest was to be the state's next line of action regarding the Meredith case, and there is no doubt that University officials knew about it. . . .
>
> In order to protect my position here, I request that you make certain that no information regarding this letter is communicated to the Federal Bureau of Investigation. One official here who knew of the state action is a former Director of the FBI academy, and I feel certain he would receive notification of the letter.

This remarkable letter makes several points of obvious significance, but one matter may not be so obvious: the fear shown by the faculty member who wrote it—and other faculty members concerned about the problem were even more afraid than this one.

This fear can only be understood in terms of the controversy and pressure over academic freedom at Ole Miss which continued during 1962. It centered around the "Murphy case," which culminated in William P. Murphy's resignation in March. He was a Professor of Law whose earlier difficulties were multiplied as a result of charges made in 1958 by two Citizens' Council activists, one a state legislator, against the chancellor and fourteen faculty members, including Murphy, James W. Silver, and myself. The charges were a hodgepodge alleging that those accused promoted apostasy, subversion, and integration. The Board of Trustees investigated in a manner which the faculty members agreed was fair and concluded that the charges were "sensational" and "without foundation in fact." In its report the board gave a somewhat backhanded endorsement of academic freedom, stating that "there should be an atmosphere of freedom" in research and teaching but that "academic freedom does not mean license" and "there should be no political or subversive propagandizing in the academic programs." There was no defense of specific faculty members against even the most ridiculous of the charges by either the chancellor or the board, a galling fact to most of those attacked and particularly so to Murphy. He had been subjected to the most vicious of the attacks, which continued even after the investigation ended. He finally issued a factual reply which was temperate except for his accurate description of the critics as "willful ignoramuses." The controversy also included unwillingness of the chancellor to grant Murphy's tenure, indications that the board would not reappoint him, and a surprisingly weak effort by the Association of American Law Schools to defend him. The American Association of University Professors was watching developments closely through reports from Murphy and from me as president of the Ole Miss chapter, but Murphy's resignation ended the matter. The entire incident is relevant to the problem of integration, since Murphy had been criticized mainly for teaching that the 1954 Supreme Court decision was law. Even though Murphy could probably have won reappointment with a determined but painful battle, the fact was that we had lost one part of the fight for the peaceful integration of Ole Miss.

Also during the summer of 1962, Chancellor Williams included in his speeches to alumni groups a strong appeal for academic freedom. After asking for financial support, he concluded:

> Finally, we need your help in a way less tangible, but no less important. We need your courageous support in helping keep for us the freedom of thought that is the very life of a great university.
>
> New ideas are almost always controversial, but it is out of controversy that truth emerges. Lasting progress comes only when we are free to investigate *all* ideas, good and bad. Truth has nothing to fear where study and discussion and thought are free. It is where thought is not free that truth withers, while error festers and grows in malignity. . . . With your aid, we shall have our "Margin for Greatness."

It may not be apparent to the non-Mississippian, but "new ideas" in this state always means "integration," and the chancellor was appealing for support in the controversy that would come with integration. He was alone among heads of the state schools in pressing the point, and he could truthfully say that there was almost complete academic freedom in the classroom. Except for a few professors, freedom did not extend very far outside of the classroom, but those with thick skins and tenure had considerable freedom. Their numbers included history professor Silver, law dean Farley, and, less frequently during this period, myself. In a book published with state funds in 1960, I wrote that Mississippi voting laws were designed to discriminate against Negroes and recommended numerous changes ranging from abolition of the poll tax to simplification of the registration forms.[24] I did this as a conscious test of my freedom at the University, and the only adverse result was one speech in which a legislator deplored the fact that a professor could criticize state laws and customs. The critics of the chancellor and the fourteen professors were right in charging that integration—an American idea considered foreign in Mississippi—was being promoted in varying degrees by those accused. The real difficulty is that integration was not promoted successfully enough.

Upon Meredith's arrest, his attorneys asked the Court of Appeals to issue an injunction against prosecution on the voter registration charge. The court on June 12 ruled that the allegation of false registration was one of the questions which it would decide after hearing the appeal and ordered the Hinds County Attorney not to prosecute Meredith on the criminal charge. The court stated that the prosecution was a "punitive action" which would interfere with its decision in the case.

On June 25 the Court of Appeals presented James Meredith with a birthday present by upholding his right to be admitted to Ole Miss.[25] The opinion, four and a half months in the making, noted that Meredith filed a class action, and the decision was clearly directed against discrimination in all institutions operating under the Board of Trustees. Judge Wisdom wrote the opinion, supported by Judge John R. Brown, and Judge Dozier A. DeVane filed a dissenting opinion. Under the court's order the next step would be the issuance of an injunction for admission by Judge Mize. Wisdom wrote a sharply worded opinion which criticized the procedural and legal delays of the University and the Board of Trustees and at ten different points cited errors in Judge Mize's conduct of the trial. Describing Meredith as "a Negro in search of an education," Wisdom wrote, "A full review of the record leads the Court inescapably to the conclusion that from the moment the defendants discovered Meredith was a Negro they engaged in a carefully calculated campaign of delay, harassment, and masterly inactivity. It was a defense designed to discourage and to defeat by evasive tactics which would have been a credit to Quintus Fabius Maximus."

On the central question of discrimination the court concluded that James Meredith's application "was turned down solely because he was a Negro." Instead of "valid, non-discriminatory" reasons for rejection, there was "a well-defined pattern of delays and frustrations, part of a Fabian policy of worrying the enemy into defeat while time worked for the defenders." Referring to Judge Mize's conclusion that there was no "custom or policy" of segregation, Wisdom wrote, "This about-face in policy, news of which may startle some people in Mississippi, could have been accomplished only by telepathic communication among the University's administrators, the Board of Trustees of State Institutions of Higher Learning." The court cited several erroneous rulings by Mize, including his exclusion of evidence regarding institutions other than Ole Miss and his failure to permit examination of admission records before the summer of 1961. The opinion listed segregation statutes which Mize had neglected to mention and quoted from a state publication which specifically described five institutions as "White" and the other three as "Negro." On the basis of Dean Love's oddly inaccurate testimony that there were as many male students on the campus in February, 1961, as in September, 1960, it rejected the contention that crowding was the reason for the "cut-off" telegram sent a few days after receipt of Meredith's application. Wisdom cited repeated delays in the handling of Meredith's application as proof of discrimination. In response to what he termed the "eloquent silence" of the University, the judge described Meredith as "a man of perseverance, but a man of patience and politeness."

The court referred to other decisions outlawing the requirement of letters of recommendation in Alabama, Georgia, and Louisiana, but to clarify its earlier ruling it stated, "The requirement of recommendations, whether from alumni or from citizens generally, attesting to an applicant's good moral character or recommending an applicant for admission, is unconstitutional when, as this case demonstrates, the burden falls more heavily on Negroes than on whites." Wisdom pointed out that the University permitted white students to register before receipt of the letters, but added, "No such latitude was extended Meredith." He concluded that "continued insistence" on the letters from Meredith further proved the application of the segregation policy to Meredith.

The court finally discovered what had happened on the denial of Meredith's transfer, that the Board of Trustees and Committee on Admissions had changed the rules after he applied. Judge Wisdom ruled that the accreditation of Jackson State made denial of transfer "no longer valid," and said further, "The reason was never valid, and again demonstrates a conscious pattern of unlawful discrimination." He pointed out that the admission records showed no other student had been denied admission who had attended as many admittedly accredited schools as Meredith. The court gave no weight to a favorite argument made by the registrar, that a student must transfer from the last school attended, and "inferred" that it was "a trumped-up excuse without any basis except to discriminate." (Although other rulings made the question pointless, this happens to be one rule that the University applies with almost complete consistency, even though it may be a foolish rule.) When the registrar wrote his letter denying admission on May 25, concluded Judge Wisdom, "the University had no valid, non-discriminatory grounds for refusing to accept Meredith as a student."

Finally, the court took up what it termed "the ex post facto rationalization of the turndown." It ruled that Meredith made "no false statement" on his voter registration application, that the contention of false registration was "frivolous" and part of "a determined policy of discrimination by harassment." On the contention that Meredith was a "troublemaker" with "psychological problems in connection with his race," the court stated that "admittedly incomplete" Air Force records, when "taken out of context . . . lend some support to the defendants' position." But it concluded that when the reports were considered as a whole, they provided "no basis for downgrading Meredith as a psychological risk on the campus." Wisdom stated that "Meredith's record shows just about the type of Negro who might be expected to try to crack the racial barrier at the University of Mississippi: a man with a mission and with a nervous stomach." Referring to the affidavits indicating some withdrawal of support by Meredith's character references, the court pointed out that they did not withdraw their certification as to his moral character, that the affidavits were secured by persons "representing, to a country Negro, the power and prestige of The Establishment" of white Mississippi, and that the defense attorneys gave no explanation for "failing to call these affiants as witnesses." He also rejected several other allegations of immorality as "trivia."

In its conclusion the court emphasized the importance of (1) looking at "the case as a whole"; (2) considering the "immediate facts" in terms of "past and present policy" as indicated by statutes, regulations, history, and common knowledge; (3) measuring "sincerity of purpose against unreasonable delays and insubstantial reasons" for University actions; (4) comparing actions taken on Meredith with those on others in the same category; and (5) piercing "the veil of innocuity when a statute, regulation, or policy necessarily discriminates unlawfully or is applied unlawfully to accomplish discrimination." When these questions were asked, said the court, "The defendants fail the test. There are none so blind as those that will not see. . . . The hard fact to get around is that no person known to be a Negro has ever attended the University." Since Meredith was rejected "solely because he was a Negro," concluded the court, "we see no valid, non-discriminatory reason for the University's not accepting Meredith." They directed that the district court issue the injunction "as prayed for in the complaint." The injunction as requested would prohibit the Board of Trustees and "all persons in active concert and participation with them" from refusing to "consider and act expeditiously" on the applications of Meredith and other Negroes "to the University of Mississippi, and other state institutions of higher learning, solely because of race and color."

With this decision the Court of Appeals cut through "the veil of innocuity" which had been created partly by itself, but mainly by Judge Mize, the Board of Trustees, the University, the state politicians, and the whole structure of a society which had attempted to erect a pattern of segregation immune to assault. James Meredith had won his case, and in every state but Mississippi that would have solved the matter. Instead it soon became clear that he had reached but one more detour of the many that remained.

4 BLUEPRINT FOR RIOT

The events of James Meredith's admission to the University of Mississippi culminated in violence carefully produced by forces which could not anticipate the destructiveness of the explosion. It was said by some that Governor Ross Barnett "only wanted a little riot" and by others that the United States government could not act decisively until the situation "got out of hand." Neither wanted what happened, yet neither was willing to prevent it. Given their respective positions, neither was able to prevent it. The executive branch of the United States was bound to enforce the law and therefore to make the necessary preparations for enforcement. Governor Barnett was personally and politically committed to resist enforcement, by lawful means if possible and by unlawful means if necessary. At no point was there really any doubt that he would ultimately resort to the latter.

But the riot, the insurrection, was produced not only by the executive leaders of the United States and Mississippi. Its roots lay in Mississippi's rebellious Constitution of 1890 which put the Negro back in "his place." The subsequent triumphs of white supremacy cannot be detailed here, but their importance cannot be overestimated. The U.S. Supreme Court entered the educational field in 1938 with a series of integration decisions which apparently outlawed school segregation in 1954. This decision mobilized the forces of resistance in Mississippi, and the weakness of the 1955 ruling inspired these forces with the illusion of success. Those on both sides who might have prevented violence lost their chance when they succumbed to the illusion of gradualism. To those who favored integration, gradualism was an excuse for delay and even for lack of preparation. To those who favored segregation, gradualism meant permanent delay.

For reasons which have already been explained, Mississippi was less amenable to integration in 1962 than it had been in 1954. The forces of segregation had prepared their defenses and even their offenses, while those willing to accept either token or real integration had done nothing. Thus politicians, judges, educational administrators, professors, newspapers, churches, business organizations, and the Citizens' Council had worked to produce a pattern and policy of resistance. They had gone so far that by June 1962, Erle Johnston, the segregationist editor of the *Scott County Times*, charged that a "handful of leaders" in the Citizens' Council had taken over. He editorialized that Council leader William J. Simmons wanted "strife, confusion, and violence." The fact was that the Citizens' Council was in control of Mississippi.[1] At the federal level the Supreme Court, and in states other than Mississippi the lower courts, had moved steadily ahead, but the legislative and executive branches had done little. The U.S. Department of Justice had made only a modest start on Negro voter registration cases in Mississippi, and the expedient of appointing segregationists as U.S. district judges promised little. The forces of segregation in Mississippi rightly believed they were winning, and the slow pace of the Meredith case gave them hope. Even when the Court of Appeals decided in favor of Meredith they did not give up hope, partly because they believed they could not lose and partly because Judge DeVane's dissenting opinion bolstered their arguments.

Although DeVane's dissent was based on no substantial facts, it provided a straw which was eagerly grasped by the board attorneys, some University officials, and all of the other individuals and organizations who refused to lose. In what was mainly a concurring dissent, he stated:

> Considered as a brief in support of the appellant's case, the decision of Judge Wisdom is a masterpiece. I agree with almost everything he has to say in the opinion about the defenses advanced by appellees and I further agree that appellees scraped the "bottom of the barrel" in their efforts to keep Meredith out

> of the University of Mississippi. In so doing appellees weakened their case very much before this Court for on every ground save one the defenses advanced are not deserving of serious consideration by this Court.[2]

Except for this paragraph DeVane limited his comments to "the fear expressed by the appellants that Meredith would be a troublemaker." He claimed that Judge Mize "was correct in finding and holding" that Meredith "bore all the characteristics of becoming a troublemaker." Mize did not make such a finding, but rather based his decision against Meredith almost entirely on the ground that Meredith "failed completely" to prove that he was denied admission because of his race. Judge Mize did refer to the registrar's testimony challenging Meredith's morality and psychological characteristics, but he did not mention the "troublemaker" question in his decision. It appears that Judge DeVane must have based his dissent on the brief of the attorneys for Mississippi, and the dissent would have been more convincing if he had candidly admitted it. DeVane made it clear that he disapproved of the Supreme Court's integration decisions and intimated that integration should not have been ordered in some instances. He argued:

> I do not consider that we have a right to ignore what the effect of this decision could be upon the citizens of Mississippi and I feel that it is the duty of our Courts to avoid where we can incidents such as the Little Rock case and I fear that the result of this decision may lead to another comparable situation, particularly for "a man with a mission and with a nervous stomach." Integration is not a question that can ever be settled by Federal Judges. It is an economic, social, and religious question and in the end will be amicably settled on this basis.

Although it is true that the integration problem cannot be solved solely by court action, the recent American experience is that much of the solution has been forced on the courts because the "economic, social, and religious" forces referred to by Judge DeVane were not doing the job. Whether he realized it or not, DeVane's dissent was a contribution to the continued failure of Mississippi to settle the problem. In the context of the developing conflict it was even more, because it gave the forces of segregation in Mississippi a legal thread on which to hang their arguments.

On July 8, the same day that Judge DeVane filed his dissenting opinion, the Court of Appeals refused James Meredith's request for immediate issuance of the court's mandate. In doing so it contributed yet another delay of the type it had criticized Judge Mize for using and effectively said to James Meredith, "You cannot enter Ole Miss during the summer session." Since registration for the second summer session was to take place on July 13, I conferred with other faculty members and decided that something should be done. On July 9 I sent to Burke Marshall at the Justice Department the following letter:

> You have not received a phone call from here because there has been nothing in the way of new information. However, you may find it worthwhile to note the following, which summarizes opinions or information from several individuals.
>
> There is almost complete agreement here, among both those who know the legal procedures as well as others, that Mr. Meredith will not be entering the Second Summer Session for which registration takes place on July 13. Almost no one feels that a court order is likely to be issued before then, and most seem to feel that a Supreme Court appeal is likely to delay the order for admission. On the other hand, there is almost complete agreement that the appeal will fail and that the order will be issued.
>
> There is also almost complete agreement that the Summer Session would be a better time for admission, considering such matters as housing and the attitude of the student body. There are only about ⅓ as many students here as during the regular academic year, and the students are on a very tight schedule, both of which facts should keep things more calm.
>
> It should be realized that University officials on the campus have almost nothing to say about the policies to be followed on these matters, which are determined by the Board of Trustees of the Institutions of Higher Learning and by the State Attorney General. The University officials are on a tightrope between the officials just referred to and their own educational responsibilities. The University is in a difficult competitive position with other state schools (Mississippi State and Mississippi Southern, both of which have recently been named "universities" by the state legislature and both of which are more popular with the above-mentioned officials and the Citizens' Council). University officials are afraid to appear "willing" to see Mr. Meredith enrolled, since this would be used as an argument that the University is pro-integration.
>
> All this helps explain an attitude that has been expressed by several university officials, that when the order is issued it should by very specific in enjoining any and all types of possible inter-

> ference with the order by University officials, state officials, local government authorities, faculty members, or the student body or general public *and* that the Department of Justice should be well represented and should make it clear that no interference with the order will be tolerated. . . .
>
> Finally, it should be pointed out that the plan which was in readiness for last February is not now an active plan, perhaps mainly because of the belief that the order will not be issued this summer. In any case, there is complete agreement that the Department of Justice should have an impressive number of representatives here when the order is issued. There is considerable fear that violence may be attempted and that state and local law enforcing officers may not be all that is required, and there is some doubt as to whether their main interest would be in protecting Mr. Meredith.

The dispatching of that letter was a calculated risk, yet developments during the next three months demonstrated that it was a reasonably accurate summary of the situation and of likely developments. Of all the mistakes which I and others feared, the greatest was the failure of the Court of Appeals to order James Meredith's admission to the summer term. Instead, those interested in law and order delayed while the promoters of resistance took heart and continued to prepare for battle. On July 17 Hinds County Judge Russell Moore announced that twenty-eight county officials had signed a pledge to go to jail rather than surrender to the Court of Appeals' "insidious attack" on constitutional government.[3]

On July 18, the final date for late registration at Ole Miss and four days after the beginning of summer classes, Judge Mize received the mandate from the Court of Appeals. The bureaucratic mill had ground out notification of the June 25 decision just late enough for Mize to avoid issuing the order. On the same day I received word from Burke Marshall that there would be no action until September because the Court of Appeals had refused to expedite its mandate. Considering the many problems which would accompany the enrollment of the first Negro at Ole Miss, it was too late academically and otherwise for successful implementation of the order. It is clear that the Court of Appeals knew or should have known that its delaying of the decision until June 25 would prevent Meredith's admission during the summer, since its own rules provided that the order would not be sent to Judge Mize for twenty-one days—and he had not yet acted promptly at any stage of the case.

Also on July 18 Judge Ben F. Cameron, another member of the Court of Appeals for the Fifth Circuit, had been at work early and the Mississippi attorneys had labored even earlier. At 9:30 A.M. an attorney presented to the clerk of the court in New Orleans an order signed by Judge Cameron in which he granted a stay in enforcement of the order for Meredith's admission. The stay was to remain in force until the U.S. Supreme Court decided finally on Mississippi's appeal against the June 25 decision, a delay which would keep Meredith from entering Ole Miss for the fall semester. Of course Meredith's attorneys had not been given the chance to appear before Judge Cameron, who acted with a degree of speed usually reserved for saving convicted murderers from the gas chamber. In the odd world in which they lived and which they helped create, the Mississippi defendants and their attorneys felt their position was precisely that.

James Meredith's attorneys went before the Court of Appeals to appeal the stay, and on July 27 the court produced its fourth major decision in the case. The three judges vacated Cameron's stay, recalled their original mandate, and issued a new mandate "forthwith." They ordered Judge Mize to issue the order for Meredith's admission immediately—the twenty-one-day delay would not apply. Judge Wisdom wrote that time had been "of the essence" since Meredith's application in 1961, but that it was now "of the quintessence." He quoted from Rule 32 of the Rules of the Fifth Circuit:

> Mandate shall issue at any time after twenty-one days from the date of the decision, unless an application for rehearing has been granted or is pending If such application is denied the mandate will be stayed for a further period of ten days. *No further stay will be granted unless applied for within the delay given above.* [his emphasis] A mandate once issued will not be recalled except by the court and to prevent injustice.

Wisdom pointed out that the Court of Appeals is "bigger than a single judge," and the court ruled that it had power to review Cameron's action. "A contrary position," he declared, "would allow a judge in the minority, were he a member of the panel deciding the case, to frustrate the mandate of the majority. *And it is unthinkable that a judge who was not a member of the panel should be allowed to frustrate the mandate of the Court*" [his emphasis]. Continuing his polite but sharp rebuke of Judge Cameron, Wisdom stated in judicial language that Cameron was ignorant of the facts and law in the case. He pointed out that this was not a Chessman or Rosenberg case and emphasized a point not made by the judges before: "It is not a matter of life or death to the University of Mississippi. Texas University, the University of Georgia, Louisiana State University, the University of Virginia, other Southern universities are not shriveling up because of the admisson of Negroes."

With the issuance of the new order of the Court of Appeals, a case which had hardly been simple became extremely complicated. The order stated:

> The case is reversed and remanded with directions to the District Court forthwith to grant all relief prayed for by the plaintiff and to issue forthwith a permanent injunction against each and all of the defendants—appellees, their servants, agents, employees, successors and assigns, and all persons acting in concert with them, as well as any and all persons having knowledge of the decree, enjoining and compelling each and all of them to admit the plaintiff-appellant, James H. Meredith, to the University of Mississippi under his applications heretofore filed, which are declared by us to be continuing applications. Such injunction shall in terms prevent and prohibit said defendants-appellees, or any of the classes of persons referred to from excluding the plaintiff-appellant from admission to continued attendance at the University of Mississippi. Pending such time as the District Court has issued and enforced the orders herein required and until such time as there has been full and actual compliance in good faith with each and all of said orders by the actual admission of plaintiff-appellant to, and the continued attendance thereafter at the University of Mississippi, this Court herewith issues its own preliminary injunction enjoining and compelling each and all of said parties to admit plaintiff-appellant to, and allow his continual attendance at the University of Mississippi, further prohibiting and preventing said parties or any of them from excluding said plaintiff-appellant from attendance to and continued attendance thereafter on the same basis as other students at the University of Mississippi.

This order in several important ways went beyond the order of

June 25, but most importantly it was a preliminary injunction from the Court of Appeals itself.

The next day, Judge Cameron issued a second stay which canceled the above order. But Cameron was having difficulty keeping up, and on the same day the Court of Appeals issued another injunction which was more specific. It ordered the Board of Trustees and the University to admit Meredith immediately, or if Meredith thought the summer session too far gone (it was one-third gone), to admit him in September. It also ordered prompt evaluation of his transfer credits on a non-discriminatory and reasonable basis and continued its earlier order against prosecution of Meredith on the voter registration charge. It would have been difficult and probably impossible for Meredith to make up the time already missed in summer school, and he announced that he planned to enroll on September 21. Meredith made one of his few comments: "I'm not getting any younger, there's been so many decisions. I hope this is the last." But Judge Cameron was still active, and on July 31 he issued his third stay.[4]

On August 4 the Court of Appeals issued an order setting aside all of Cameron's stays on the ground that they were "unauthorized, erroneous and improvident." Stating that it might seem unnecessary to issue further orders, the court issued this one "to make certain that the record is kept straight," and it demanded "full and immediate obedience and compliance."[5] On August 6 Judge Cameron continued his defiance by issuing a fourth stay. Since it was apparent that Cameron would never back down, Mrs. Motley announced that she would petition Supreme Court Justice Hugo Black to throw out his stays.[6] On August 31 the U.S. Department of Justice entered the case for the first time by filing a "friend of the court" brief with Justice Black in support of Meredith's petition. The Mississippi reaction was summed up by Attorney General Joe Patterson when he compared U.S. Attorney General Robert Kennedy to a "jackass" braying at "a great American eagle."[7] Apparently he considered Mississippi the eagle.

Justice Black on September 10 issued an order vacating all four of Cameron's stays and requiring that the judgment of the Court of Appeals be made effective "immediately." He also enjoined the Board of Trustees and University officials "from taking any steps to prevent enforcement" of the judgment, pending the Supreme Court's action on their appeal. In a brief opinion Black stated, "I agree with the Court of Appeals that the stays issued in this case can only work further delay and injury to movant [Meredith] while immediate enforcement of the judgment can do no appreciable harm to the University or the other respondents." He further stated what everyone familiar with the case knew, that the Supreme Court was very unlikely to grant *certiorari* for review of the case, since it "essentially involves only factual issues." To put the matter beyond doubt, Black pointed out that he had submitted the question to all other Justices of the Supreme Court and that each of them agreed "that under the circumstances I should exercise that power as I have done here." Mississippi had reached the end of the long legal road.

On the Ole Miss campus the situation before September 10 was outwardly calm, although there was an electric kind of interest in the developments. After Justice Black issued his order, reported Dean Love, "the campus began to seethe with excitement—but there was no disorder whatsoever."[8] Just before 1:30 A.M. that night about fifteen students and outsiders set up a large cross near Fraternity Row, but the campus police arrived before it could be set on fire and persuaded the students not to light it. When Dean Love arrived they told him "they merely wanted to protest the admission of Meredith." The dean made some point of the fact that *the students* took down the cross and loaded it on a truck to be hauled away, but there was no disciplinary action against them. Although the campus police prevented the situation from getting out of hand, this episode was the first of many in which a low-key and permissive policy on student discipline encouraged a bolder protest of James Meredith's admission and impending arrival on the campus.

The University policy to be followed was formulated at an off-campus workshop on September 5 and 6, at which twenty-five student leaders met with various administrative officials. According to Dean Love, the problems discussed were those of keeping the University open, avoiding violence, and dealing with "the probability of outside interference." The decisions were "to conduct an educational campaign," mainly through the campus newspaper, and for each student leader "to do everything possible to maintain law and order." Dean Love's report, as well as later events, indicate this was to be the main approach. University officials were terrified—because of outside pressures—at the thought of punishing students for protesting or impeding Meredith's admission, so the students were expected to discipline themselves. Even though I and others were critical of the approach, there was no doubt that those controlling Mississippi would have done all in their power to eliminate a tough disciplinary policy. These outside forces made it clear then and later that Ole Miss students should be able to resist by using threats, profanity, bricks, Molotov cocktails, and even guns.

On September 11 Chancellor Williams and Dean Love met in the afternoon with fraternity presidents, and that night Love and the director of men's housing met with the fifty dormitory managers. Four days later Dean of Women Katharine Rea and Dean Love met with presidents of sororities and women's residence halls. The purpose of these meetings was to secure student cooperation in avoiding violence and keeping the University open. About half of the students were already on the campus for fraternity and sorority rush activities before the opening of the fall semester, and new students would begin arriving for orientation on September 15. The hope was that personal contact with student leaders would keep the other students under control so that the University would not have to use disciplinary measures.

The night of September 11 supplied proof that outside forces were not about to permit the University to operate normally. At about midnight someone fired a cross in a vacant area behind Fraternity Row. As several fraternity members went to investigate, they saw a camera flash and four or five figures run away. The next day the *Jackson Daily News* carried a page-one picture with the headline, MEREDITH CROSS BLAZES AT OXFORD. The news story stated erroneously that one hundred students and campus police watched the blaze and that police and University officials broke up the crowd with "threats of expulsion." The facts were that the students phoned the police and put out the fire, and there was no crowd to break up. Dean Love later reported—and I agree—that the cross-burning was staged to produce a newspaper story so written as to inflame feelings at the University and throughout the state. This was only part of a steady stream of articles and letters published during September by the two leading Jackson newspapers which caused difficulties for the University and attacked both the U.S. courts and the Kennedy administration. In a letter printed in the *Jackson Daily News* on September 10, Presley J. Snow of Philadelphia criticized "outside" attacks against the "law-abiding" people of Mississippi. "But the citadel will resist," he proclaimed, explaining in justification, "and if it needs added incentive to resist, let it be remembered that much of the hogwash known as the 'law of the land' in the nation today is a crime against the American people." It was all part of the blueprint.

On September 13 Judge Mize issued a permanent injunction for James Meredith's admission, but the press paid more attention to Governor Ross Barnett's interposition address, delivered on television the same evening. The *Jackson Daily News* headlined its story, ROSS RISKS JAIL TO HALT MIXING.[9] In his sepulchral voice the governor intoned, "We must either submit to the unlawful dictates of the federal government or stand up like men and tell them 'NEVER.' " In words capitalized in the news stories he promised, "NO SCHOOL WILL BE INTEGRATED WHILE I AM YOUR GOVERNOR." After calling for refusal "to submit to illegal usurpation of power by the Kennedy administration," he continued, "I especially call upon all public officials both elected and appointed to join hands with the people and resist by every legal and constitutional means [and here he departed from his prepared text and inserted "and every means"] the tyrannical edicts which have been and will be directed against the patriotic citizens of our State." Barnett said he was prepared to go to jail and called for the resignations of any officials "not prepared to suffer imprisonment for this righteous cause." In a statement which increased the fears of University officials, he promised that schools "will not be closed if this can possibly be avoided—but they will not be integrated." His proclamation of interposition included the words, "Therefore, in obedience to legislative and constitutional sanction I interpose the rights of the sovereign State of Mississippi to enforce its laws and to regulate its own internal affairs without interference on the part of the federal government or its offices." Although the doctrine of interposition had been rejected by the U.S. courts as recently as 1960 in the Orleans Parish school case as "illegal defiance of constitutional authority," Governor Barnett was determined to resist.[10]

The reaction to the governor's message was a wave of approval which drowned out the few voices of dissent, plus silence from some who feared what lay at the end of Barnett's road. Senator Eastland said, "I certainly support him to the limit." Lieutenant Governor Paul Johnson echoed, "He stated the position of the state very well," and added, "There is unity among all officials on this question." State Senator Hayden Campbell of Jackson called the speech "historic, masterful, and courageous."[11] The *Jackson Daily News* ran a brief front-page editorial headed, "We Support Gov. Barnett."

On the other side, State Representative Joe Wroten of Greenville accused Barnett of calling for "anarchy and defiance" and for Mississippians "to bear arms against the United States government"—and he believed they did not want that. The editors of small-town newspapers already mentioned criticized the governor's position, as exemplified by Ira Harkey of the *Pascagoula Chronicle*. In an editorial on September 14 headed "Governor Reaches Point of No Return"—one of several which won him a Pulitzer Prize—he stated what could have been the situation: "Mississippians are mature enough to recognize the inevitable, to accept it and adapt to it with good enough grace. The political faction that rules them, however, is not." He criticized Barnett's "blazing advisers" and concluded with the most perceptive of the contemporary comments:

> But it is not "the Kennedy administration" that is making demands upon Mississippi. It is the United States of America, it is democracy itself, it is the whole of humanity. These surely will not back down either. Barnett has asked them to force us to comply. They will, and the process can ruin Mississippi.

But Mississippi would not listen to reason or accept the inevitable, and instead editor Harkey eventually left the state.

Those who cheered Ross Barnett the night of September 13 had forgotten that when a group of editors by a nine to seven vote chose him as the man who "made the greatest impact on the state in 1960," one who voted *for* him explained that Barnett "set the state back at least fifty years." Another claimed that he had "erased virtually all the prestige Mississippi had enjoyed in eight years under his predecessors."[12] In 1960 Barnett was booed loudly by Ole Miss students at a football game and plans to have him speak on the Forum Series were dropped for fear the students would be impolite to "their governor." But this was 1962, and Ross Barnett had hit the mark in battling the United States.

The sparseness of news coverage may indicate that Mississippi newspapers were reluctant to admit that a native Mississippian such as Judge Mize could play the role of "traitor" by ordering the admission of a Negro to a white school. But he did, and his order read:

> Now, therefore, it is here ordered, adjudged and decreed that the plaintiff, James Howard Meredith, be and he is hereby granted all the relief that is prayed for by him in his complaint and that the defendants, . . . and their agents, servants, employees, successors, attorneys and all persons in active concert and participation with them be and they hereby are permanently restrained and enjoined from:
>
> (1) Refusing to admit plaintiff, James Howard Meredith immediately to the University of Mississippi and that they shall each of them be, and they are hereby required to admit him to the University of Mississippi upon the same terms and conditions as applicable to white students;
>
> (2) From interfering in any manner with the right of plaintiff, James Howard Meredith to matriculate in, or attend the University of Mississippi;
>
> (3) From taking any action or doing any act or being guilty of any conduct which will impair, frustrate or defeat his right to enter the University of Mississippi;
>
> (4) Refusing to admit the plaintiff, James Howard Meredith to the University of Mississippi upon his applications heretofore filed, all of which are continuing applications.
>
> It is further ordered that said defendants, or any of the classes of persons referred to, are prohibited and enjoined from excluding the said James Howard Meredith from admission to continued attendance at the University of Mississippi.

> It is further ordered that the defendants, their servants, agents, employees, successors and assigns, and all persons acting in concert with them, are enjoined to admit the plaintiff, James Howard Meredith to the University of Mississippi upon his applications heretofore filed and they are enjoined from excluding the said James Howard Meredith from admission to continued attendance at the University of Mississippi or discriminating against him in any way whatsoever because of his race.

Since the meaning of court orders is not self-evident, it must be noted that the relief "prayed for" by Meredith was "On Behalf of Himself and Others Similarly Situated"—it was a class order. Mize did not issue the injunction against "any and all persons having knowledge of the decree," as instructed by the Court of Appeals. Even though he quoted that portion of the court's instructions in his order, he left room for a doubt expressed later as to whether the injunction also covered Ole Miss students and the general public. But the order was issued and was filed on September 14. It remained for the U.S. government to enforce it and for Mississippi to resist it. For James Meredith the question was, "When do I enroll?"

One of several secret meetings which took place on September 14 was a three-hour session of the Board of Trustees with Governor Barnett's executive assistant, Attorney General Patterson, and two state attorneys who had worked on the Meredith case attending. As with most secret meetings in Mississippi the results were soon known to newsmen, and they were that the board members opposed closing the University and had pointed out that "defiance of the injunction would subject them, not the Governor, to any contempt action which would carry a jail sentence." The governor met for more than an hour with the heads of the Mississippi National Guard and the Highway Safety Patrol. Apparently they discussed the "possible use of patrolmen and deputized Guardsmen. . . ." In Washington both Mississippi senators and four of its five congressmen joined in sending a telegram to Governor Barnett: WE CONGRATULATE YOU ON YOUR EFFORT AND DETERMINATION TO PRESERVE THE SOVEREIGN RIGHTS AND PRIVILEGES OF OUR STATE AND PLEDGE YOU AND THE PEOPLE OF MISSISSIPPI OUR FULL AND UNQUALIFIED SUPPORT. Congressman Frank

E. Smith, who had been defeated in the Democratic party primary in June, refused to go along with his colleagues' support of resistance. He charged that Barnett was leading Mississippi "down another blind alley" with a policy which "threatens our great university" and added, "Whether we like it or not, the question of state versus federal law was settled one hundred years ago." While increasing numbers of state politicians and newspapers announced their support of Barnett, State Representative Karl Wiesenburg of Pascagoula denounced his stand as "bordering on treason."[13]

In Oxford on Sunday, September 16, eight ministers representing five denominations read a joint statement in their churches in which they "solemnly and prayerfully" urged:

> 1. That the entire population act in a manner consistent with the Christian teaching concerning the value and dignity of man.
> 2. That Christians exert whatever leadership and influence possible to maintain peace and order among us.
> 3. That we all pray unceasingly for God's guidance of the leaders in this community and in our beloved state and nation.
> 4. That we make every effort to resist the pressures placed upon us by emotionally excited groups and uphold the honor and good name of the University of Mississippi.

In the face of the attitudes rampant in Mississippi, this statement should have produced some kind of award for courage for these men: Don H. Anderson (Methodist), Duncan M. Gray (Episcopal), Walter L. Maloney (Catholic), Wayne Coleman (Baptist), Clifford A. McKay (Presbyterian), Wofford K. Smith (Episcopal), Murphey C. Wilds (Presbyterian), and William A. Pennington (Methodist).

Several ministers went beyond the statement in their messages that Sunday, and the brief excerpts which follow do not tell the whole story. In his "pastoral word," Episcopal Rector Duncan M. Gray, Jr., pointed out that each "professing Christian bears a *heavy responsibility* to see that no acts of intimidation or violence take place," and called for "the leadership necessary to assure the peaceful admission of James Meredith to the University, insofar as we have the power to do so." University Episcopal Chaplain Wofford K. Smith warned of the "catastrophe" that would come if "the mob replaces law and order," and suggested that the simple way out "is to bring Christian principle to bear upon the issue." Presbyterian Murphey C. Wilds spoke of peacemakers and told James Thurber's story of the "Peaceful Mongoose." From students he specifically called for (1) recognition of the "voices of authority" on the campus, (2) "refusal to stand by and watch any disorder which might come about at the instigation of others," and (3) speaking in a voice which would be "one strong for peace," emphasizing that "there can be no such thing as a prank in this situation." He urged adults to speak out for Christian behavior, to "break the silence which would give consent for others to do what they would not do themselves."

On September 20 Duncan Gray repeated on the Oxford radio station a sermon he had given when James Meredith's enrollment seemed imminent in February, 1962. After warning against violence and calling for upholding "the *law* as it is interpreted by our courts," he concluded, "As Christians, we will have the *continuing* duty to see that this new student is accepted and treated *as a person;* that he is not exposed to badgering, torment, or ridicule; that he is given the opportunity to stand on his own merits as a student among students, person among persons, regardless of the color of his skin. Ultimately, this is where the real test of our Christianity will come." In the words of Murphey Wilds, these men were attempting to "break the silence" of the forces of law and decency, but they were shouted down by the voices of violence.

On the Ole Miss campus most students and all faculty and administrators were worried. Fraternity and sorority leaders were discouraging demonstrations, and there were none of consequence during the week before registration. At about 2 A.M. on September 14 a small cloth dummy bearing the sign "Hail Barnett" was found hanging near the Student Union Building, but it was not clear whether the perpetrators were for or against the governor. It was reported that on September 16 a forty-two-car caravan of Ku Klux Klan members had started for Mississippi from Tuscaloosa, Alabama, but it never arrived.[14] In the early morning hours of September 18 the supporters of resistance distributed a "Liberty Bulletin" on the campus which urged students to place themselves "under the direction of Gov. Barnett" and not to "engage in force or violence unless he calls for it." It challenged the chancellor's policy by warning students not to be "intimidated by any leftist school administrator."[15] The unsophisticated zealots who prepared the "Liberty Bulletin" were no doubt unconscious of their grim humor, since leftist administrators are a nonexistent species at Ole Miss. On the same day the chancellor, in a speech to new students who had come early for the orientation program, cautioned them to refrain from violence and demonstrations and to "go about your business as normal." At the opening faculty meeting on September 15 Chancellor Williams announced that he had talked to student leaders and was encouraged by their responsiveness. The University, he said, had two things to do: avoid any action that would contribute to closing the University, and avoid any demonstrations or violence. He stated that the issue was now between the state and federal governments and that decisions regarding the University would be made in Jackson. He concluded by reading Judge Mize's injunction which had been served on him and other officials. There were no instructions to read the injunction in classes, although some professors did so.

When the Board of Trustees met again on Monday, September 17, it became apparent that the breaking point was near. These men had been willing to defend segregation with every available legal device, but a contempt citation was the end of the road. Board Chairman Thomas J. Tubb had invited the press to the meeting and Tally Riddell made a motion that they be allowed to attend, in order to publicize some pro-education arguments to rebut Barnett's counsel of destruction. But the governor and his supporters applied pressure, and the motion for a public meeting was withdrawn. No policy was announced after the two-and-a-half-hour meeting, but it was clear that the governor outlined his plan for trying Meredith on the voter registration charge.[16] In a statement which placed him with the small group willing to defend education, board member Dr. Verner Holmes of McComb announced that he would not "vote to close the university."

The state legislature met on September 18 in a special session called by Governor Barnett, and after a call to battle by Barnett the legislators resolved:

> That we do now commend Governor Ross R. Barnett for his fearless and courageous stand against political aggression, abuse and misrepresentation designed to disrupt and destroy Southern institutions, traditions, and way of living, and which do violence to fundamental principles of our constitutional republican form of government which is guaranteed to each state by Article IV of the Constitution of the United States, and particularly the rights of states to solve their domestic problems and adopt laws and policies for local self-government; and we, the duly elected representatives of the people of the State of Mississippi, do hereby join our Governor and pledge our full support in the staunch stand he has taken to uphold and defend by every lawful and honorable means available the laws and sovereign powers of our state against unlawful, unwarranted aggression and usurpation by the federal government.[17]

This resolution of rebellion talked of "lawful and honorable" resistance, yet the legislators knew that interposition was unlawful, that the governor had not committed himself to use only lawful methods, and that words such as "lawful and honorable" had a meaning peculiar to Mississippi. There was not a dissenting vote on the resolution in the Senate, and in the House of Representatives only Wroten of Greenville and Wiesenburg had the courage to vote "no"—but there were many who knew they should have opposed. Speaker Walter Sillers answered one representative's question by stating that the resolution did not endorse the closing of schools but that each member would have to construe it for himself. But the resolution backed Barnett completely, and he had threatened to close the University. Even though former Governor J. P. Coleman had termed interposition "legal poppycock" before he signed the interposition law of 1956, he put his name on the side of rebellion in supporting "the Governor and all elected and appointed officials in this matter."[18] As he and those who read between the lines knew, this was a politically expedient and equivocal statement, because the Board of Trustees and Attorney General Patterson had already begun withdrawing support for Barnett behind the scenes. But public courage and acceptance of responsibility during these days was a rare commodity among politicians, newspaper editors, and educators.

By September 19 an unusual assortment of groups was arriving on the Ole Miss campus. It included Citizens' Council leaders, officers of the Highway Safety Patrol, county sheriffs and deputies, news reporters from the press, radio, and television, worried alumni, and students. It was a grotesque sort of homecoming, and the University was faced with an impossible task in trying to produce an equal welcome for all. Apart from the students, for whom the routine was well established, University officials worried most about the newsmen. The primary image of Ole Miss nationally—not entirely of its own making—was that of a producer of Miss Americas and football teams. Descending on it were hordes of skeptical journalists. With the opportunity for striking paydirt in favorable publicity went the nightmare of reaping the worst. At first there were reports that the University might exclude newsmen, but they were ultimately welcomed with "red carpet" treatment, which meant turning the board room of the Lyceum (administration) Building into a newsroom. Additional telephones—not enough—were moved in; desks, typewriters, and dictionaries were provided; the cafeteria brought free box lunches and coffee; an information brochure on Ole Miss was hurriedly produced; and University public relations men were on hand to provide ambiguous answers to impossible questions. The reporters were provided with everything but news.

Most administrators and faculty members were afraid to comment, partly because the University was rapidly being eased out of the minor policy role it had played. For the next two weeks the real newsmakers were to be in Jackson, Mississippi, and Washington, D.C., although an illusion persisted that the University had more than a bit part. One reporter found a professor who would comment that Ross Barnett was "the worst governor Mississippi ever had." I ran into an American Broadcasting Company television reporter in the hall on September 19 and suggested that he come to my office when he had time and if he wanted some comments—I never saw him again. But this wasn't much, and it is no surprise that the newsmen welcomed—and in some cases encouraged—the early signs of rebellion among some students.

The *Mississippian*, the student newspaper, in its first fall edition on September 18 published stories calculated to carry out the previously adopted policy of encouraging calmness and normality. The front-page lead story reported that "students have almost overwhelmingly expressed a desire to continue their education without interruption." After referring to "rumors and sensational stories" in some newspapers, the *Mississippian* gave a rigorously factual account of the cross-burnings and other events on the campus during the preceding week. In addition to the chancellor's standard message of welcome, there were three editorials which emphasized the importance of friendliness to newcomers on the campus, the educational purposes of the University, and the need for accurate and responsible reporting of the news. On September 20 editor Sidna Brower wrote a front-page editorial in which she criticized the reporting of the campus situation in the Mississippi daily press and specifically attacked "the screaming headlines and sensationalized stories" of the *Jackson Daily News*.

The first day of registration, Wednesday, September 19, was almost normal, partly because Thursday was the day scheduled for registration of new students, including James Meredith. The only important departure was the presence of guards at the five entrances to the campus. In Jones County, Chancery Judge L. B. Porter, on behalf of the parents of forty-six students, issued an injunction prohibiting Meredith's enrollment, listing as defendants University, board, and federal officials. In an unworried interview in Memphis on Tuesday, Meredith had said he expected no trouble from Ole Miss students and had explained, "Students at the university are the same as those elsewhere. Negroes are attending other Southern colleges without trouble and I can't see that Mississippi is any different."[19]

By this time some in Mississippi realized that closing Ole Miss would mean: (1) disbanding the football team and losing the players to other colleges, (2) paying financial obligations for faculty salaries and federally financed dormitories, (3) the end of ROTC programs and the immediate draft of some students for military service, (4) the postponement of education for many students because of their inability to gain admission to other colleges, (5) the closing of the School of Medicine and the large hospital operated by it, (6) damaging the state's economy in many ways, and (7) the loss of several sell-out football games in Jackson's brand new Memorial Stadium, which still had to be paid for out of revenues from ticket sales. These and other more personal problems had been discussed at length on the Ole Miss campus and elsewhere in the state, and officials had publicized these very arguments in subtle ways. Of course the irresponsible legislature which had proposed the closing of schools had not considered the real meaning of the policy. The absence of serious *public* discussion of the problem *in Mississippi* clearly indicated how far Ross Barnett and his supporters had led the state toward public insanity. Ira Harkey, in an editorial on September 19 in the *Pascagoula Chronicle*, predicted Barnett would resort to violence: "A pall of contradiction covers our state as if every one of us had developed schizophrenia. . . . In a madhouse's din, Mississippi waits. God help Mississippi."

A busy September 20 began at 12:25 A.M. with the burning of a 14-by-27-foot cross made of cloth sacks, laid out on a street between the men's dormitories. The first students to crawl out of bed saw a car drive away just after the lighting of the cross. Firemen extinguished the fire in ten minutes, while a small crowd of students cheered. At about the same time in Jackson, the legislature completed action on Senate Bill No. 1501, which denied admission to any state school to any person "who has a criminal charge of moral turpitude pending against him" or "has been convicted of any criminal offense and not pardoned." To protect their friends, the legislators carefully provided that the law would not cover "any charge or conviction of traffic law violations, violation of the state conservation laws and state game and fish laws, or *manslaughter as a result of driving while intoxicated or under the influence of intoxicants.*" The unbelievable exemption indicated by my emphasis was included to cover a student who had an undergraduate degree from Ole Miss and now wanted to get into the School of Law. The law also provided a fine and jail sentence for anyone attempting to enroll in violation of it or for anyone abetting such enrollment—meaning board or University officials.

The immediate reason for the new law was soon clear. Although the Court of Appeals' July 28 order against such prosecution was still in effect, James Meredith was tried in absentia on September 20 by a Jackson Justice of the Peace on the charge of false voter registration. He was found guilty and sentenced to pay a fine of $100 plus costs and to serve *one year* in the county jail. This was a considerable penalty—but not for a Mississippi Negro—since the Hinds County registration clerk had testified in *Meredith v. Fair* that Meredith was "qualified to vote in Hinds County." But now Barnett's supporters were not really after Meredith but were executing a conspiracy against the Board of Trustees and University officials to prevent them from carrying out the court order for Meredith's admission. These officials had made it clear privately that they would not go to jail in response to Barnett's invitation; he now proposed to make them violate either the state law or the federal admission order.

On September 19 Robert Kennedy had sent a long telegram to the Board of Trustees and University officials in which he outlined the federal government's views on the "legal position." After pointing out that the court orders prevented any hindrance of compliance and that he had cooperated and would cooperate to "avoid law enforcement problems," he stated, "It is our purpose to see that the orders of the Court are complied with peacefully." He added that since neither he nor Meredith had received any commitment that Meredith's registration would take place in Jackson "without evasion or delay," Meredith would go to Oxford on September 20 to register with other transfer students. Kennedy warned that "any orders or other steps by the Board of Trustees intended to prevent the officials of the University at Oxford from registering Meredith in the regular course would be in violation of the orders" of the courts. He concluded: "I respect the State of Mississippi whose citizens have made many contributions to the country, and the great University which you are privileged to serve. Historically, American citizens have freely and frequently disagreed with or disapproved of laws and court decisions but have obeyed them nevertheless. The federal courts have spoken unequivocally on this matter. All of us as citizens of the United States have a responsibility to obey the law and I as Attorney General have the responsibility to enforce the law. I am confident that you will act in such a way not only as to preserve order but as to assist in meeting our responsibilities." This telegram was based upon knowledge that the Board of Trustees was likely to take action to divest University officials of responsibility, and was a thoughtful plea that they not do so. I found at least one University official who received the telegram, but it is odd that it was never delivered to the office of the Board of Trustees. This breakdown in communication encouraged board members to believe that federal officials were bypassing them and dealing directly with Governor Barnett, who was not yet a legal party in the case.

The Board of Trustees had notified Meredith to present himself at the board office in Jackson at 3 P.M. on September 20 "for registration or other disposition of his application." At its meeting at 10 A.M. the board was informed officially of the two state court actions and of the legislature's "Meredith law." During its lunch break the board learned that Meredith would go to the University instead of to Jackson to confront Barnett's interposition. There had been several conferences between the governor and the board. Chancellor Williams, Registrar Ellis, and the board members all had refused to perform the task of rejecting Meredith, even though Barnett suggested they would not suffer financially. He had then suggested he could propose at least a hundred "stalwart" individuals who would be proud to serve as special registrar to reject Meredith. Although Barnett had assured board members he knew of "lawful ways" to keep Meredith out, Attorney General Patterson advised that there were none and that a contempt citation and jail would be the next step. Carrying out an informal decision made the night before or earlier, the board voted on the afternoon of September 20 "to invest Honorable Ross R. Barnett, the Governor of the State of Mississippi, with the full power, authority, right and discretion of this Board to act upon all matters pertaining to or concerned with the registration or non-registration, admission or non-admission, and/or attendance of James H. Meredith at the University of Mississippi."[20] Barnett now had power not only under his proclamation of interposition but also as the replacement for all board and University officials for purposes of Meredith's enrollment. As such, he was the "successor" to the position of Registrar Robert Ellis, and Judge Mize's injunction would apply specifically to him.

Also on the 20th Governor Barnett secured from the Hinds County Chancery Court an injunction which prohibited the Board of Trustees from registering Meredith. His request for the order included a remarkable statement which made his position completely clear and further cut the ground from under the board: "It is against the public policy of the State of Mississippi as well as its laws for any colored person to be admitted as a student at said institution and his enrollment and entry therein would be in direct violation of the laws of the State of Mississippi." The Hinds County court order was lost in the shuffle of events, but it added another complication to the legal situation.

On the Ole Miss campus excitement and concern grew throughout the day of the 20th. There was a changing crowd of fifty to two hundred students, faculty, and newsmen in front of the Lyceum Building most of the day, and its numbers increased sharply during the afternoon. At one point a group of students led by a well-known troublemaker attempted to haul down the American flag at the center of the circle and to replace it with the Confederate "stars and bars." Other students led by Associated Student Body Vice-President Gray Jackson broke through the newsmen surrounding the flagpole and raised the flag again. University officials made no attempt to apprehend the demonstrating students, and from this point on they had no disciplinary control over the students. Later in the day I heard the A.S.B. President, Dick Wilson, telling another student not to raise the Confederate flag he was carrying—again no suggestion of disciplinary action. What amazed me and several other faculty members was that the control of discipline seemed to be entirely in the hands of student leaders. They worked hard and with remarkable success by means of persuasion, but when that method failed they had no real power to fall back on. Early in the afternoon I asked Dean Love whether something could not be done to control the clearly explosive situation. He replied in a tired and almost desperate voice, "I wish something could be done, but no one will make a decision." His reply revealed another segment of the blueprint which was rapidly developing.

James Meredith had been staying with friends in Memphis during the week before September 20, and he spoke and acted as though less worried than most. He commented, "It is indeed a unique and unusual thing that a person wanting only an ordinary education should find himself the top news story of the day." He pointed out that his wife Mary June and two-year-old son would join him in June after her graduation from Jackson State College. Meredith explained that she had not joined in applying to Ole Miss because "this is a man's business. I don't think it is the duty or responsibility of a woman to get out in the forefront. I've had several people tell me it would be easier if a woman were making the first entry, but I think it is a poor man that stands behind his woman." Meredith dismissed the possibility of personal danger, saying it "has always been there, and will always be there whether I enter or not. So, I have nothing to lose." He pointed out that he had secured admission to Atlanta University in case his Ole Miss attempt failed.[21]

Governor Barnett arrived from Jackson by plane at 2:30 P.M. and went to the University Continuation Center. When asked at the airport if Meredith would enter the University, Barnett replied, "Hell, no." A deputy sheriff in charge of a group of local law enforcement officers said that their orders were to arrest Meredith, and, if necessary, to shoot it out with the federal marshals. Meredith was brought to the campus just before 5 P.M., accompanied by Department of Justice attorney St. John Barrett, Chief of the Executive Office of U.S. Marshals James P. McShane, and two U.S. deputy marshals. Highway patrolmen escorted them onto the campus and along a road lined with patrolmen to the Continuation Center. As Meredith entered there were some boos and mild epithets, and during his twenty-minute stay the mixed crowd of students and outsiders chanted "We want Ross" and the Ole Miss "Hotty Toddy" yell:

> Hotty toddy, God A'mighty,
> Who in the hell are we,
> Flim flam, bim bam,
> Ole Miss, by damn.

The brief drama inside began as James Meredith said, "I want to be admitted to the University." Registrar Ellis then read the board order which transferred his authority to Barnett. The governor read his interposition proclamation and denied admission to Meredith. The Department of Justice attorney then asked, "Do you realize that this puts you and the other officials in contempt of a federal court order?" Barnett replied coldly, "Are you telling me I'm in contempt, or does it take a judge?"

Meredith emerged, showed no reaction to the chorus of jeers, and drove off with U.S. deputy marshals. A few minutes later the governor and lieutenant governor appeared and were greeted with a roar of approval. Barnett waved to the crowd of about a thousand and announced, "The only comment I have to make is that the application of James H. Meredith has been denied." Registration was just ending in the Gymnasium, and it was rumored there that Meredith was coming over to register. In the building during the afternoon registration there were several young Oxford businessmen—deputized by Lafayette County Sheriff Joe Ford—who said they were there to keep out the "rednecks." We learned later that Meredith had left the campus immediately after his rejection, and it was clear that he would miss the first day of classes on Friday.

The federal courts had been even busier on September 20 than those of Mississippi. The U.S. District Court enjoined the prosecution or arrest of Meredith, set a hearing for September 24 on a request for injunctions to prohibit enforcement of the moral turpitude law and the civil suit against Meredith's enrollment (*Meadors, et al v. Meredith*), accepted transfer to itself of the Meadors suit, and issued a "show cause" order for trial of three University officials on charges of contempt. The Court of Appeals issued its own order against prosecution of Meredith or anyone aiding his enrollment under the moral turpitude law and against enforcement of the injunction under the Meadors case. The Department of Justice was acting in these moves under a Court of Appeals order of September 18 which designated it as a friend of the court. James Meredith and the University were definitely back in court, although at this point University officials were ready to register him.

On September 21 Judge Mize cleared the University officials of contempt on the ground that the power to admit Meredith had been taken from them—actually the board had withdrawn such power on September 4. The Department of Justice then sought contempt citations against both the board members and University officials in the Court of Appeals, and trial was set for September 24. In failing to seek immediate action against Governor Barnett the Department of Justice insured further delay of Meredith's enrollment. News reports were that U.S. officials considered Barnett's action as "politically motivated" and that they did not intend to "oblige" his wish to go to jail. At the University I and several other faculty members wondered why the federal officials were refusing to take Barnett into court, since this played into the hands of the standard Mississippi tactic of delay. One official told me later, "The problem of Meredith's missing classes never occurred to us. Our problem was to get him enrolled." If Barnett thought delay would prevent the admission of Meredith, he might well have read an official release from the Department of Justice: "It is our responsibility, together with the courts, to see that these orders are obeyed no matter what course is ultimately necessary."[22]

A brief item from Miami, Florida, received little emphasis in the press at this moment but provoked much discussion among those concerned about the future of Ole Miss. Dr. Henry King Stanford, president of the University of Miami and chairman of the Commission on College Accreditation of the Southern Association of Colleges and Schools, announced that his commission was "watching events at the University of Mississippi with grave concern," but that steps would be taken only after all the facts were established.[23] This, plus growing concern over student discipline—not yet really bad, but potentially dangerous—led me to spend Sunday working on a statement which I hoped the Faculty Senate would adopt. I had been chairman of a special committee appointed by the chancellor in 1961 to recommend a constitution for the senate. As elected, the senate was broadly representative of various points of view among the faculty, which means that it was cautious and not inclined—especially under the circumstances—to be bold.

The draft resolution which I produced was essentially a list of truisms, stated in moderate language. I include it here not because of its braveness or brillance, but because it demonstrates how mild a statement could be and still horrify our administrators. After some toning down on the advice of other faculty members, it read:

> The Faculty Senate of the University of Mississippi affirms its support of the following principles:
>
> 1. The primary purpose of the institutions of higher learning is education, and the continued carrying out of this purpose should not be interfered with by other controversies or considerations.
> 2. The present controversy over the admission of students to the University constitutes interference with this primary educational purpose. When a clear and final legal determination on the controversy has been made, it should be accepted and implemented in a manner which will not interfere with the process of education.
> 3. Accreditation of the University of Mississippi and other institutions of higher learning is absolutely essential to their educational purpose. The costs of denial of accreditation 30 years ago are still being paid, and the lesson should not be forgotten. A spokesman for the major accrediting organization has stated that actions already taken raise the question of the status of Mississippi educational institutions. The present controversy should be settled in a manner which will not further endanger the accreditation of Mississippi institutions of higher learning.
> 4. The administrative officials of a university should be in a position to carry out their responsibilities of educational leadership. The Chancellor, the Registrar and the Dean of the College of Liberal Arts have been placed in a position which prevents them from fulfilling their educational responsibilities. They deserve the understanding and support of everyone who believes in the value of education.

Dr. Karl Morrison, a Professor of Economics since 1939 and more conservative than I, was a member of the senate, and he wrote a draft stronger than mine in that it specifically criticized Barnett's actions. But the executive committee of the senate would not even call a special meeting, so the faculty's representative body went through September without considering the fate of the University. I decided to have one last attempt to interest someone in a faculty statement, so I showed my draft to Provost Charles F. Haywood (head of the academic division) at a meeting of the executive committee of the Graduate Council on September 28. His face reddened, his hands quivered, and he said, "This would ruin the University." I replied, "It is going to be ruined anyway, unless something is done." I told him that it was likely that the local chapter of the American Association of University Professors would take some action, but he said we should inform the administration before we took public action. We moved on to other matters.

On Monday, September 24, University officials and members of the Board of Trustees, represented by a total of sixteen attorneys, appeared before the eight judges of the Court of Appeals. The array of attorneys resulted from the desires of the various defendants to be represented by their own attorneys, rather than by those from the State Attorney General's office. Registrar Robert Ellis clarified one major question promptly when he stated that "when the decision became ours, that we would do exactly what the Court told us to do, and that meant registering Meredith."[24]

The other question, what the board would do and when, took the rest of the day. As attorney Charles Clark attempted to justify the board's failure to comply with the order, the judges deflated his arguments with pointed comments and questions. Judge Brown remarked that the Hinds County justice of the peace—who convicted Meredith on the voter charge—"is in violation of the order too, isn't he?"[25] Chief Judge Tuttle inquired whether there was "any way we can enjoin all of" the Mississippi chancery judges.[26] Regarding Attorney General Patterson's advice to the board, Judge Joseph C. Hutcheson asked, "Did you advise them that this monkey business of coming around pretending to take over the school was legal?"[27] While an attorney for the University officials was explaining the role of Governor Barnett, Judge Hutcheson commented, "That is a misconception of the Governor's powers. In our state we impeach the Governor for interfering, and you all look like you are going to reward him. . . . What I mean to say: Were you relying on the doctrine of interposition, which was knocked out at Appomattox?"[28] When another attorney attempted to continue the hopeless argument, Hutcheson asked, "Counsel, would you first state where in the law an injunction goes off or on according to the opinion of the enjoined person as to whether they are acting in good faith?"[29]

The court came to the central issue when Mrs. Motley moved that "the appellant be registered right here and now in open court by the Registrar of the University of Mississippi."[30] U.S. Assistant Attorney General Burke Marshall supported her and added, "The action the court has to consider has to go beyond the registration of Meredith. The basic problem is not just the act of registration, but accepting him as a student on continued attendance at the University. . . ."[31] Regarding possible contempt on the part of University officials, Marshall stated that "they should, when faced with the dilemma that they were faced with, they should have applied to this Court for relief. I do not think that they were justified in, as Mrs. Motley says, 'experimenting with contempt' of this Court's order upon the basis of instructions from their superiors, which were designed to make it impossible . . . to comply with the court's order. . . . The first step should be to make the Board of Trustees face up to its responsibilities, and, if they do that, there isn't going to be any problem with the University officials."[32] Defense attorney Clark raised the question of possible action by Barnett with the statement, "You have the solemn declaration of the Governor of the State of Mississippi that he is going to close that institution." Judge Tuttle replied, "We have heard that of every state in the South." Judge Wisdom added, "We are not foreclosed from proceeding against the Governor of Mississippi by what we do today." Tuttle suggested before declaring a twenty-minute recess that the defense attorneys learn from their clients whether "they will immediately comply with whatever order the Court issues."[33]

When the hearing reconvened, Judge Tuttle announced that "the Court has unanimously concluded that the twelve members of the Board of Trustees have willfully and intentionally violated the Court's order." Board Chairman Tubb announced that the board. members "will enter any order and do any act that this Court may direct them to do, as, if, and when the Court directs them to do it." Tuttle then stated that the court would not issue a contempt order, but would specifically order them to carry out the court's orders, including the rescinding of board orders against Meredith's registration and appointing Barnett as registrar. There was agreement that Meredith's request for a dormitory room would be handled in the same manner as for white students and that he would be registered in Jackson by 4 P.M. the next day, September 25.[34]

Governor Barnett now issued an executive order calling for the arrest of any federal official attempting to prevent any state official from carrying out his "official duties." In the State Senate E. K. Collins proclaimed, "We must win this fight regardless of the cost in time, effort, money and in human lives." He promised that Meredith would not be enrolled at Ole Miss "as long as there are red corpuscles in the bodies of true Mississippians."[35] On the Ole Miss campus a student commented, "I'm so tired of this mess, I don't care whether they let fifty [Negroes] in." In New York City a light-skinned Negro, Harry S. Murphy, Jr., revealed that he had attended the University as a Navy V-12 student during the 1945-1946 academic year.[36] On September 25 the Board of Trustees moved to carry out the court orders with instructions to University officials to admit Meredith and to distribute to all University personnel copies of Judge Mize's order of September 13. In the *Mississippian* Sidna Brower cautioned students to "think before acting" so that Governor Barnett would have no reason to close Ole Miss and the U.S. government no need to send U.S. marshals "to preserve peace."[37]

When Registrar Ellis arrived in Jackson on Tuesday the 25th he was summoned to appear before a state legislative committee, and the governor met James Meredith and Department of Justice attorney John Doar at the entrance to the meeting room of the Board of Trustees. An "angry, taunting" mob of more than two thousand greeted Meredith and his escorts—Barnett and his advisers had made certain there would be an impressive gallery for the next act in the show. John Doar attempted to hand the governor an order from the Court of Appeals which restrained him and other Mississippi officials. After Doar suggested that they get on with the business of registering Meredith, Barnett read a statement and concluded, "I do hereby, finally deny you admission to the University of Mississippi." Meredith left the building, protected from the surging mob by highway patrolmen and Patrol director Colonel T. B. Birdsong. (On this same day the National Aeronautics and Space Administration announced that Mississippi's Americanism would be rewarded by the construction of a one-half billion dollar test facility for rocket engines.[38]) The Court of Appeals issued a "show cause" order for contempt of court against the governor and scheduled a hearing for Friday; it also agreed to include the governor as a defendant in Meredith's original suit. Governor Barnett asked after this second rejection of Meredith, "How many times do we have to do this?" The answer was his to determine.

At the Ole Miss campus on September 26 the *Mississippian* ran two stories on Tuesday's events headlined BARNETT REJECTS MEREDITH. Under much smaller headlines it printed Judge Mize's order for Meredith's admission, plus the order from the Board of Trustees to the chancellor that all University personnel were to comply "strictly" with that order and the Court of Appeals order of July 28. Although Sidna Brower pointed out at the end of a story that the injunction applied to students, the emphasis was on Barnett's rejection of Meredith. The University distributed copies of the board order and Mize's injunction to all faculty and staff, taking great pains that it went to the lowliest typist or paper-grader. It was not distributed to students, although it was posted on dormitory bulletin boards in addition to its publication in the *Mississippian*. There were no instructions for faculty members to read the order to their classes, although some did so. The message could not have gotten over very powerfully to the students, particularly with the governor's defiance dominating the news.

The Department of Justice brought Meredith to the campus at about 10 A.M. on Wednesday, September 26, for his third rejection, this time by Lieutenant Governor Johnson. After Johnson said, "We do not intend to allow Meredith to enter," there was an almost comic elbowing match between federal officials Doar and McShane and several highway patrolmen. McShane said, "You understand that we have got to break through." Johnson replied, "But you can't. If there were any violence you and Meredith would be responsible." His logic was as bad as his law, but Meredith again left, and in a few minutes the tardy Barnett was at the Alumni House to congratulate Johnson on having "stood tall" against the U.S. government.[39] The lieutenant governor also won a contempt order from the Court of Appeals, and his hearing was set for September 29. At the airport James Meredith commented, "Well, at least there is one good thing; I am getting in lots of flying hours."

On the same afternoon seven ministers sent a telegram to Governor Barnett:

> WE, THE FOLLOWING MINISTERS OF OXFORD AND CHAPLAINS TO THE UNIVERSITY, FEARFUL OF THE ANARCHY UPON US AND OUR PEOPLE THROUGH CONTINUED DEFIANCE OF FEDERAL COURT ORDERS AND CONVINCED OF THE CHRISTIAN'S CALL, BOTH TO OBEY THE LAWS OF THE LAND, AND TO BE HIMSELF A PEACEMAKER, DO HEREBY CALL UPON YOU ABOVE ALL ELSE TO AVOID THE CLOSING OF THE UNIVERSITY, TO PROTECT ITS ACCREDITATION AND TO UPHOLD THE GOOD NAME AND DIGNITY OF THE UNIVERSITY.

Two days later the all-Negro Baptist Ministers' Union of Jackson issued the strongest statement of all, in part of which they declared: "With a dictator like Mr. Barnett, we are helpless. The decent people of Mississippi both young and old can see nothing but destruction, humiliation, fear, and we are discouraged, insulted, and tired of such Democracy, if that's what he calls it."

Thursday, September 27, was supposed to be the day that Governor Barnett would bow to federal force. Barnett was to face his contempt trial on Friday, which was also the deadline for late enrollment at Ole Miss. In lengthy and repeated telephone conversations Attorney General Robert Kennedy, Barnett, and Johnson arrived at a shaky agreement which fell apart as the day progressed. The conversation which began at 12:50 P.M. was a verbal duel:

KENNEDY: I just talked to Mr. Watkins and we were going to make this effort at 5 o'clock this afternoon your time. . . . Is that satisfactory?

BARNETT: Yes, sir. That's all right.

KENNEDY: I will send the marshals that I have available up there in Memphis and I expect there will be about twenty-five or thirty of them and they will come with Mr. Meredith and they will arrive wherever the gate is and I will have the head marshal pull a gun and I will have the rest of them have their hands on their guns and their holsters. And then as I understand it he will go through and get in and you will make sure that law and order is preserved and that no harm will be done to Mr. McShane and Mr. Meredith.

BARNETT: Oh, yes. . . . General, I was under the impression that they were all going to pull their guns. This could be very embarrassing. We got a big crowd here and if one pulls his gun and we all turn it would be very embarrassing. Isn't it possible to have them all pull their guns? . . .

KENNEDY: You will make sure not the marshals but the State Police will preserve law and order?

BARNETT: There won't be any violence.

The next conversation was at 1:35 P.M.

KENNEDY: Governor, now he is on his way and should be there about 5:30. . . . The thing is we just received a report from the FBI regarding instructions to state police down there and they have been told these marshals are coming and told that you want to preserve law and order and there is not to be any disorder, and that once this fellow gets into the University it is the responsibility of the marshals to preserve law and order. I didn't want a misunderstanding—

BARNETT: After he gets in you certainly don't expect us to guard him all the time. . . . I declare I don't think I could agree to guarantee the man after he gets in. When he gets in he is one boy—. . . . General, wait a minute here. The lieutenant governor has an idea here.

JOHNSON: General, our local officers are here on the campus and in the county and in the city. They are the ones who would be responsible here. . . .

KENNEDY: We had over a period of the last four or five days in conversations with the governor, he always assured me law and order will be preserved. Can I have the same assurance?

JOHNSON: We do that everywhere in our state.

In a conversation at 1:50 P.M. Barnett attempted to convince Kennedy that his contempt trial should be postponed, but the Attorney General argued that he would look good at the trial if Meredith was enrolled by then. After Barnett explained to Kennedy the problem of outside law enforcement officers and others who had come to Oxford and over whom he had little control, he said he could talk with two or three people he was "worried about." The governor said he would talk to these "people" to get the situation under control and would call back in "thirty or forty minutes." The next discussion was at 2:20 P.M.

BARNETT: General, we will be here at 5 o'clock and I hope they get here by that time. We are going to put forth every effort and I don't think there will be any violence whatever.

KENNEDY: Do you think we should take the chance? I don't think we should take the chance if there is any question about it.

BARNETT: I don't think there is any question about it. There were a couple of fellows I was worried about. We know them so well and we will get them straightened out. . . . Our people are going to be law abiding.

The final conversation was at 4:35 P.M.

BARNETT: General, I'm worried—I'm nervous, I tell you. You don't realize what is going on. There are several thousand people in here in cars, trucks. Several hundred are lined up on the streets where they are supposed to land. We don't know these people.

KENNEDY: I had better send them back.

BARNETT: There is liable to be a hundred people killed here. It would ruin all of us. Please believe me. Talk to the lieutenant governor, he'll tell you.

KENNEDY: I just have to hear from you, governor.

BARNETT: There are dozens and dozens of trucks loaded with people. We can't control people like that. A lot of people are going to get killed. It would be embarrassing to me.

KENNEDY: I don't know if it would be embarrassing—that would not be the feeling.

BARNETT: It would be bad all over the nation.

KENNEDY: I'll send them back.

Robert Kennedy's repeated demands for assurances that Meredith would be protected resulted partly from the fact that Barnett had planned to go back on an agreement for safe passage made the day before. When Mississippi Attorney General Patterson learned of the plan to have Meredith arrested, he notified Burke Marshall. This accounted for Kennedy's conversations with attorney Tom Watkins, a conservative but honorable segregationist who wanted to avoid damage to the University and to Mississippi.[40] The question was always whether Barnett would accept the advice of men like Watkins or of the radical wing of the Citizens' Council. By not siding firmly with those interested in legality, the governor gave most of his support to those who promoted violence.

On the University campus the numbers of highway patrolmen and crowds of students and outsiders increased as afternoon approached. At about noon Dean of Women Katharine Rea suggested to Associated Student Body President Dick Wilson that it might be a good idea to get the women students back to their residence halls. He replied, "No, this is not what we want. We would rather have them here." Apparently he feared that such a move would upset what was not yet a dangerous situation. The fact was that the chancellor had asked students not to assemble in large groups, and they were not complying. But until the middle of the afternoon most of those watching the situation, including myself, believed that Meredith would enter after a token confrontation between state and federal forces.

The crowd grew larger and more boisterous after Barnett arrived, although the lieutenant governor had cruised around the area in a loudspeaker-equipped car requesting students and outsiders to leave the scene, and explaining, "This is for your own safety. We want you out of the line of fire." He also said, in less polite phrases, "If you want this nigger to get in, just stay here." By late afternoon the crowd had grown to a size variously estimated at 1,500 to 5,000, but the lower figure was nearer the mark. There were large numbers of adults, probably half the total, and the mob —for it could now be called that—reached a pitch that could not be controlled. There were shouts of "We want Ross" and the "Hotty Toddy," but full wrath did not develop because Meredith and his federal escorts were not there.[41] A former *Mississippian* editor wrote: "After a couple of wars and a revolution, you learn how to smell death and danger. And that smell was in the air between 5 and 5:55 P.M. yesterday on the street corner. The trouble was that too few people realized it—too few people could recognize the smell." Stan Dearman quoted numerous students who were worried about their academic future, yet most of them supported

Barnett. He also quoted Sterling Slappey of *U.S. News and World Report:* "I swear that at one minute it was a bunch of happy, good-natured school kids—but the next minute it was a mob. Even in Moscow, I never saw it happen so fast. But if you say that, you're not telling the whole story."[42] He meant that no more than a third of the students were there and that other forces had produced the situation.

By about 6 P.M. it was clear that Meredith would not come; he and his escorts turned back near Batesville, twenty-three miles west of Ole Miss. The decision had been made in the last Kennedy-Barnett phone conversation—4:35 P.M. It was clear that Barnett had not been willing or able, in the situation which he and his advisers had produced, to maintain order and carry out his agreement. That night I wrote another letter to the Department of Justice and among other things stated, "We have watched the tragedy of a University being destroyed by total disregard of the importance of education in a democratic system. We would like to see a real attempt made to uphold the principles of law against those who violate them." The University deadline for late registration had been September 24, and Meredith had already missed a week of classes.

In Dallas former General Edwin A. Walker said that if federal troops moved into Mississippi, "I will be there." He called for "10,000 strong, from every state in the union" to "rally to the cause of freedom." Pointing out that at Little Rock in 1958 he was on the "wrong side," he declared, "This time I am on the right side and I will be there."[43] In Washington two senators and four congressmen from Mississippi telegraphed President Kennedy: A HOLOCAUST IS IN THE MAKING. YOU ARE THE ONLY PERSON WHO CAN STOP IT. Congressman Frank Smith did not join them, because he knew that the President must enforce the law and that the only one who could stop the "holocaust" was Ross Barnett. It was announced that the President was conferring with military advisers on plans for the use of troops.

In New Orleans on September 28 the Department of Justice and Meredith's attorneys asked the Court of Appeals to convict Governor Barnett of contempt.[44] Chief Judge Tuttle emphasized that the burden of enforcing the court orders was now on the executive branch and suggested that there should be no more delay. Burke Marshall explained that the federal executive had acted to give state and University officials "every opportunity . . . to meet their responsibilities," but that "there is no question but that the executive branch of the government will use whatever force, physical force, is required, if that is required to enforce the order of the Court." On the problem of continued defiance by Governor Barnett, Marshall declared, "The Court order will be enforced whether he purges himself or not." The Court of Appeals found Barnett guilty of civil contempt, gave him until 11 A.M. Tuesday to purge himself, and levied a fine of $10,000 daily until he complied. Marshall pointed out that the United Mine Workers had once been fined $2,800,000 for civil contempt, and that Barnett's fine was mild in comparison. The Court specifically ordered the governor to cease resistance to the court orders and "to maintain law and order at and around the University and to cooperate with the officers and agents of this Court and of the United States in the execution of the orders . . ." Lieutenant Governor Johnson was convicted the next day, and the Court imposed a daily fine of $5,000.

The Ole Miss chapter of the American Association of University Professors met at 5 P.M. for an hour and a half on September 28. James Silver and a few others were in favor of issuing a public statement similar to that of the Oxford ministers, but a large majority were inclined to be cautious. The result was the appointment of a committee to prepare a statement and a decision to meet again on Monday, October 1. I was asked to invite the chancellor to attend the Monday meeting in order to explain the situation and answer questions. He told me on Saturday morning that it would not be proper for him to attend such a meeting of the A.A.U.P. —I never understood why—and we ended up with an agreement to call a general faculty meeting on Monday where he would answer questions. The events of Sunday were to change both the time and nature of that meeting. Although the A.A.U.P. was later accused by the Citizens' Council of being radical, the fact is that it was excessively conservative during the week before September 30.

The executive council of the Southern Association of Colleges and Schools announced on the 28th that it would consider the accreditation of all public colleges in Mississippi at its November meeting. The council said it had "reached the conclusion that the integrity of the institutions of higher learning in Mississippi is threatened" and that both the Board of Trustees and the governor had violated the standards of the Association.[45] Related to this was a telephone call from Hugh Clegg, University Director of Development and former FBI official, to Congressman Frank Smith. He asked Smith to "pass along to the President and the Attorney General the threat that Ole Miss would have the Southern Association of Colleges and Schools on them for citing the University officials in a motion of contempt."[46]

There was a belated private effort on the part of business leaders and Ole Miss alumni to put pressure on Barnett against the possible closing of the University. Some of these leaders made the obvious point that closing Ole Miss would mean undoing the work of many Mississippians over the past century to build a good university. Although most of these men were segregationists, they knew that such a step would mean depriving five thousand white students of an education in order to keep out one Negro. Few of these leaders were willing to say anything publicly before September 30, but it is clear that their private pressure did influence Barnett's decision not to close the University.

As the Jackson daily press continued its emotional reporting, Ole Miss students went to Jackson on Saturday for a football game with the University of Kentucky. To a halftime crowd which looked like a sea of confederate flags, Governor Barnett spoke words not calculated to promote law and order: "I love Mississippi! I love her people—her customs! And I love and respect her heritage!" The response was reminiscent of Nazi rallies thirty years earlier. The crowd also joined in a song which violated the court orders in spirit if not in law, "Never, No, Never":

> Never, Never, Never, Never, No-o-o Never Never Never,
> We will not yield an inch of any field,
> Fix us another toddy, ain't yieldin' to nobody,
> Ross's standin' like Gibraltar, he shall never falter,
> Ask us what we say, it's to hell with Bobby K,
> Never shall our emblem go from Colonel Reb to Old Black Joe.

A few people left the game early in disgust at the display of mass hysteria and anarchy. Most stayed and cheered for riot.

By the time the students returned to the University on Sunday, September 30, most of the blueprint had been drawn. Its architects were those whose roles have been described; some contributed by action, others by inaction. They included Ross Barnett and his forces of resistance, the Citizens' Council, the political leaders, the dominant press, and some from fields of education and religion. They also included those in Mississippi who had been unenthusiastically pulled along in the tide. They included the forces of the U.S. government, which had been slow to move effectively partly because of Mississippi perfidy and partly because the system works slowly. They included James Meredith, who said his mistake was in waiting until he was twenty-eight years old to apply for admission to Ole Miss. They included the University, which not only made mistakes but also was not immune to massive political pressure. Finally, these architects of disaster included faculty members like myself, who waited too long and then did too little. The diverse Americans who drew the plan knew little of its consequences, but they drew it well.

"Violence No Answer" was the headline of an editorial in the *Memphis Commercial Appeal* on September 28: "Playing politics and waving the Bonnie Blue Flag are not answers. The answers may be unpalatable. But not so bitter as hatred and violence. Finally, it is the young students—those now in the university and those who may attend in years to come—who must be considered. Mississippi needs their talents and services. It should not drive them away." The students were the last ingredient in the blueprint, and their educational interests should have been uppermost. Yet they were led into tragedy by their elders, and the greatest tragedy is that many of them welcomed their own educational destruction.

5 A NIGHT OF VIOLENCE

Until Sunday morning, September 30, Attorney General Kennedy and Governor Barnett had agreed that James Meredith would be brought to the University on Monday morning. All of the available information makes it clear that the decision to bring him on Sunday instead resulted from the governor's argument that this would be less dangerous. In a speech televised nationally on Monday Barnett confirmed that on Sunday he had advised, "It would be better to place him on the campus by helicopter Sunday than to force him in with widespread bloodshed Monday." The governor justified this stand by arguing, "I realized that Oxford would be crowded on Monday and that hundreds of people would probably be killed." Yet Barnett also claimed that the decision to put Meredith on the campus on Sunday "was that of the federal government," that he had urged "a cooling off period"—presumably one long enough to prevent Meredith's enrollment for the fall semester.[1] This was hardly convincing for a man who had led a lengthy "heating up period" and had been convicted of civil contempt; he was to be arrested and fined if he did not discontinue his contempt by Tuesday. Even as he was negotiating an irresponsible surrender, the governor could not see that the whole strategy of delay was at an end.

Neither Governor Barnett nor the federal government has yet released an authoritative description of the hectic negotiations which concluded with a shaky agreement to bring Meredith to the University. (A *Look* magazine article has been described as "accurate" by the Department of Justice.[2]) As on earlier days, there were no established lines of communication between the participants. At any given time there might be telephone calls between Attorney General Kennedy and Barnett, but both resorted to phoning others who acted as formal or informal advisers. There was no clear channel of communication between the University and either federal or state officials. Anyone who saw a possibility of affecting the outcome was likely to telephone or telegraph anyone else with power or influence. The conflicting pressures on the main participants complicated the negotiations between them. Throughout these negotiations the governor emphasized three points: first, there would have to be a "show of force" so that he could say he was "overwhelmed"; second, he was not sure he could control his own supporters and even some law enforcement officers; and third, he was reluctant to promise maintenance of law and order. The President and the Attorney General insisted repeatedly that Barnett commit himself to the maintenance of order, although they were willing to take him "off the hook" with a show of force. On Saturday the President sent a telegram in which he demanded by that evening an answer on that point, and shortly before 10 P.M. (midnight, Washington time) the governor telephoned that he could *not* make the commitment. An Associated Press story from Washington reported, "Barnett repeatedly told Kennedy that he 'could not and would not' assume responsibility for preserving law and order at the University town of Oxford. This source said Barnett informed Kennedy the situation was beyond his control."[3] Barnett's refusal demonstrated the failure of ten days of attempts to secure Meredith's enrollment by the use of marshals, and the answer to the governor's decision took the form of preparations to use military forces. Soon after midnight Saturday the President issued a proclamation stating that the governor had not given "adequate assurances that the orders of the courts of the United States will be obeyed and that law and order will be maintained," and which went on to command all persons engaged in "obstructions of justice to cease and desist therefrom and to disperse and retire peaceably forthwith." The President implemented this with an executive order which federalized the Mississippi National Guard and directed the Secretary of Defense to take "all appropriate

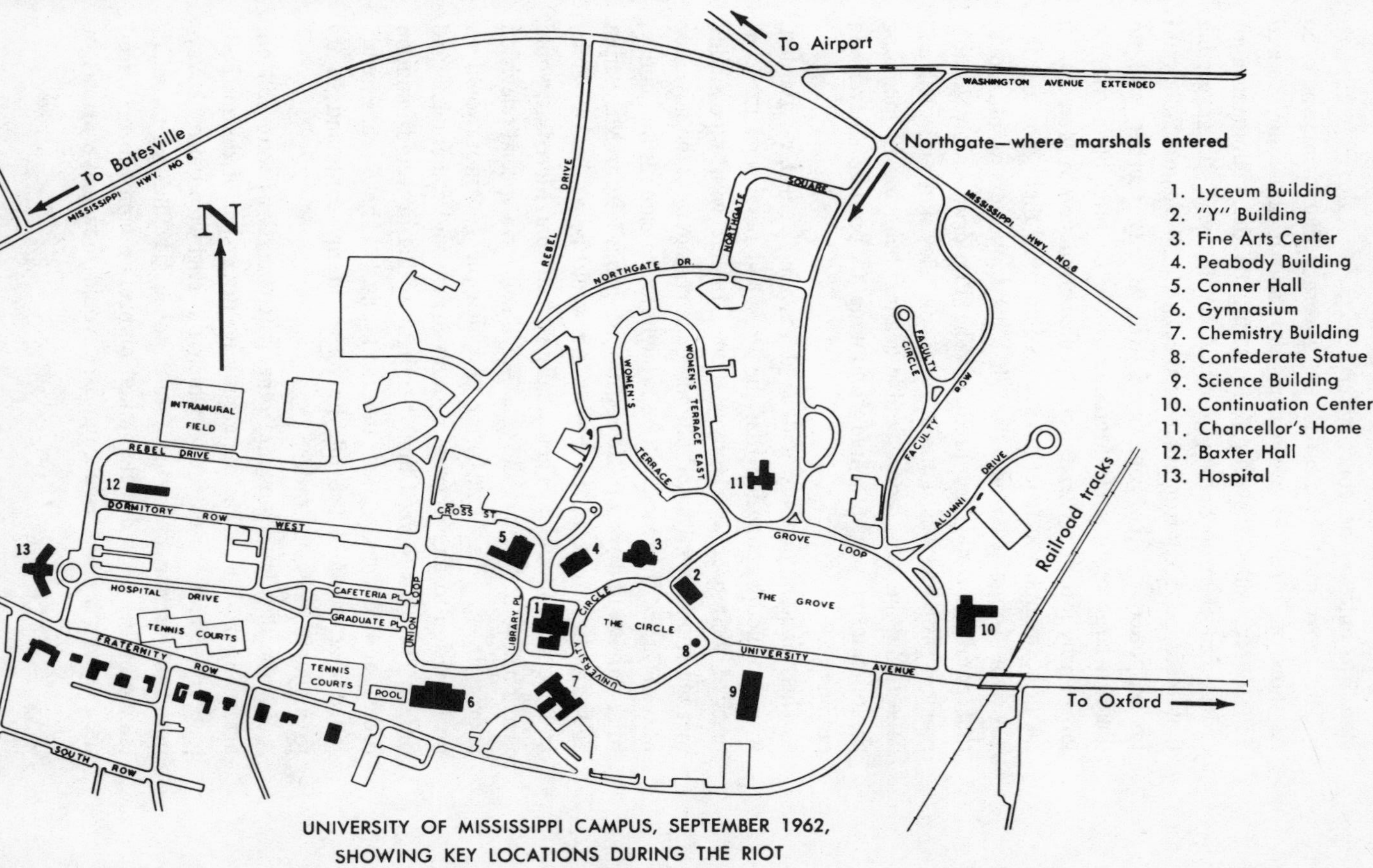

UNIVERSITY OF MISSISSIPPI CAMPUS, SEPTEMBER 1962,
SHOWING KEY LOCATIONS DURING THE RIOT

steps" to enforce the court orders.

This move made it clear to the governor that there would be "a show of force" to overwhelm him, and it apparently caused him to reconsider his refusal to guarantee the maintenance of order. But even on Sunday morning Barnett was still suggesting that there be a confrontation at the University gate. He would be supported by the Highway Patrol, county sheriffs, and no doubt a large mob, while Meredith would be brought in with "a large Army force." After Barnett denied admission to Meredith on his fifth attempt, the federal forces would draw their guns and the governor would "step aside." What his supporters would do at that point he could not predict. The President's reply to this reckless proposal was a threat to go on television and "tell all" concerning the governor's double-dealing behavior of planning capitulation in private while continuing to promise "never" in public.[4]

This threat apparently had a "devastating" effect on Barnett, who repeatedly requested that the President not reveal the contents of their telephone conversations. In line with a possibility that the two Kennedys had already been considering, the governor next suggested that Meredith be brought to the campus on Sunday, since large numbers of "segregationist gangs" from Mississippi and elsewhere were on their way and would be at the University in force on Monday.[5] They finally agreed that Meredith would arrive before 5:30 P.M., the time scheduled for a special television address by the President, prior to which the governor would go on television to announce Meredith's arrival and call for law and order. They also agreed that the Highway Patrol would maintain order, and Barnett stated the next day, "I have consistently stated that I would use all the forces at my command to try to maintain law and order."[6]

But the details on this and other vital questions were still not agreed upon. There was apparently no discussion of the methods to be used and the extent to which the Highway Patrol, always mistakenly reported as the "state police," would go in maintaining order. Would their limited numbers attempt to or indeed be able to "seal off" the campus? Would they make arrests or otherwise attempt to control the inevitable mob in order to prevent violence? Would they make it clear that they were on the campus on this day of Mississippi's capitulation to assist the federal government and to insure Meredith's enrollment, rather than to resist as they had done before? The replies to these and other questions came later, but it is clear that the "agreement" made on Sunday morning did not include the answers.

Another unanswered question was whether Barnett, who still controlled the University—practically if not legally—would immediately notify University officials to make plans to handle Meredith's arrival *on Sunday* instead of on Monday as originally planned. Although the decision to bring Meredith on Sunday apparently was made at least by 11 A.M., no one seemed to think of notifying the University until several hours later. Yet another unanswered question was whether the governor would make his new position clear, even if only secretly, to his Citizens' Council advisers, and more importantly still to the four state officials—and Council members—whom he had appointed for the explicit purpose of exercising his authority on the University campus.

One answer to the deficiencies in this pact is that federal officials knew they could get only a "gentleman's agreement" from Barnett, and they were well aware that his end of the bargain was at best an unknown and at worst a minus factor. Yet, as several Department of Justice officials explained, the nature of the federal system required that a commitment from a state governor—even Barnett—must be accepted and acted upon until events demonstrated it to be worthless. They also pointed out that the Highway Patrol had maintained order on previous days, although the disturbing facts were that it had lost control on September 27 and that its "maintenance of law and order" thus far had been *to keep Meredith from registering*.[7] The other and related answer to the problem of maintaining order is that federal officials had already set in motion the arrangements for military forces large enough to handle a substantial insurrection. Their see-saw negotiations with the governor had produced the maximum agreement possible, and the federal deadline for moving from negotiation to action had arrived. They feared that the governor would fail to follow through on this plan as on several previous ones, but they had to move.

The Department of Justice had announced at about 9 P.M. Saturday that any necessary portion of the more than eleven thousand members of the Mississippi National Guard would be used to "keep the peace" in Mississippi, while regular federal troops, consisting of about a thousand infantrymen and five hundred military police, would be in reserve at Memphis.[8] More than one hundred Army engineers from Fort Campbell, Kentucky, moved in to set up a "tent city" and handle housekeeping arrangements for about seven hundred federal marshals in a camp at Holly Springs National Forest, north of Oxford.[9] Deputy marshals, Border Patrolmen, and prison guards were ordered to Memphis from San Francisco, Fort Leavenworth, Chicago, Denver, St. Louis, and federal installations in several other localities. A contingent of twenty-six prison guards was called back from vacation Saturday afternoon and traveled by bus from Fort Leavenworth.[10]

Under the agreement with Governor Barnett, the Highway Patrol would guarantee the safe entry of the marshals and Meredith onto the campus and would cooperate with the marshals in maintaining order. The element of surprise—and of danger—was an important part of the plan: that Meredith would already be on the campus before the proponents of resistance learned the fact from the television appearances of Governor Barnett and President Kennedy. If the federal officials had known how limited would be Barnett's arrangements and instructions for maintaining law and order, they might well have sent a military force ahead of the marshals and Meredith.

On Tuesday, September 25, the governor had issued a directive to county sheriffs called to the University and to three state officials, Lieutenant Governor Johnson, Highway Patrol Director T. B. Birdsong, and Hinds County Judge Russell Moore, the last presumably selected because he was a close associate of the governor and an activist in the Citizens' Council. The purpose of the directive was "to secure the people of the state and to prevent violence and a breach of the peace and to assure that the peace

KENNEDY
is a Rat Fink!

MADE IN
OCCUPIED
MISSISSIPPI

HELP ROSS
KEEP
MISSISSIPPI
SOVEREIGN

THE CASTRO
BROTHERS
'Have Moved into the White House'

YANKEE GO HOME

A representative sampling of bumper stickers which appeared on cars in Mississippi during the integration crisis.

On September 26, 1962, at Ole Miss, Lieutenant Governor Paul Johnson confronts Chief U.S. Marshal James P. McShane, Department of Justice attorney John Doar (background), and James H. Meredith—and rejects Meredith on his third attempt to register at the University. *(Flip Schulke, Black Star)*

A determined James McShane arrives at the Oxford-University airport to lead U.S. marshals onto the Ole Miss campus, Sunday, September 30, 1962. *(Fred Ward, Black Star)*

At 4 P.M., on September 30, the first truckloads of marshals pass faculty apartments after entering the University campus. *(UPI)*

At 5:10 P.M., Chancellor J. D. Williams (in suit at left) talks with students in the crowd in front of the Lyceum Building. *(Flip Schulke, Black Star)*

By 5:40 P.M., marshals have surrounded the Lyceum Building and at this time Mississippi highway patrolmen are holding the crowd back. *(Flip Schulke, Black Star)*

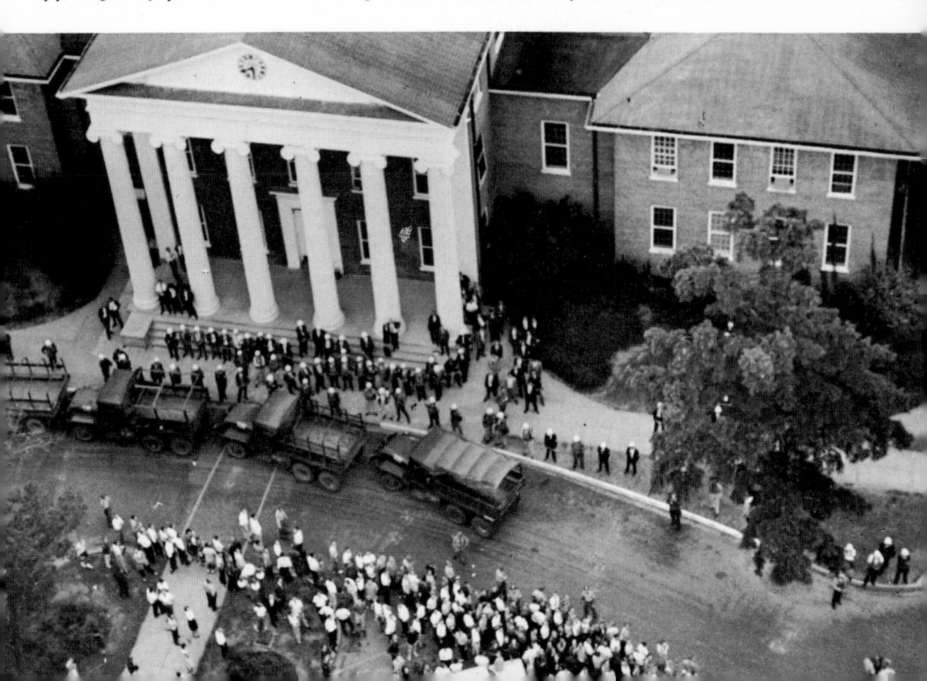

A youth shouting at the marshals is ignored by Mississippi highway patrolmen. *(UPI)*

The mob attacks the car of photographer Gordon Yoder as highway patrolmen help Yoder and his wife (far right) out of danger. *(U.S. News & World Report)*

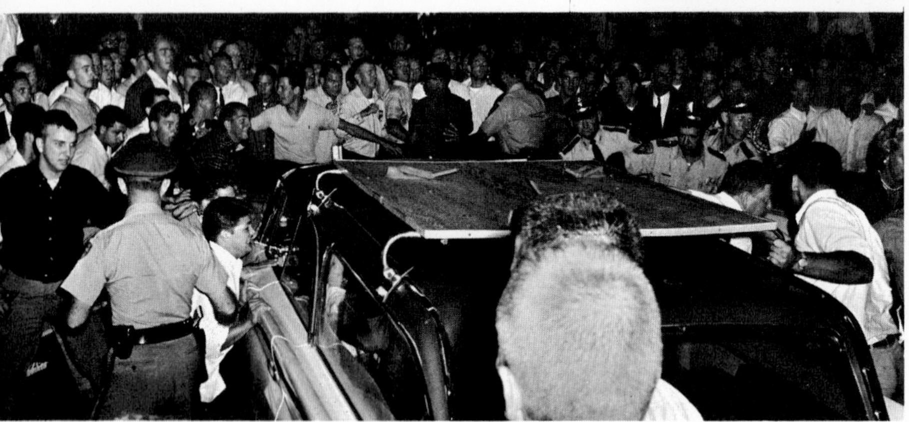

As President Kennedy issues a television plea for compliance with the law, U.S. marshals unleash the first barrage of tear gas and await the reaction of the rioters. *(Flip Schulke, Black Star)*

Troops begin clearing the rubble from the gas-laden riot area on October 1, the morning after. *(U.S. News & World Report)*

Faculty members' cars, burned by the rioters, block a campus road the morning after the riot. *(UPI)*

McShane (left) and Doar escort James Meredith to his first class after his registration on October 1. *(Fred Ward, Black Star)*

Soldiers take prisoners into custody after the spread of rioting to downtown Oxford on the morning of October 1. *(Flip Schulke, Black Star)*

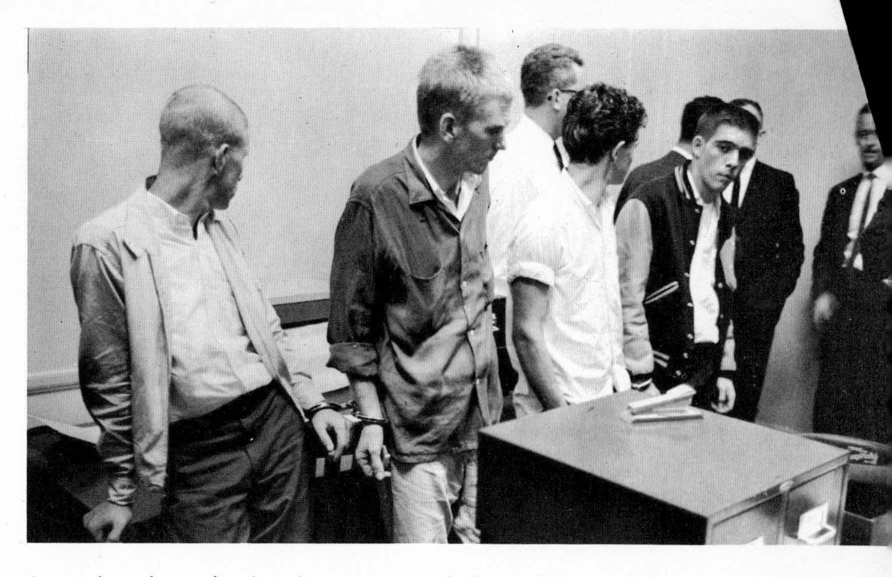

Arrested youths are lined up for appearance before a U.S. commissioner on October 1. *(Fred Ward, Black Star)*

With Confederate flags in the background, Governor Ross Barnett cheers at the Ole Miss homecoming game on October 7. *(UPI)*

James H. Meredith marches in the commencement procession on August 18, 1963, the first Negro to win a degree at the University of Mississippi. *(Russell H. Barrett)*

and security of the state are fully protected." The directive provided specifically for "the protection of all citizens of the state and all others who may be within the confines of the state." It concluded, "You are authorized to cooperate and work with all other duly constituted officials of the state and to do all things necessary in the premises."[11]

On Saturday, September 29, the governor issued to George M. Yarbrough, president pro tem of the State Senate, a similar order except for omission of the last sentence. Senator Yarbrough was designated to head the governor's representatives for Sunday, who included Judge Moore, State Senator John C. McLaurin, and State Representative C. B. (Buddie) Newman. The choice of such men to supervise the protection of the federal forces about to integrate the University could only have been matched by the selection of a team of Holy Crusaders to propagate the Islamic faith. Although these four were to represent the governor in carrying out his agreement with federal officials, and although he must surely have conferred with them before they left Jackson on Sunday, there is not the slightest indication that he told them of the agreement not only to accept integration but to provide protection for the integrationists. The governor certainly did not give them specific instructions on how far they were to go and what methods they were to use in maintaining law and order.

The pattern of behavior in Mississippi required that those who challenged the traditions of the state be harassed or arrested, and that above all they be denied the protection of law. Despite the Kennedy-Barnett agreement, it would have taken completely clear and explicit instructions to the governor's representatives for them to follow the reverse of the pattern. Yet they were to be responsible for giving orders to the Highway Patrol in fulfillment of Barnett's promise to maintain law and order. That they did not receive the necessary instructions is apparent from their actions.

Senator McLaurin was quoted as saying, "We were going up there to get the defenses prepared" for Meredith's arrival on Monday, presumably to resist his entry as had been done before. Senator Yarbrough sent word for the Highway Patrol to come to

Oxford, and Judge Moore is reported to have called seventy county sheriffs to come to Oxford with deputies by 10:30 Sunday night. Three high-pressure pumper fire trucks were to be ready to move on short notice. It was significant and potentially ominous that the sheriffs had been called, because the governor had stated on several occasions that he could not control them. In any case, these four representatives of the governor agreed to meet at the University at 6:30 P.M. on Sunday, apparently unaware that the main goal of getting Meredith onto the campus was to be accomplished before that time.

Colonel Birdsong of the Highway Patrol, supposedly under the control of Senator Yarbrough and his three colleagues, obviously had received entirely different instructions sometime on Sunday from Governor Barnett. There had been some hint of this possibility in the Sunday edition of the *Memphis Commercial Appeal*. Staff writer William B. Street wrote, in an article that was prophetic on several points, "There are shades of disagreement between some of Governor Barnett's planners and certain high officers of the Highway Patrol. Differences are said to center mainly on whether disposition of patrolmen is to be handled by the Patrol's regular officers or by the governor's personal advisers." Colonel Birdsong apparently believed that he would have control over the Patrol and that it would be effective. He told a federal official there would be "no need for federal aid in maintaining law and order around the campus."[12]

Early on Sunday afternoon highway patrolmen began manning the entrances to the University campus and refusing entrance to those who did not have identification showing they were entitled to be on the campus. There were not enough patrolmen to "seal off" the unfenced and wooded campus, and there was no serious attempt to prevent entry at points other than regular entrances. Some "unauthorized" newsmen and others were escorted off the campus during the afternoon, but it later became clear that there were too few patrolmen and insufficient determination to keep the campus clear of outsiders. Apparently the patrolmen had no orders to make arrests or to use any enforcement measures stronger than telling people what they could and could not do.

But it is also clear that Colonel Birdsong had been instructed by the governor to cooperate with federal officials and to maintain order, even though Senator Yarbrough still had contrary instructions on the mission of the Highway Patrol when he arrived on the campus about 6:30 P.M. on Sunday. There is no way to escape the conclusion that this confusion had been created intentionally by the governor as part of his attempt to surrender while feigning resistance. Apparently he did not want Senator Yarbrough and his Citizens' Council colleagues to know of his instructions to Colonel Birdsong until Meredith was already on the campus. It was risky deception, and obviously Barnett had not explained to federal officials this part of "his plan."

Although the University was a key factor in the situation, neither Governor Barnett nor federal officials had consulted with University officials in negotiating the "agreement" for Meredith's arrival. These officials later blamed the Department of Justice for the decision to bring him on Sunday and for failure to give adequate notice of the change in plans, but the main responsibility for both alleged shortcomings rested with the governor. Apparently the main disputants were so preoccupied with the problem of reaching some kind of agreement that they regarded the University's role as inconsequential. Ole Miss officials had encouraged this situation by meekly awaiting the outcome of federal-state negotiations. As Chancellor Williams explained later in a speech before the Commonwealth Club of California, he looked upon the University as "a sparrow caught in a badminton game." It would have been better for the University to act like an eagle, but that would have meant a total and considerably difficult change in attitude. Certainly there should have been much more communication between the University and the two main participants, and the University should have anticipated a confrontation on Sunday, but effective communication was a major problem in the whole operation and Governor Barnett avoided it as much as possible. It is unbelievable but apparently true that no one informed the University of Meredith's impending arrival until just before 4 P.M. on Sunday.

The University did have a plan, but neither University officials nor anyone else in authority had bothered to coordinate it with federal or state plans as they developed. The weakness of the Ole Miss plan was that it assumed outsiders would be kept off the campus by someone, most likely the Highway Patrol, and that the University would have to control only its own students. Yet a high University official told me that he had calculated the number of officers necessary to surround and really seal off the campus, and it came to 1,500, at least five times more than the entire strength of the Highway Patrol. The University plan provided for placing Chief Burns Tatum's force of University policemen, which had been augmented by police from surrounding cities, in "strategic places" on the campus when Meredith arrived. A special issue of the *Mississippian,* the student newspaper, would be in every student's room on Monday morning, and it would contain "statements from the chancellor and a number of other prominent and influential persons intended to give a sense of direction to students and to instruct them in the conduct that was expected when Meredith arrived."[13] Tape recorded messages from the chancellor and the dean of students were to be broadcast over the campus radio station. As during the preceding two weeks, student leaders were instructed to help keep other students under control. Apart from its failure to provide for control of outsiders, this was a minimum plan even for controlling the students. In the face of the steadily increasing buildup of public and student resistance under the leadership of the governor and others, and of the certain movement of large numbers of outsiders into the Oxford and University area, neither of which the University could or would do anything to control, the Ole Miss plan could have had only a limited effect. It is clear that the federal and state planners regarded the University's role as irrelevant, and the "sparrow" made no attempt to make its proposals relevant.

Operating under a "plan" which left major details undetermined, the architects of an unconsciously contrived blueprint followed its fuzzy outlines to riot and catastrophe. Who was to tell insurrectionists in Mississippi and other states that Governor Barnett had negotiated surrender with the enemy? Who, and on what public address system, was to tell students and outsiders at the University that they should accept the enrollment of James Meredith with no further protest? Who was to control them by arrest and other means when they moved from peaceful protest to riot? Who was even to determine the answers to these and other inescapable questions? No one knew who would answer, any more than they knew what the answers would be. They came with the events of Sunday, September 30, 1962.

The day in Oxford began calmly enough. About half the students had gone to Jackson for the football game on Saturday and were not yet back. I drove from Oxford to the University and spent most of the morning writing up the minutes of the local meeting of the American Association of University Professors which had been held on Friday. On my way home at about noon, Paul Hahn, Assistant Professor of Anthropology, stopped me in front of his apartment at the east end of the campus to express his concern over what might happen. He knew of the large number of outside toughs who were already in Oxford and in some cases already on the campus, and he was worried that the Department of Justice might try to bring Meredith to the campus on Sunday. Agreeing that it would be a mistake to try on Sunday, I said I didn't think they would but added that the people handling the situation were out of my league, and there was nothing I could do to influence developments. We talked about the value of a telephone call, and I finally gave him the number of the Department of Justice and Burke Marshall's extension. He later attempted to telephone his warning against the Sunday plan, but the lines were so busy that he could not get through. Obviously the warning would have had no effect, but it is worth noting that someone made the attempt.

After driving home by way of the Oxford square following more work on the campus early in the afternoon, I remarked to my wife, "There sure are a lot of bums in town." Music professor Parks Grant, who lives on east University Avenue, reported, "Commencing around 2:30 that afternoon there was a constant procession of cars toward the campus. I would say that westbound cars outnumbered eastbound by about six to one. What struck me as peculiar was that many of these cars bore out-of-state license tags and many contained nothing but men—four or five men. Now, a car containing nothing but men is a most unusual sight, especially on a Sunday afternoon."[14] The governor had warned that Oxford would be crowded on Monday; it was already crowded on Sunday.

At morning services Oxford ministers repeated the call for Christian behavior which they had made the preceding Sunday. With but one exception these ministers had spoken strongly before September 30, although news reports in Mississippi and elsewhere gave almost no coverage to their statements. Many students and others were absent from church because they had not returned from the Saturday night football game in Jackson, so they did not hear the call of their religious leaders. Of more importance is the likelihood that most of those who were to riot later in the day either do not go to church anyway or would not have been convinced of any connection between their religion and acceptance of Meredith's enrollment at the University. Still more important is that the inability of church leaders to produce a sane response in Oxford was a much more pronounced deficiency in other parts of the state. If most churches throughout the state had spoken out for application of their religious principles, they might well have had a decisive influence on the public conscience. Instead the Oxford ministers were a small collection of voices who, with one exception, pleaded courageously but vainly against the majority attitude of resistance.

Where were the newsmen, who later bemoaned the absence of moderate voices, when Rector Duncan M. Gray, Jr., delivered a powerful sermon in St. Peter's Episcopal Church on Sunday, September 30? In this church, which many Americans had seen in the filmed version of "Intruder in the Dust," this soft-spoken man asked, "Are we really sufficiently aware of the *deadly serious* nature of our present predicament?" The strength of his answer is weakened by partial quotation, but the following is illustrative:

> We do *not* have the right to defy and disobey the law when it is established and in force. In trying to do this, we have brought upon ourselves the threat of *anarchy;* and, as Christians, we

cannot and *must* not support this alternative to the democracy under which we live. . . .

We do not want troops in our state, and we can be thankful that the federal government has been as patient as it has in not taking this step so far. However, we may well see troops here in the next few days. But when this happens we will have only ourselves to blame. Ultimately, the federal government cannot be asked to withhold such measures if we refuse to give in, any more than a policeman cannot be told to avoid the use of force when a lawbreaker resists arrest and continues to break the law. . . .

Our governor has said that the state's cause on this score is righteous and just; and I'm sure he is sincere in his belief, as are many other Mississippians who share it with him. But in the name of reason and in the name of Christian standards of freedom and justice, I ask you to consider the fact that *no university in the world would defend this position rationally, and no Christion Church in the world would defend it morally*. . . .

Surely, most of us realize by now that there can be only one resolution to this crisis: the admission of James Meredith to the University. Our leaders have tried to make us think it could be otherwise, and they have succeeded in convincing many people that this is possible. This is especially tragic, because it will make our adjustment to the new situation all the more difficult. But we, as Christians, should now accept this fact, if we have not already done so. Not only is this the only practical and reasonable solution, but it is also the only answer that is just and right. It is our business now to get to work at once to do all that we can to make the adjustment to this new situation as peaceful and orderly as possible on our campus and in our community. . . .

For these are times which not only *try* men's souls, but also *infect* and *poison* them. The seeds of anger and hatred, bitterness and prejudice, are already widely sown, and, as Christians, we need to do our utmost to uproot them and cast them out. You and I have heavy responsibility in the days and weeks to come. . . .[15]

Reverend Gray's call for proper behavior was effective among his own church members, but it went unreported and unheeded among those who most needed to hear it. The same was true of the somewhat less challenging sermons by most other Oxford ministers, including one in which Presbyterian minister Murphey C. Wilds criticized the concept of Mississippi sovereignty emblazoned on automobile bumper stickers and argued that "God is sovereign." There were not enough of these messages throughout the state, and there were not enough people prepared to comply with them to avoid tragedy.

The train of events which began Sunday afternoon was no simple confrontation between unified and well-organized forces of resistance and their equivalents on the side of law. The story is not a tidy chronology; it must include many elements of confusion and contradiction. There were attempts at organization on both sides, but these were repeatedly challenged by the tendencies of many groups and individuals to act independently. I tell the story as I saw it, sometimes as a sequence of events and sometimes as a sudden reality of factors which developed.

At 2:30 P.M. Edwin O. Guthman, in charge of public information for the Department of Justice, met on the campus with Colonel Birdsong. They agreed that the marshals would come to the Lyceum Building. This was hardly a surprising decision, since it was the administration building and the assumption was that James Meredith would register Sunday afternoon. The campus was quiet, and at this point neither saw any signs of impending difficulty.

Soon after 3 P.M. Sunday transport planes left the Memphis Naval Air Station with the first group of marshals, and they began landing at the Oxford-University Airport at about 3:30. An Air Force Jetstar flew in with Deputy Attorney General Nicholas Katzenbach and other representatives of the Department of Justice. All boarded seven Army trucks for the two-mile drive to the University along a road that was jammed at some points with cars and onlookers. Colonel Birdsong met the convoy on the highway and served as an escort. There were some cheers but mainly jeers as they rode the crowded trucks, and "nigger lover" was the worst language directed at the marshals and truck drivers. Many newsmen and others still thought the marshals were bound for a temporary tent camp at Holly Springs National Forest. Instead they turned in at the north entrance of the University, and the highway patrolmen waved them through on the road that goes up Sorority Row.

Also at 3 P.M. Chancellor Williams met at his home with Dean of Students Love and Director of Development Hugh Clegg, whose advice the chancellor often asked on difficult problems. Their purpose was to complete the University's plans already referred to for Meredith's arrival. Although the marshals had already left Memphis, these officials still thought they were planning for events on Monday which in fact were to begin in only an hour. At a few minutes before 4 P.M. there was a call for the chancellor from Attorney General Kennedy, who delivered the news that James Meredith would arrive that afternoon. The chancellor was astounded and called Hugh Clegg to the phone in a fruitless attempt to get the plans changed. Clegg explained that nothing at the University was open, that the necessary officials could not be gotten together, and that there would be no time to put the University's plan into operation. Failing in this line of argument, he explained that this was the "Bible belt," and that it would upset the people to register Meredith and "desecrate the Sabbath." The Attorney General was not swayed any more effectively by Clegg's forceful and eloquent argument along religious lines, because the agreement with Barnett had been made and was already being put into effect. An inescapable side observation is that the governor, a Baptist Sunday school teacher, had demonstrated no misgivings at all about the religious aspect of bringing Meredith to the campus on Sunday, which would surprise no one who knows the governor. Soon after the phone conversation ended, the first truckloads of marshals drove past the chancellor's home. The University's plans, sufficient or not, had been superseded by events.

The trucks arrived in front of the Lyceum Building at about 4:15 P.M., and the marshals began to circle the building with most concentrated on the east side. According to Robert Kennedy, this deployment was at the suggestion of Colonel Birdsong.[16] Some reporters with overactive imaginations made much of the orange gas-grenade vests which some of the marshals wore, referring to them as "medieval," but many of the marshals during the early part of the evening wore business suits. Although their dress and equipment varied, it included arm bands, white helmets, gas mask pouches, sidearms, nightsticks, and short tear gas guns. Even so, they presented a strange picture to the students who were beginning to return to the campus, and to the outside "sightseers" who were already coming onto the campus by the many routes not guarded by highway patrolmen. The marshals were the visible embodiment of an unpopular court decision, and their dress had little to do with their reception.

Although most observers did not know it, most of the non-military federal personnel who came to the campus were not marshals—in fact there were no actual marshals. There were 123 deputy marshals, 316 border patrolmen, and 97 guards from federal prisons, a total of 536, and not all of them came onto the campus. Under the orders of the Attorney General, marshals and their deputies have general authority to enforce the law, including specific authority to make arrests without warrant and to exercise the same powers as a county sheriff in enforcing state laws.[17] All of the marshals and prison guards had gone through special riot training programs, and those sent to Ole Miss had been screened to eliminate those not graded "satisfactory" or better. The border patrolmen had gone through their own training program, based upon the training manual prepared by the executive office for U.S. Marshals.

The federal officers initially brought three types of gas grenades and one type of cartridge. There was no use of "sickening gas"—I was told it would have ended matters rapidly. All grenade canisters were about the size and weight of large frozen orange juice cans. The training instructions state that they should not be thrown at a low level into a crowd—common sense should tell members of any crowd to keep a safe distance away from law enforcement officers who may have to resort to gas. But the members of mobs do not read the training manuals.

Within a few minutes after the arrival of the marshals a crowd began gathering at the west end of a tree-filled area called the Circle. This crowd grew steadily throughout the evening, and estimates of its size varied with the time and the imaginative powers of the observer. One reporter stated that it reached four thousand, but a more accurate guess is that it was two hundred at the beginning and eventually grew to about two thousand. Marshal Al Butler, an hour after his arrival, estimated it at five hundred.[18] In the afternoon it was small enough so that individual jeers could be heard, and after reaching the noise level of a football rally, it declined in the late stages so that individuals could again be heard.

The timing of the crowd's remarks to the marshals is difficult to determine, except that they became more bitter and filthy as the crowd grew larger and began to change to a mob. Early remarks directed at good-natured Al Butler suggested with no attempt at consistency that his wife was "home with a nigger" and that he had a "nigger mistress" and "nigger children."[19] A faculty member reported some unprintable vituperation, but the milder epithets included "lousy nigger lover," "goon squad," and "— — son of a bitch."[20] Some witnesses referred to this as a "football" type of cheer, an interesting commentary on that aspect of American life, and there was indeed the chanting of the Ole Miss "Hotty Toddy" yell. There were several varieties of "Two, one, four, three, we hate Kennedy." More menacing were the calls, "We want Meredith. Get a rope."[21] The jeers and threats were reinforced by scores of Confederate battleflags which draped automobiles and hung from dormitories, and a variety of bumper stickers along the lines of "Help Ross Keep Mississippi Sovereign." The "rebel" aspect of the scene was heightened also by the members of the Ole Miss band, who returned from the Jackson football game in their Confederate-type uniforms which some newsmen thought they had acquired especially for the demonstration against Meredith's arrival. Most members of the crowd during the early period probably were of the "football set"—rude, boisterous, and smart alecky, but not violent. But this was no football game.

Where had the crowd come from? It is clear that at the beginning most were students, although not 95 percent as one estimate stated.[22] My estimate, based on examination of many photographs, is that at least one-third were not students. It is also clear that the proportion of students decreased steadily throughout the evening and night. Deputy Marshal Duane Caldwell said later that by 8 P.M. "youths of student age were in the minority."[23] The most objective information is that of those arrested during the riot, less than one-sixth were Ole Miss students.[24] There is no difficulty explaining how the non-students were able to get onto the campus. Although soon after 2 P.M. the Highway Patrol had set up roadblocks at the five "gates" to the campus (there are no gates) and had patrolled the campus in an attempt to eject outsiders, it was impossible for them to have cleared the campus of outsiders by the time the marshals arrived.

One newsman said that "anyone" could get on the campus, and several faculty members who live in the apartments near the main north entrance observed groups of up to thirty or forty coming through the wooded area to the west of that entrance.[25] A faculty member noted that one of these groups wandered around trying to find the way to the center of the campus, an indication it was not familiar with the terrain. Others recalled that the highway patrolmen were checking University windshield stickers on cars but not the identity of all occupants. A teenage Nationalist party supporter, who later testified in favor of Melvin Bruce, one of those arrested in the riot, said that the patrolmen at the east entrance were doing "the best they could" at about 7 P.M., but that they were only checking cars going onto the campus and were making no effort to identify those on foot.[26] When Professor William Strickland drove onto the campus at 7:30 no one checked his identity.[27] I noticed that when Professor William Crowder and I entered the campus at 8:15 P.M. the patrolmen checked our identification cards, but they were making no attempt to control those who were walking on, even though there were eight or ten patrolmen standing around and doing nothing. These and other observations indicate clearly that by 7 P.M. there were several hundred outsiders on the campus who had no good reason for being there.

Within five minutes after the arrival of the marshals, Dean Love and Hugh Clegg arrived at the Lyceum Building, and with Colonel Birdsong and Chief Tatum they conferred with several officials of the Department of Justice, including Deputy Attorney General Katzenbach, Attorney John Doar, and Chief Marshal James McShane. The University officials agreed, although not very happily, that the federal officials would take over the offices of the Dean of Students and later of the Dean of Women. A direct telephone line to the White House was provided, and it became the main channel of communication for federal, state, and University officials. Dean Love later complained with considerable justification that it was almost impossible for his staff to function, a difficulty understandable enough in view of the limited office space and the general pattern of confusion. He did manage to get five of his staff members to the scene, but they could hardly have been expected to stem the tide that was developing.

The highway patrolmen took positions more or less between the marshals and the jeering students and "others." Occasionally some members of the crowd would move across the street to direct jeers and profanity at the marshals at close quarters, and a few actually tried to engage in friendly conversation with the marshals. With varying degrees of success and with varied determination the patrolmen talked to these students and moved them back across the street. It seems clear that different patrolmen had different ideas about their role, or at least different degrees of willingness to perform their duties.

As the crowd grew in size and explosiveness Chancellor Williams circulated among groups of students, as did several other University officials and faculty members, telling them that the marshals and the Highway Patrol were working together and that any student who got out of line would incur the wrath of both groups. He warned that misbehavior would be contempt of court and subject to legal action, but he did not threaten disciplinary action by the University. He pointed out that if the students behaved properly, the University could be kept open and also keep its accreditation. Some students suggested that the chancellor should call the students together around the flagpole in the center of the Circle and speak to them as a group. But he was afraid this might concentrate the scattered groups of troublemakers and make them even more dangerous. Only a few minutes after this a highway patrolman was telling a student that the marshals had entered the campus without the knowledge or cooperation of the Highway Patrol.[28]

The picture of the situation as it came across to the students during the three hours after the arrival of the marshals was confusing and contradictory. University officials, student leaders, and faculty members were attempting to calm the students, mainly by warning them that misbehavior would damage the University, particularly by causing it to be closed or to lose its accreditation. Some students creating the most trouble replied that they couldn't care less if there was to be a "—— nigger" student.[29] Other students were desperately trying to find a way to stop the disturbances. There were no attempts by University officials, highway patrolmen, or marshals to isolate leaders of the troublemakers and to identify or arrest them. As the temper and behavior of the crowd grew worse, the disappointment and frustration of those few interested in maintaining order increased. Attempts to control the mob by persuasion could not match those factors which promoted violence.

At about 5:30 P.M. a Border Patrol plane from Memphis landed at the Oxford-University Airport with the passenger whose desire to attend the University was now provoking the last throes of resistance. With an escort which included federal officials, Highway Patrol officers, and University Police Chief Tatum, James Meredith and his guard of twenty-four marshals came into the campus through a back entrance and went to Baxter Hall. Federal officials agreed not to force his registration that night, since they had other problems and University officials were adamant about registration on Sunday. Registration at Ole Miss, as at other universities, is no simple procedure. There are many forms to be completed, fees to be paid, and academic advice to be given, all of which requires the presence of numerous officials. Meredith had said several days before that he had no physical fear, and he demonstrated none that night. He did say that he found it unreal that this gigantic operation was necessary to get him into Ole Miss, but James Meredith had become accustomed to accepting almost anything during the preceding twenty months. He made his bed, read a newspaper, and went to sleep. He was awakened but a few times by the noise of the riot—most of which was a quarter of a mile distant—and by students who threw bottles into the dormitory hallways to keep him awake.

Meanwhile, the first violence occurred at about 7 P.M. when a man in his late thirties took some stones from his pocket and threw them at a truck; he then picked up a handful of gravel from the gutter and threw it at another truck. Now the complexion of the crowd began to change. "It was no longer comprised largely of students, but of young people not dressed like our students, and of older people. Many were dressed like farmers."[30] A University staff member said there were many who were not students and quoted a newsman as saying he had entered the campus with no difficulty through the main entrance. One of the crowd called out to a patrolman, "Why don't you do something or take the guns away from the marshals?" The patrolman replied, "We can't do anything, but you can." One student, obviously drunk, was sitting on the back of a Highway Patrol car shouting the worst kind of profanity at the marshals. Two students attempted to get him to leave, but he would not. Meanwhile the patrolmen were laughing at him and encouraging him to continue his insults. One of the many students who were dismayed at the course of events asked one of the marshals to help control the students, but the marshal replied that he had orders to stay where he was. The student then complained to a University employee, "Someone in authority has got to step in. This crowd has gone crazy. They don't care about the University. These highway officers—they're not interested in this University or in keeping it open."[31]

At this same time the previously banned reporters were permitted to enter the campus. There are numerous reports that the Highway Patrol also abandoned its control of the entrances at this time, and that a few minutes later a large number of Patrol cars left the campus. Reporter Wayne King of the University of North Carolina *Tar Heel* stated that the ban on non-students entering the campus was dropped at 7 P.M. William B. Street reported, "Mississippi highway patrolmen were ordered returned to their home districts at 7 Sunday night in an order broadcast on the Patrol radio network. The order said the 'University campus has been taken over by federal forces.' "[32] Although there is confusion on the point, it is clear that many patrolmen did leave but others did not. The University entrances were left either unguarded or poorly guarded, and large numbers of outsiders were able to get onto the campus.

In the Lyceum Building Katzenbach and Birdsong were arguing about the return of the patrolmen. The Patrol director maintained that he did not have enough patrolmen to guard the campus—although his instructions were to enforce order with the state's two hundred-plus force—and he offered to send patrolmen to the "gates" if they were accompanied by marshals. Katzenbach countered that he "couldn't spare" the marshals. During the argument Birdsong reportedly stated that he had only twenty-five cars and fifty patrolmen, although there were many more in his force and there must have been more than that on the campus.[33]

Another Mississippi official now entered the picture—Senator Yarbrough, described by some as "a man of awesome presence." Governor Barnett's chief emissary had been joined at the Alumni House at about 6:30 P.M. by Judge Moore, Senator McLaurin, and Representative Newman. The last three had landed at the airport at about the same time as Meredith, and McLaurin remarked, "It's completely occupied." They telephoned Governor Barnett to report the "early invasion" by federal forces, but as McLaurin remarked later, "Apparently he knew about it already."[34] Senator Yarbrough took his group to the Lyceum and informed Katzenbach that he would have to withdraw the Highway Patrol "to avoid bloodshed." Katzenbach explained that the presence of federal marshals "in no way displaces the state authority." Despite word on the White House line from Attorney General Kennedy that the President would describe Yarbrough's action on television, he was unconvinced. President Kennedy then phoned Governor Barnett, who ordered Yarbrough to keep the patrolmen at the University. Although this was after 7:30 P.M., it was apparently the first time that Senator Yarbrough learned of the governor's "agreement" with the President.

The crowd became particularly nasty and violent from 7:30 P.M. onward. The patrolmen moved closer to the Army trucks and the mob swarmed onto the road, while the patrolmen made no attempt to restrain it. Sometime between 7:00 and 7:30

the crowd had definitely become a mob. By this time the photographers who had entered the campus at 7 P.M. were at work, and many in the mob were hardly eager to have their actions recorded for posterity. A group of about thirty-five moved in on a photographer from Dallas who was attempting to reach his wife waiting in their car. He apparently "asked for it" by asking some of the rioters, "When are you boys going to start demonstrating?" Considering the events of the last three hours, the question was hardly appropriate. The "boys" screamed at his wife (of Jackson, Mississippi), "Nigger-lovin' Yankee bitch." A girl expectantly asked her boyfriend, "Lord, Joe, what are they gonna do to that woman?" Her escort replied, "Kill her, I guess. She's a nigger lover, isn't she?"[35] Reporter Wayne King described the scene: "Yelling and cheering, they began to rock the car, smashing the windows with rocks and bottles. Some tore off chrome ornaments with their bare hands, while two Mississippi patrolmen made an obvious point of looking the other way, drawing cheers from the mob."[36] Several patrolmen finally rescued the photographer and his wife. Another photographer was shoved by the crowd and his camera smashed. A faculty member's wife asked a group of five patrolmen to help the injured man. One patrolman told her, "I don't see anything, lady," and again the patrolmen smiled at each other. Soon several patrolmen did investigate and two of them grabbed the photographer's arms while the mob continued to attack him, although the patrolmen finally tore him away.[37]

Chemistry professor William Herndon, who tried to help one of the photographers, was beaten by the mob and was saved only when the University chief of police took him into the Lyceum Building. Twice he was slugged from behind with enough force to knock his glasses to the ground, and he finally left without them. As he went into the Lyceum some of the students were still trying to attack him, and one of them said, "Give him back to us, chief, and we'll take care of his ass."[38] Inside the Lyceum Building he asked a University official, "Can't you do something to stop this?" The official, apparently in a state of bureaucratic shock, replied, "There is nothing we can do."[39] No highway patrolmen or anyone else made any attempts to arrest or even identify any of those committing violence against photographers or others.

On television at about 7:30 P.M. came an odd statement of "compliance" from Governor Barnett. The governor undermined his call to "avoid violence" with so much rhetorical advocacy of resistance that it must be quoted in full:

> As Governor of the State of Mississippi, I have just been informed by the Attorney General of the United States that Meredith has today been placed on the campus of the University of Mississippi by means of government helicopters and is accompanied by federal officers.
>
> I urge all Mississippians and instruct every state officer under my command to do everything in their power to preserve peace and to avoid violence in any form. Surrounded on all sides by the armed forces and oppressive power of the United States of America, my courage and my convictions do not waver. My heart still says, "Never," but my calm judgment abhors the bloodshed that would follow. I love Mississippi. I love her people. I love those ten thousand good Mississippians in the National Guard who have now been federalized and requested to oppose me and their own people. I know that we are completely surrounded by armed forces and that we are physically overpowered. I know that our principles remain true, but we must at all odds preserve the peace and avoid bloodshed.
>
> To the officials of the federal government, I say: Gentlemen, you are tramping on the sovereignty of this great state and depriving it of a prestige of honor and respect as a member of the Union of states. You are destroying the Constitution of this great nation. May God have mercy on your souls. Mississippi will continue to fight the Meredith case and all similar cases through the courts to restore the sovereignty of the state and constitutional government.[40]

It is doubtful whether many of the rioters on the Ole Miss campus heard this statement, but it is equally doubtful whether its equivocal language would have in any way dissuaded them from resistance and violence.

Meanwhile, an episode of almost comic opera proportions resulted from a tardy decision to acquire a public address system. The University failed in its attempt to move in a system; the Department of Justice was promised one from the Army, but it never arrived; and the state officials who were supposedly responsible for maintaining order apparently had not even thought of the problem and had none available. At various times throughout the evening and night a loudspeaker system at the Student Union Building did deliver forlorn messages from the chancellor and the dean—"You are instructed to stay in your dormitories"—but this was two hundred yards from the riot.

In the early evening members of the mob threw small objects at the marshals—gravel, eggs, pennies, and lighted cigarettes. The marshals remained passive, and the highway patrolmen made no attempt to stop what columnist George Sokolsky termed "teen-age fun."[41] Realizing that they were getting away with their "fun," and perhaps frustrated because the marshals did not react, the mob grew bolder. A marshal reported, "The rocks got bigger and they started throwing coke bottles."[42] Numerous faculty members and reporters saw members of the mob throw rocks, bricks, and bottles.[43] Occasionally there was the sound of broken glass as an Army truck windshield shattered. There were attempts to burn the canvas tops of the trucks by throwing cigarettes and lighted paper on them. Those who attempted to extinguish the smoldering fires were stoned or sprayed with other fire extinguishers. A rioter climbed onto the running board of a truck and sprayed a fire extinguisher into the face of the driver. The mob slashed the tires of the trucks, put dirt and grass into the gasoline tanks, and let the air out of tires. One student who was having difficulty in releasing the air from a truck tire talked with a highway patrolman, then tried again with more success. Another student later asked whether the patrolman had done anything to him. "Hell no," he replied, "he showed me how."[44] Reporter Wayne King said later, "The attitude of the Mississippi state police appeared to be divided between 'let the students go' and 'encourage them.' "[45] Someone threw a flaming torch on the top of a truck, another threw it to the ground, and still another threw it back on the truck. Those who attempted to extinguish the fire were squirted with a fire extinguisher.[46] At least two of the marshals' group leaders requested permission to use tear gas after 7 P.M., and the marshals put on their masks and prepared to fire ten minutes before gas was actually used.[47]

At about ten minutes before 8 P.M. Senator Yarbrough came

onto the front steps of the Lyceum to talk to the crowd and was at first booed. Although some reports said the crowd quieted down, others have said there was still so much noise that few heard him. Yarbrough attempted to influence the mob: "We don't want any violence. Get back off the street and, if you will, go back to your dormitories." They responded, "We want Ross." Department of Justice officials in the Lyceum now requested more action by the patrolmen in controlling the mob. While some patrolmen remained back in the crowd, University Police Chief Tatum and several patrolmen moved along the road in front of the Lyceum. As they moved the crowd back at any given point and continued along the street, the crowd pressed back on the street behind them. At the same time thirty or forty patrolmen were standing to one side and doing nothing. One said, "They're out of control. No one can control them any more." From the crowd someone threw a two-foot iron pipe, producing the eighth casualty among the marshals. "As though on signal," according to *U.S. News & World Report,* "there erupted a rain of rocks, bricks, bottles—anything that could be thrown. The calm turned to chaos."[48] A University staff member said that "bricks and bottles were in the air almost constantly."[49] Several faculty members saw the marshals put on their masks and heard someone shout, "They're going to gas us; go!"[50] Someone ordered the reporters to get out of the line of fire, and Chief Marshal McShane gave the order for gas.[51] Wayne King of the University of North Carolina said he "felt the marshals had reason to start the tear gas barrage, but that if they had known what would follow they wouldn't have done it."[52] What followed was unbelievable.

There is considerable disagreement about the precise time the tear gas was fired. About two-thirds of the witnesses agree with Department of Justice Attorney John Doar that it was at 7:57 P.M., before President Kennedy began his television address. In any case, the disagreement points up the confusion of events; even a few minutes delay indicates that the marshals were willing to wait until the last possible moment before resorting to the use of gas. Lieutenant Colonel Whitney Stuart, Army ROTC commanding officer at the University, told me he was absolutely certain that he was listening to the President's speech on a portable radio at the corner of the Lyceum Building when the first gas was fired. Several witnesses have said that after the first gas they went into the "Y" building and that the President "had just started" or "was just starting" to speak. One significant fact is that the University clocks are always about three or more minutes slow, and anyone who observed the time of the gas firing as 7:57 should have read it as 8 P.M., or slightly after. Having read and listened to a few positive statements and many uncertain ones, I would place the event at the moment the President began speaking or slightly later. One thing is certain: few on the scene thought the question of time was of any importance. John Doar, relying on the Lyceum clock, noted it in a timetable of events which he kept, and Nicholas Katzenbach phoned Robert Kennedy, who in turn attempted to get word to the President, but he was already on the air.[53]

President Kennedy delivered a plea for moderation and cooperation which had been carefully drafted to have the maximum appeal to Mississippians. There was no hint of triumph or vindictiveness in the words or in his voice, although some thought his voice implied uncertainty about the events in Mississippi.[54] Even though the message came too late, it was heard by those who crowded into the "Y" building after the first gas, by others with portables or car radios, and by many in their homes in the Oxford-University area. Because it cannot really be summarized, the whole text must be given:

> Good evening, my fellow citizens.
>
> The orders of the court in the case of *Meredith v. Fair* are beginning to be carried out. Mr. James Meredith is now in residence on the campus of the University of Mississippi. This has been accomplished thus far without the use of national guard or other troops—and it is to be hoped that the law-enforcement officers of the State of Mississippi and the federal marshals will continue to be sufficient in the future. All students, members of the faculty, and public officials in both Mississippi and the nation, it is to be hoped, can now return to their normal activities with full confidence in the integrity of American law.
>
> This is as it should be. For our nation is founded on the principle that observance of the law is the eternal safeguard of liberty

—and defiance of the law is the surest road to tyranny. The law which we obey includes the final rulings of our courts as well as the enactments of our legislative bodies. Even among law-abiding men, few laws are universally loved—but they are uniformly respected and not resisted.

Americans are free, in short, to disagree with the law—but not to disobey it. For in a government of laws, and not of men, no man—however prominent or powerful—and no mob—however unruly or boisterous—is entitled to defy a court of law. If this country should ever reach the point where any man or group of men, by force, or threat of force, could long defy the commands of our courts and Constitution, then no law would stand free from doubt, no judge would be sure of his writ, and no citizen would be safe from his neighbors.

In this case—in which the United States government was not until recently involved—Mr. Meredith brought a private suit in federal court against those who were excluding him from the University.

A series of federal courts—all the way up to the Supreme Court, repeatedly ordered Mr. Meredith's admission to the University. When those orders were defied and those who sought to implement them threatened with arrest and violence, the United States Court of Appeals—consisting of Chief Judge Tuttle of Georgia, Judge Hutcheson of Texas, Judge Rives of Alabama, Judge Jones of Florida, Judge Brown of Texas, Judge Wisdom of Lousiana, Judge Gewin of Alabama, and Judge Bell of Georgia, made clear the fact that the enforcement of its order had become the obligation of the United States government.

Even though this government had not originally been a party to this case, my responsibility as President was therefore inescapable. I accepted. My obligation, under the Constitution and the statutes of the United States, was and is to implement the orders of the court with whatever means were necessary, and with as little force and civil disorder as the circumstances permit.

It was for this reason that I federalized the Mississippi National Guard as the most appropriate instrument should any be needed to preserve law and order while United States marshals carried out the orders of the court, and prepared to back them up with whatever other civil or military enforcement might have been required.

I deeply regret the fact that any action by the executive branch was necessary in this case, but all other avenues and alternatives, including persuasion and conciliation, had been tried and exhausted.

Had the police powers of Mississippi been used to support the orders of the court, instead of deliberately and unlawfully blocking them, had the University of Mississippi fulfilled its standard of excellence by quietly admitting this applicant in conformity with what so many other Southern state universities have done for so many years, a peaceable and sensible solution would have been possible without any federal intervention.

The nation is proud of the many instances in which governors, educators, and everyday citizens from the South have shown to the world the gains that can be made by persuasion and good will in a society ruled by law.

Specifically, I would like to take this occasion to express the thanks of the nation to those Southerners who have contributed to the progress of our democratic development in the entrance of students regardless of race to such great institutions as the state-supported universities of Virginia, North Carolina, Georgia, Florida, Texas, Louisiana, Tennessee, Arkansas, and Kentucky.

I recognize that the present period of transition and adjustment in our nation's Southland is a hard one for many people. Neither Mississippi nor any other Southern state deserves to be charged with all the accumulated wrongs of the last hundred years of race relations. To the extent that there has been failure, the responsibility for that failure must be shared by us all, by every state, by every citizen.

Mississippi and her University, moreover, are noted for their courage, for their contribution of talent and thought to the affairs of this nation. This is the state of Lucius Lamar and many others who have placed the national good ahead of sectional interest. This is the state which had four Medal of Honor winners in the Korean war alone. In fact, the guard unit federalized this morning early, is part of the 155th Infantry, one of the ten oldest regiments in the Union and one of the most decorated for sacrifice and bravery in six wars.

In Mississippi in 1945 Jake Lindsey was honored by an unusual joint session of the Congress. I close therefore with this appeal to the students of the University, the people who are most concerned.

You have a great tradition to uphold, a tradition of honor and courage, won on the field of battle and on the gridiron as well as the University campus. You have a new opportunity to show that you are men of patriotism and integrity. For the most effective means of upholding the law is not the state policeman or the marshals or the National Guard. It is you.

It lies in your courage to accept those laws with which you disagree as well as those with which you agree. The eyes of the nation and all the world are upon you and upon all of us, and the honor of your University and the state are in the balance. I am certain the great majority of the students will uphold that honor.

There is in short no reason why the books on this case cannot now be quickly and quietly closed in the manner directed by the court. Let us preserve both the law and the peace, and then, healing those wounds that are within, we can turn to the greater crises that are without and stand united as one people in our pledge to man's freedom.

Thank you and good night.

On the basis of hindsight it is arguable that it was a mistake to delay the President's speech from 5:30 until 8 P.M., even though the reason for the delay is clear enough. The plan was that neither Governor Barnett nor the President would deliver their public statements until James Meredith had been safely brought to the campus, and the reasoning was that people would thus be presented with an accomplished fact and would not be inclined to protest strongly. From Barnett's special point of view it would have been both risky and contrary to his own tactics to let his radical or "white Muslim" supporters know in advance that Meredith and the marshals would enter the campus with the protection of the Highway Patrol. It is no great tribute to the perceptiveness of these supporters that they did not figure out before 6:30 P.M. what was to take place, but they cannot be blamed too much for believing that their hero would play fair with them. University officials also seemed to believe—or had to believe—that the governor would tell them what was to happen, and they did not have, and perhaps could not have had, a backstop plan in the event of Barnett's non-cooperation. Even the federal officials at least tentatively accepted the governor's assurances to maintain law and order, although they had the military in reserve. But the plan was made, and so many of its pieces had to be put together that delay of the speech seemed necessary. The television time had to be reserved in advance with enough margin to allow for delays in getting Meredith on the campus. Even after the governor had finally "agreed" at 11 A.M. Sunday, the pieces to be put together included the Department of Justice team, the marshals, the military, the Highway Patrol, and, belatedly, the University. In some respects it was a more forbidding job than the Normandy landings, and it may be remarkable that it was all accomplished in eight hours. In any case, the "plan" did not envision the situation which existed in front of the Lyceum just before 8 P.M., and

I know of very few people who thought beforehand that such a situation would develop.

At the end of the President's speech the network announcer reported that there was a disturbance on the campus and that the marshals were using tear gas. My wife and I were watching the television coverage at our home in Oxford, two miles from the campus, and I immediately went next door to suggest to Professor William F. Crowder that we go to the campus to see what we could do. We went in his car—later burned by the rioters—after I stopped long enough to get a coat so that I would look more "like a professor." We drove onto the campus through the confusion of cars and people on foot, and he parked the car near the "Y" building. He went immediately to Peabody Building, because he was afraid the gas might harm the many rats which the Department of Psychology was using for federally financed experiments. I started to walk to Conner Hall to get a camera from my office. On the sidewalk north of the Lyceum I was almost run down by three men, and I found myself running with the mob to escape a gas barrage which had just been fired. One of these men was carrying a long two-by-four and the rest of the mob hardly looked friendly, so I headed back to the car. Since there were many people milling around in the area between the Fine Arts Center and the women's dormitories, I decided to talk with some of them and try to get them to go to their dormitories. I did this with scant results for a few minutes—most in that area did not want to riot but could not control their inquisitiveness—and I then went to Conner Hall through the back entrance. From the third floor I took a Polaroid picture of the Lyceum and by phone arranged to meet Bill Crowder at the east end of Peabody, so we could drive home. We decided that those who were going to control the riot would not want us in the way. When we met at about 8:45, the space between us and the car was filled with gas and rioters, so we decided to wait in Peabody Building. We waited for more than six hours.

When the gas was first fired part of the mob was surging forward toward the marshals and others were trying to get out of the way. Although critics later said the gas was fired without warning, there was enough advance notice so that several wives of faculty members were able to get out of the way after the marshals donned their masks and heard the order to fire. Many in the mob avoided the first gas, and many others obviously were not interested in avoiding it. Anyone in the mob must have known that after the marshals first put on their masks the use of gas became more likely with each passing minute of mob attack. Among those retreating before the gas firing was Professor James Silver, who was accidentally tripped by the staff of a "rebel" flag in the hands of a student. It may seem odd that in this mad scramble the student came back to help him up. Advance notice or not, it was probably inevitable that the firing of gas would cause some injuries, partly from carelessness in a tense situation and partly because of the crowding and shoving of the mob. None of the gas devices used in the early evening was explosive, but they could cause painful injury if used at very close quarters. One highway patrolman almost died from the worst of such injuries; he was probably hit by the canister the moment before its gas was expelled. Dangerous and unbearable as the gas might have seemed, many in the mob showed amazing resistance to it. With one exception, the really serious injuries were not a result of the gas.

After the first gas the mob reassembled in several locations, but a large group was near the partially constructed science building. At least two men unfamiliar with the campus began to assume leadership of the rioters; they asked what kind of riot material could be found in the two buildings to the left of the Lyceum and were told they were the chemistry and engineering buildings. One of these would-be leaders shouted, "All right now, we've forced them to fire their tear gas. Now let's keep on attacking until we make 'em fire all they have and then we'll get the bastards. We'll keep on attacking until the bastards run out of gas and then we'll kill the bastards." This man with the limited vocabulary shouted orders to any who would listen and told different groups to advance to certain points and wait for the signal so all could attack together. A student rioter was working hard at organizing the gathering of bricks from the construction site. Still another boy made a point of moving from group to group to spread the lie that a coed had been killed by the marshals. Soon after this a man in a black and white car was sending out a radio broadcast that he had "personally" watched three marshals beat a student to death and leave him "dead" on the ground.[55] These are but two of the many inaccurate stories—and sometimes outright lies—that were spread both on and off the campus during the night and the following day.

The highway patrolmen left the scene of the rioting almost immediately after the gas firing. They were understandably angry about the gas, although some of their action and inaction had made its use inevitable, and their superiors had been warned of its impending use. Here were law officers in a state where arrests were common for "breach of the peace" or "failure to move on" when ordered to do so. Yet wholesale violations of state and local laws had occurred under the very noses of the patrolmen, who made not a single arrest or identification during the night. It is probably unfair to place all the blame on them; apparently they had not been instructed to make arrests or identifications. The buck passes right up the line to the governor, and there the responsibility rests. The highway patrolmen were hampered because their World War I gas masks were not effective, yet they could have operated as effectively as the rioters without masks.

Governor Barnett's four stand-ins left the campus for Jackson soon after 8 P.M., leaving in charge Colonel Birdsong, who by this time could not be blamed for being the most confused, badgered, and double-crossed man in the picture. The Patrol director has a reputation as a competent and sincere law enforcement officer, yet he had little reason to believe that he was in charge of his force. After telephone conversations between the President, the governor, the Attorney General, Burke Marshall, and attorney Tom Watkins, one of the governor's moderate advisers, the Highway Patrol finally began to make some efforts to keep additional rioters from getting to Oxford and onto the campus.[56]

At about 9 P.M. General Edwin Walker rose to brief eminence with a typically confusing appearance in which he complimented the rioters on their "protest," stated that this was not the route to Cuba, accused Colonel Birdsong of having "sold out," and unintentionally complimented Episcopalian Rector Duncan Gray and his church by saying he was ashamed to be an Episcopalian. There is some disagreement on whether he did or did not "lead a charge," but his presence hardly served to control the insurrection. He did add confusion and an odd type of drama to a scene that needed no more of either.[57]

Soon after this Episcopal Chaplain Wofford Smith, having heard that the marshals had wounded a student with a shotgun, waved a white handkerchief to get inside the Lyceum. After learning that the report was untrue, and seeing the array of bloodied marshals and newsmen, he went outside with a marshal to confer with students who wanted to talk peace. After some discussion football player "Buck" Randall told the mob that the marshals would stop using gas if the rioters would stop throwing things. Someone from the mob demanded Meredith; then a shower of bricks and bottles came from the rioters; and the marshals responded with more gas. Too many of the mob wanted no truce.[58]

There are no details to indicate who shot French reporter Paul Guihard and Oxford bystander Ray Gunter, although both were killed by .38 caliber bullets. Guihard was shot in the back at close range, and his body was found near the Fine Arts Center before 9 P.M. Gunter was hit by a stray bullet at about 11 P.M. while watching the riot from a point near the science building, then under construction. There were so many wild stories of death and injury that neither of the actual deaths seemed to have any particular effect on the course of the riot. The reported death of Director of Student Activities Tom S. Hines illustrates the confusion and uncertainty. At about 8 P.M. a network radio broadcast stated that he had died of a heart attack on the campus, and several neighbors went to his home to comfort his wife. George Street, Assistant Director of Development, drove through the rioting to check at the Lyceum Building and then back to assure the wife that Hines was alive and well. When Hines's daughter got home about an hour later, she insisted on driving to the campus to check. She arrived in front of the Lyceum during a lull in the rioting at the very time her father came out to survey the situation. She then drove home in the Hineses' new station wagon and left their older car, a fortunate move because the car was later burned by the rioters.

At about 9:30 P.M. graduate student Edward R. Gaines heard a curious two-way radio conversation from a "black Mercury" with a covered license plate, parked between the chancellor's home and Ward Dormitory. The man in the car was talking both with someone in Alabama and with a woman parked east of the railroad bridge on the campus. The other voice asked, "How are you doing?" He replied, "OK, but we could use some help." The reply to that was, "Just sit tight. Eighty cars just left here." Another student heard someone in a different car talking to what he called the "Alabama Volunteers," but he could not hear the details of the conversation.[59] These conversations indicate that the rioters were in some respects almost military in their organization. Border patrolman Melvin Moore said members of the mob "made frontal attacks and flanking attacks, like they were being directed by a military tactician. They weren't just a bunch of mad college kids."[60] Deputy Marshal James McKeigue said, "They were organized ruffians prepared and equipped for battle. Barnett and his state cops spurred them on."[61]

Members of the mob brought two odd vehicles into the assault, first a bulldozer and then an old University fire truck, but the marshals repulsed them by what amounted to hand-to-hand combat. Rebel snipers were active with both rifles and shotguns, and they fired at marshals, soldiers, military vehicles, the Lyceum, and almost anything in sight. One faculty member saw a man firing a rifle in the general direction of the Lyceum from two hundred yards away. He asked if the rioter was not afraid of hitting those on his own side, and the man replied, "I hadn't thought of that." Two University policemen arrested and identified two men who were shooting out street lights with a rifle, but the Lafayette County Grand Jury afterward failed to indict them. Members of the mob burned a variety of automobiles, all belonging to Mississippi residents, and the owners included a University staff member and four faculty members, two of them staunch segregationists. In addition to the standard bricks, bottles, and rocks, the mob used Molotov cocktails, pieces of concrete from broken blocks and benches, spears fashioned from iron rods and lumber, and acid presumably obtained from the chemistry building. Chemistry professor Bill Herndon had locked the doors early in the evening, but rioters broke through outside windows into two basement rooms, one of which was the physical chemistry laboratory and a probable source of a limited amount of acid. Contrary to some reports, the mob did not gain access to the chemistry supply room. A staff member of the Navy ROTC saw and heard a highway patrolman explaining to some of the rioters how to make a Molotov cocktail.[62]

An uncooperative breeze played tricks with the gas used by the marshals. Sometimes it was blown back in their faces and at other times it was blown north into the women's dormitory area, but in both cases it was blown away from the mob. There have been allegations that the marshals deliberately fired gas into the dormitories, but Dean Katharine Rea states this was not true of the women's dormitories. The insidious gas did seep in around doors and windows, and the students who went in and out of doors did not realize that they were letting gas in and were also carrying it in on their clothing. There were more persistent claims—probably true—that gas was fired into at least one men's dormitory. Knowing this particular dormitory, my guess is that the marshals tossed a grenade through the door after being angered by taunting from the occupants. The student manager was an active leader of Patriotic American Youth, a junior version of the John Birch Society and Citizens' Council combined, and a major opponent of Meredith's enrollment. The marshals certainly knew that gassing a dormitory would force the occupants into the street, and it is difficult to believe they would—without provocation—consciously add to the mob's numbers. I saw a group of marshals chase some rioters into the men's dormitory area and fire gas at them sometime before 9 P.M., and intermittently during the night I saw similar instances near several of the women's dormitories. Gas fired near any open doors or windows would soon fill a building. The real difficulty was that too many of the students and other rioters were willing to protest in the face of the uncomfortable and sometimes dangerous effects of the gas. They had an easy method of avoiding it—to stop demonstrating and rioting—but their mental state prevented that.

Our small group of refugees in Peabody Building spent the night in an acceptable state of discomfort, although this building is about twenty-five yards from the Lyceum and was in the center of much of the rioting and gassing. Our band included, in addition to Crowder and myself, a Clarksdale policeman, a staff member of the Division of Student Personnel, and two psychology graduate students. We first set about picking a room on the north side of the building which could be entered only through an entry hall and another room, and thus could be kept free of gas. We then stuffed toilet paper into the cracks around the windows and a north-facing door, and we agreed that anyone entering or leaving would open and close doors very carefully so that a minimum of gas would enter. Someone produced a radio, and we listened to some remarkable coverage of the situation. A graduate student phoned his wife and asked her to phone the homes of the others, since it was difficult to get a line out of the campus. We did not know that the White House had taken over one line completely. The wives were worried, and my wife ironed clothes desperately through much of the night to relieve her anxieties. Early in the evening one student obtained a mattress and proceeded to sleep through the whole noisy night. My tobacco pouch happened to be full, and I did not run out until about 2:30 A.M.

We were careful not to turn on lights in rooms facing the riot area, and at intervals throughout the night I covered my face with a wet handkerchief and went into these rooms. From there I could see the rioting—the burning cars, the Molotov cocktails, the screaming members of the mob, the methodical marshals—all through the ghostly clouds of gas. Occasionally I could hear the firing of weapons other than gas guns, which caused me to do my looking through venetian blinds. Several times I saw the Volkswagen of University official George Street as he took an indirect route to bring medical supplies to the Lyceum. More than once during that long night the Clarksdale policeman criticized the deficiencies of the Highway Patrol in controlling the crowd. "You can't control mobs that way," he said. We phoned the Lyceum several times that night to ask about the safety of going home and about when the troops were coming. Once we reached Nicholas Katzenbach and another time Tom Hines, both of whom put in a long hard night. Both times we were told that troops were "on their way," but to stay put. Sometime after the troops came, at about 3 A.M., we started to leave Peabody Building by the west basement door, and a soldier suggested, "You'd better go out the other end; there's live firing out here." We said the mob was still at the other end, and we cautiously worked our way to a car in an outlying parking lot, leaving behind the tired soldiers and Crowder's burning car,

The first troops on the campus were fifty or sixty Mississippi National Guardsmen, led in by Captain Murry Falkner (nephew of the author) at about 11 P.M. The rioters greeted these local folks by breaking Falkner's arm, wounding others, firing live ammunition into their jeeps, and breaking most of the windshields. Apparently without ammunition—which they could not have used anyway—and without training in dealing with unprincipled rioters, the guardsmen stood alongside the marshals and took part of the punishment which brought them honor from Americans and derision from some fellow Mississippians.[63] At the request of Nicholas Katzenbach, Captain Falkner tried to reason with the rioters over two electric megaphones, but as he said, "It just made the mob mad." When guardsmen made an attempt to take portable lights to an athletic field to prepare for a helicopter landing, rioters set fire to the canvas cover of one truck and put a bullet hole through the radiator of another. Officers who were trying to plan operations from the Oxford Armory had no map of the Ole Miss campus and worked from a rough sketch on a blackboard. George Fielding Eliot wrote later that the Mississippi guardsmen "were faithful to a noble heritage."

When Lieutenant Governor Johnson came to the campus at about midnight, he gave orders for more action from the Highway Patrol. Johnson asked Birdsong, "Where are your men?" When Birdsong replied that they were "billeted in the Gymnasium," the lieutenant governor responded, "Well get them the hell up and out there to set up road blocks." But the next morning Johnson told the legislature what a good job the Highway Patrol did. Even after midnight some patrolmen were telling potential rioters at the east side of the campus, "We can't let you in here, but if you break up into small groups you can sneak in across the railroad tracks."[64] Although it is clear that Patrol road blocks did turn back large numbers, a federal official told me that military road blocks—not the Highway Patrol—kept most of the late rioters from reaching the campus.

At about 2 A.M. the first regular troops arrived and received the standard greetings of bricks, Molotov cocktails, bullets, and vile language. This platoon of the riot-trained 503rd Military Police Battalion had been flown in by helicopter. One helicopter had circled low over the campus at about midnight in an unsuccessful attempt to find a place to land, and finally went to the Oxford-University Airport instead. After riding to the Northgate entrance of the campus in Navy buses, the soldiers marched to the Lyceum in "V" riot formation, most carrying rifles with bayonets fixed and some with riot shotguns. These were the men who performed the tiresome and dangerous job of routing the hard-core rioters from the campus. The main body of the 503rd MP's and all of the 716th MP Battalion drove south from Memphis in two convoys. Lieutenant Henry T. Gallagher of the 716th obtained a Mississippi road map from a service station and commandeered a Navy shore patrolman who showed the way as far as Holly Springs, thirty miles north of Oxford. The convoy was impeded by drivers of several private autos, who drove slowly in front of the military jeeps and trucks and would not let them pass. The 503rd went on into Oxford and was partly immobilized when rioters dropped a railroad tie on a truck from a railroad overpass. Other rioters peppered the long line of soldiers with rocks and sticks. Lieutenant Gallagher left the 716th north of Oxford and with the aid of a city map supplied by the Army drove by a circuitous route to the airport to get orders from Major General Charles Billingslea. Gallagher's driver was hit in the face by a rock on the return trip. One platoon was sent immediately to the campus as reinforcements, while the rest lined up on a street north of the campus to await orders.[65]

Although General Billingslea declared the area "secure" at 6:15 A.M. on Monday, the remaining rioters moved into downtown Oxford to continue their insurrection to the last. They first attacked a car driven by a Negro at a main intersection, while highway patrolmen watched with pointed inaction. As reported by the Associated Press, "After some building of momentum, groups of men and youths—many carrying soft drink cartons as ammunition holders—appeared at many intersections. The bottles began to fly through windshields and bang against the side of Army jeeps, even the cars of the passing citizens of Oxford."[66] As the violence spread, Mayor Richard W. Elliott appealed to a Highway Patrol officer for help and got the answer, "We have orders not to interfere." The mayor complained, "Patrolmen actually saw cars demolished and saw mobs on the streets and did nothing about it." He then asked the local FBI agent to get help from the troops, who moved in with gas and bayonets to end the rioting.[67] Their most effective weapon was a "gas dispenser," a device like a flame thrower with which they sprayed extra-strength gas into the mob.

The end of the riot left two dead and many injured. It also left a massive cleanup job, the question of how a single Negro would fare at the University, and a long series of questions as to who caused the riot and why. It had been a long and dismal night. When James Meredith registered at 8 A.M. Monday, escorted by grim and tired federal officials, he could say only, "This is not a happy occasion."

6 INTEGRATION VERSUS DISINTEGRATION

In the early morning hours of Monday, October 1, editor Sidna Brower and the staff of the *Mississippian* published the "extra" edition which had been planned for the day of James Meredith's arrival on campus. Beneath a banner headline which read CHANCELLOR ISSUES PLEA was a reproduction of a letter signed by Chancellor Williams:

> Ole Miss is a great university. Your conduct at this time can make it greater. The finest service you may render Ole Miss is to help keep the University operating.
>
> We can maintain a normal University operation provided:
>
> 1. Those who live on campus stay on campus.
> 2. Avoid congregating in large groups.
> 3. Do not participate in demonstrations of any kind.
> 4. Identify and report agitators to campus police.
> 5. Keep away from points of danger.
> 6. Cooperate fully with campus police.

A message to students from Dean Love requested that they listen to the campus radio station and read the *Mississippian* for announcements, and included a statement which had been superseded by events:

> For your protection and that of this University, there will probably be about 100 highway patrolmen stationed on campus at our request to properly deal with any outside person or groups who come here to cause trouble. They are not here to resist the Federal government.

On an inside page was an up-to-the-minute editorial, VIOLENCE WILL NOT HELP:

This is an appeal to the entire student body and to anyone concerned with the present situation. Not only do the students chance forfeiting their education by participating in riots, but they are bringing dishonor and shame to the University and to the State of Mississippi.

When students hurled rocks, bottles, and eggs the federal marshals were forced to resort to tear gas to back off the crowds.

When outsiders show their objections in the form of violence, they are seriously injuring the students in their attempt to continue their education. As a student, I beg you to return to your home.

This is a battle between the State of Mississippi and the United States government; the University is caught in the middle. The Civil War was fought one hundred years ago over almost the same issues and the United States of America prevailed. The federal government is once again showing its strength and power to uphold the laws of our country.

No matter what your convictions you should follow the advice of Governor Ross Barnett by not taking any action for violence. Blood has already been shed and will continue to flow unless people realize the seriousness of the situation.

Whatever your beliefs, you are a citizen of the United States of America and of the State of Mississippi, and should preserve peace and harmony of both governments.

Directly beneath the editorial was a message in capital letters from Jack Lynch, chairman of the Student Judicial Council: ANY STUDENT CAUGHT PARTICIPATING IN DEMONSTRATIONS OR ENGAGING IN A RIOTOUS MANNER MAY BE SUBJECT TO EXPULSION. Most of these requests for peaceful behavior had been written to try to prevent violence. They were used now in an attempt to stop it.

The assortment of exhausted marshals, soldiers, students, faculty, and University officials who passed through the center of the campus Monday morning saw the remains of a battlefield. The Circle in front of the Lyceum was littered with burned vehicles, tear gas canisters, bottles, bricks, concrete fragments, and lumber. One student found a blood-stained wrench from the University fire truck. Military vehicles were still there, and pup tents had been set up by the soldiers. The interior of the recently painted Lyceum was littered with cigarette butts, coke bottles, and occasional blood stains. In outlying areas of the campus and along the roads were more tents, military vehicles, floodlights, and soldiers. Everywhere was the penetrating burn of tear gas, intensified by the humidity produced by a light rain. The mood of those present seemed to match the scene; there were no smiles to relieve the grimness of picking up the pieces. Some of the pieces were physical; the most important were educational, legal, political, and personal.

A new phase of the story now began, and it moved on different—and sometimes almost unrelated—planes. Ole Miss—like other universities—is a collection of communities whose members come together only when necessary. The circumstances added still other communities: the military, the marshals, and that odd group outside of the University which gave material and ideological support to the student rebels. All of these groups were acting under the pressure of crisis, and they acted in unusual ways—sometimes in ways which added to the crisis. The resolution of the crisis required that these communities arrive at some basis of temporary cooperation, yet their usual patterns of behavior prevented this. Of particular importance were the attempts of certain individuals to cut through the barriers which normally divided these groups. Also important was the fact that James Meredith had little contact with any of these communities whose actions were so vital to him.

When James Meredith registered at about 8 A.M. Monday, he enrolled in courses and with teachers already selected for him about ten days earlier. The problems which were to complicate his attendance would have been simpler had the academic rules been applied more loosely; but the University is demanding in the types of transfer courses it will accept in fulfillment of requirements in mathematics and science. His schedule for the fall semester included required courses in algebra, English, and Spanish, although the last was changed to French several days later when it was discovered that he had already taken an equivalent course in Spanish. His "electives"—already chosen for him—included American Political Parties and American Colonial History. All his courses had been arranged so that he would have professors mature enough to handle problems of class discipline and unlikely to discriminate for or against him. Meredith's extra-academic reception was so bad that it was some time before he realized the importance of this preparation. His justifiable complaint was that all of his University of Maryland courses in Japan were classified by Ole Miss as "extension credit," which meant that his courses in Russian language were not accepted as meeting part of the foreign language requirement. It is common knowledge at the University that courses from low-quality junior colleges are accepted at full value, yet some of Meredith's courses from a better school were not accepted. The difficulty was that he sought to transfer an odd mixture of courses, more than a year of them acquired because of his delayed admission. Moreover, he had already missed more than a week of classes, and he entered an advanced course in French two weeks late.

Meredith's first day of classes was far from normal, even though about half of the students did not attend classes at all. Escorted by John Doar, James P. McShane, and several marshals, he was followed by a group of heckling and cursing students. The continued harassment by students pointed up a problem which was not solved for weeks. University officials argued that control over discipline had been taken from them, while federal officials maintained that their only function was to protect Meredith. The result was a vacuum of authority and near anarchy which could be remedied only by cooperation between University and federal officials.

Student discipline was the major problem facing the University for the next four months, but officials were slow to tackle it even after they discovered its importance. The many factors which blocked prompt disciplinary measures included segregationist pressure from outside Ole Miss, the confusion of authority on the campus, the presence of too many newsmen, the actions of a minority of students bent on ruining the University, and an organizational set-up within the University—similar to that in most universities—which seemed designed to prevent the solution of difficult problems. It sometimes seemed that each group worked against the others to produce failure.

University officials had sent word before 8 A.M. Monday that classes would meet except where rooms were still filled with tear gas. In classes that morning, many professors made stinging comments about "those who riot and violate court orders." Since few of the rioters were present, the reception was mainly sympathetic. But some students reported their versions of the teachers' remarks to segregationist leaders, and later there were charges of attempted "brainwashing" of students by faculty members. The holding of classes was largely symbolic, but it did reflect the commendable determination of University administrators that Ole Miss would not be closed for even one day.

The 160 persons who had been arrested the night before were processed by federal officers during the day and by afternoon most had been released. Others arrested on Monday included former General Edwin Walker. Those to be held longer were lined up in the Lyceum and marched to buses for transfer to a temporary stockade at the U.S. Soil Sedimentation Laboratory near the local airport. Twenty-five of those arrested were Ole Miss students, and an equal number were from thirteen other colleges in the South. There had been an anti-Meredith demonstration on Sunday at Starkville, home of Mississippi State University, and some of the participants came to the Ole Miss campus. There were also students from Memphis State University and Southwestern at Memphis. Southwestern President Peyton Rhodes said he "hoped" his students would "stay away" from Oxford and "leave the situation alone." Memphis State President C. C. Humphreys stated more strongly, "If we learn that any student has gone to Oxford during this week, either as spectator or participant in the troubles, he will be expelled."[1] The Ole Miss Student Judicial Council later took disciplinary action against the eight students whose cases were submitted to it, although outside pressure prevented any expulsions.

On Monday at 4 P.M. the University of Mississippi faculty held a meeting which had been initiated by the local chapter of the A.A.U.P. to produce some communication between the faculty and the administration. It was a somber group which heard Chancellor Williams state that the University had attempted to prepare its personnel for Meredith's enrollment, and that all the parties involved in the case shared some responsibility for the events of Sunday night. He pointed out that Colonel Frederick Harris, a former professor of military science at Ole Miss, was among those in command of the troops, and that the safety of everyone was now assured. In response to questions from faculty members, the chancellor said firmly that the University would not be closed and that the governor and the Board of Trustees had already agreed to send letters to the Southern Association of Schools and Colleges in an attempt to preserve the accreditation of the schools under the board's control. The letters would state that there would be no more political interference in matters controlled by the board. Williams indicated the continuing confusion when he stated that the federal government had taken over "police powers" on the campus, so that the University was "unable" to exercise such power. An English instructor and I both raised the question of whether the students realized that Judge Mize's injunction applied to each of them, and the chancellor replied that additional steps would be taken to make students aware of the court order. The question of student disciplinary action had not yet become a major issue, and no faculty member raised it in a direct way.

Early on Monday morning Jackson businessman William H. Mounger had gone on television with a plea for law and order and salvation of the University. On Tuesday Mounger and 127 other business and professional leaders from throughout the state issued a strongly worded appeal for "enforcement of law and order" and against "mob rule." Although the statement reaffirmed disagreement with the Supreme Court decision of 1954, the signers called for "sane" and "sensible" rather than "inflammatory statements" from state news media, for state rather than federal investigation and prosecution (in order to uphold the state's "honor and dignity") of those who violated the law, for "restraint and judgment" from the students in all state schools, and for support of other principles which would permit the state and the University "to march forward with honor, dignity, and respect." The men who signed this statement included many of the non-political leaders of the state, who had allowed others to assume control of state policies in government and education. Now their belated public action was an attempt at remedy rather than prevention, but it was an important beginning on the long road back to "honor, dignity, and respect."

One cause of confusion and difficulty on the day following the riot and for a few days thereafter were the false reports of death and injury, always blaming the marshals. As late as October 15 the *Dan Smoot Report,* a far-right periodical published in Dallas, printed a statement credited to an anonymous student that marshals had shot two of his fraternity brothers, that another boy (presumably Ray Gunter) "was shot between the eyes in the head by a marshal," and that two girls had been shot and "one is in critical condition and the other has died." The fact is that no girls were seriously injured, and the University finally disposed of the rumors concerning the girl's death by releasing a picture of her posing with Student Body President Dick Wilson. There were actually more serious injuries to marshals and soldiers than to rioters or those who called themselves bystanders. The unfounded rumors of death and injury were part of the developing argument that the "vicious marshals" had caused the riot, and for months after September the battle of accusations and investigations continued.

The remarkable aspect of the debate over the causes and even the events of the insurrection was that no agency or group ever made an honest attempt at a complete investigation. There was a deluge of news analysis, most of fairly good quality but with all the shortcomings of brief reports for mass audiences. The University administration telephoned a curious defense of its own position to Senators Eastland and Stennis in the early hours of October 1, but on November 15 issued a different and much more complete report to protect its accreditation. Senators Eastland and Stennis sent their own staff investigators to the campus to interview rather different sets of individuals, but neither ever published a formal report. The Mississippi legislature, in special session during September and early October, first started to look at the matter as a committee of the whole house, then appointed a special joint committee after some legislators made it clear that they would reveal facts which did not follow the official state line. (Senator Herman Camp, who had come to the campus with the National Guard, made a revealing speech. A member of the state House of Representatives, Karl Wiesenburg, published his dissenting views in a pamphlet.) The Lafayette County Grand Jury investigated along lines which prevented the taking of testimony on all the facts, and for different reasons so did a federal grand jury. The Mississippi Junior Chamber of Commerce and the Citizens' Council both issued reports. The U.S. Department of Justice brought in a large contingent of lawyers and FBI agents, and no doubt acquired the largest collection of statements. Finally, the Ole Miss chapter of the A.A.U.P. issued a brief statement and then designated me to write an accurate account of the riot, but by the time it was written they had moved on to more pressing matters. I used the material as a basis for three speeches to university audiences during the year (in Columbia, South Carolina; Memphis; and Nashville), but they were not released to the press. There are also chapters on the events in several books, of which James W. Silver's is most authentic.

These investigations and reports were made for a wide variety of reasons and at different times. Some were important as events, while others were almost irrelevant. Most dealt with a group of key questions, but the answers depended on the purposes of the investigators, the sources of information, the amount of time expended, and the time at which information was secured. I found that some participants would talk most candidly immediately after September 30, and that others would not talk at all until a year later. Two kinds of reports never issued would have been valuable: one by a congressional committee composed of members representing all opinions, another a "white paper" based upon the extensive investigations of the Department of Justice and the FBI. There is no adequate explanation for lack of the former; for the latter the reason is that the contempt cases of Governor Barnett and Lieutenant Governor Johnson were—and are—still in the courts. The Department of Justice thus released only statements of its position on key questions. It would take a whole book to deal adequately with the maze of alleged facts and charges. I attempt no more than an evaluation of the major issues.

The evidence and the opinions of many observers are clear: Governor Barnett and the forces allied with him share the major responsibility for the trouble which led to riot in Mississippi. The contrary charge, as variously stated by his supporters, is that the Kennedy administration wanted to promote "dictatorship" and "to pervert to political purposes" the power of the federal government.[2] The enrollment of one Negro became part of a plot similar to those seen by the John Birch Society. The preponderant evidence against Barnett can be seen in his conviction by the Court of Appeals on civil contempt charges and in Judge Brown's statement in an October 12 hearing that the governor's interposition speech was "an open incitement to rebellion."[3] It can be seen also in the avalanche of critical editorial comment, of which a statement by Lydel Sims in the *Memphis Commercial Appeal* is typical:

> The flag of the Confederacy has become a rallying point for hoodlums and crackpots from whom men like Lee and Forrest would have turned away with cold contempt.
>
> Inflamed by pious statements that *invite violence while purporting to deplore it* [my emphasis], the mob has gathered to fight the good fight for anarchy.
>
> That they will be turned back is scant relief for the shame and anger felt by reasonable people on both sides of the now-secondary issue of integration.
>
> It will be a long time before any of us get the feel of slime off our hands.[4]

Although the primary responsibility of the Barnett administration is clear, the Kennedy administration can be criticized for considering politics as a major factor—leading it to move too late and with too little strength in enforcing the court order. Of course the aim was to avoid the type of criticism heaped upon President Eisenhower for his use of troops at Little Rock. It is ironic that President Kennedy was hurt politically by carefulness that was intended to appease those segregationists who were not willing to violate court orders, but he would also have been hurt if the choice had been to use soldiers from the beginning. There should have been a firm decision to have Meredith registered by the deadline date for late registration, Monday, September 24, but none of the participants was willing to take *effective* action to accomplish that. Nevertheless, without Barnett or his equivalent there would have been no problem.

A second cause of controversy is the charge that the federal government "rushed in" marshals and troops because of unwillingness to "await the outcome" of "judicial processes" yet to be concluded.[5] But there were numerous orders for Meredith's immediate admission, none of which had been stayed by any higher court as of September 30. In the hearing on civil contempt on September 28, the judges of the Court of Appeals demonstrated more concern over delay than did federal attorneys. On at least five different occasions one judge after another criticized the slowness of the executive branch of the federal government in enforcing the court orders.[6] In its decision of June 25 the Court of Appeals panel had stated clearly that further delay would damage James Meredith but would not be a hardship on the defendants. As court decisions after September 30 demonstrated, the Mississippi defendants had no legal arguments against Meredith's admission which even justified a full hearing. The whole Mississippi strategy had been based on delay rather than substantial legal claims, and by September 30 that strategy had given the state "its day in court" for sixteen months. Governor Barnett's attorneys claimed that he never had a "fair hearing," but as Judge Bell stated in a continuation of the hearing on civil contempt on October 12, "He could raise any type of defense he wanted to raise, but he didn't come."[7] The fact is that until September 30 Barnett had personally entered the case instead of following the usual course of allowing his subordinates to perform specific executive actions. The equivalent would have been for President Kennedy to accompany James Meredith to confront the governor. Having taken personal action, the governor refused to go before the court to accept responsibility for such action. When he capitulated on September 30, the honorable and consistent course would have been for Barnett to admit Meredith to the University campus. At least he should have informed University officials of his agreement with federal officials. Although I have covered the main legal arguments, James Silver's study of "the closed society" includes an analysis by a "Mississippi constitutional law professor" of several other legal questions.[8] Also of interest is a pamphlet by a former Mississippi legislator in which he argues persuasively that Barnett did not even uphold the constitution of Mississippi.[9]

A third question for argument was the decision to bring Meredith to the campus on Sunday instead of Monday. Although some supporters of the governor blame this on federal authorities, it has been made clear already that the primary responsibility was Barnett's. I still question the wisdom of the decision, although federal officials thought it was the only way to assure even the possibility of Barnett's cooperation. If the move could have been made earlier on Sunday, and if there had been real plans for cooperation between state, University, and federal forces, the worst of the violence might have been prevented. The speed-up probably lessened the chances for cooperation—certainly it did so as far as the University was concerned. It also changed the timing for bringing in marshals and troops, and this was especially important because of the innate slowness of military communications and operations. It might have been worthwhile for federal officials to end negotiations with the governor and to have explored possibilities of communication with the Board of Trustees and University officials. The many ifs in these questions cannot be fairly answered on the basis of hindsight, and it can only be said that different approaches on the part of federal officials *might have* produced better results. It is certain that a different approach by the governor could have changed developments, but Sunday may have been too late. I question the conclusion that the Sunday entry prevented a massacre of civilians by troops, although the point is clearly debatable.[10] If federal forces had come on Monday, it would presumably have been without Barnett's cooperation; and riot-trained troops would—or should—have been present in such numbers that resistance would have been impossible, or at least improbable.

A fourth question was the failure of a total of about one thousand federal, state, local, and University law enforcing officers to maintain order before 8 P.M. on September 30, even though the total membership of the mob could not possibly have been more than four thousand at any time. The principal explanation is that there was not even a semblance of a plan for the coordination of their efforts. The report of the Mississippi legislative committee places all responsibility for the lack of such a plan on the federal government. It correctly points out that much of the equipment necessary for riot control was not there, including such items as public address facilities, barricades, and first-aid supplies. It bases its criticism on material from an FBI Law Enforcement Bulletin, neglecting to note that the FBI is not a police organization and has never had operational responsibilities for riot control. It also neglects to look into the training programs for federal marshals and prison guards, including the training manual for U.S. marshals.[11] Those on the campus who had the most experience in riot control were the ninety-seven prison guards, but they had handled prison riots which were comparatively tidy. The federal officers did at least have riot sticks, tear gas, and workable gas masks, of which state and local officers had none. The Highway Patrol had no equipment whatsoever for riot control, not even the public address car which the lieutenant governor had used on Thursday. The University had a public address system loaded on a truck at about 7:30 P.M., ready to move to the Lyceum, but it was not sent for fear it would be damaged, plus an assurance from federal officials that they had one on the way. The whole argument over details may be irrelevant anyway, because it is clear that none of the officers had instructions to arrest anyone for anything, or even to identify troublemakers. There were wholesale violations of federal, state, and local law before 8 P.M., but there were no arrests. The only officers who consistently attempted to control matters before 8 P.M. were the University policemen under Chief Tatum, of whom one marshal said, "He's an officer. Mississippi can be proud of him."[12] Governor Barnett had promised maintenance of order by the Highway Patrol, yet the Patrol was not prepared for such action. The riot-trained and equipped military police handled matters effectively when they arrived, and they probably would have done so earlier. When federal officials finally realized that state authorities were not going to be effective, it took some time to get federal forces into action, although one official said just after 8 P.M., "The troops will have to come in now." Certainly the soldiers should have arrived sooner, and the apparent reasons for delay were postponement of the decision to order their movement, plus the normal slowness of military operations.

The University's role in the lack of planning was principally that school officials were not prepared to adopt a different approach when their original plan became irrelevant. While it is true that the governor or federal officials should have informed the University at least four hours sooner of the change in plans (to bring Meredith on Sunday instead of Monday), it is also true that the officials did little except roll with the tide when they learned of the change soon after 3:30 P.M. This does not detract from the hard work of several officials throughout the night. These men were not very happy about their role, but they gave considerable assistance to the besieged federal officials and marshals. A statement from the Department of Justice acknowledged this. What they should have done is partly indicated by the statement of Mississippi newsman Kenneth L. Dixon: "Even up to the time that the marshals started using tear gas, there was no apparent official effort to control the crowds. . . . 95 per cent of that student crowd could have been controlled with no difficulty whatsoever had one respected school official or public official been on a public address system."[13] Beyond that there should have been arrests of ringleaders in the mob, but as University officials said in their statement early Monday morning, they were not willing even to *threaten* students with expulsion for taking part in demonstrations. They did not do so until November 1. Even so, there is a bare possibility that their action might have been more effective had they learned by noon of Meredith's Sunday arrival.

The fifth question about the riot produced the most heated debate. Did the marshals fire tear gas without warning into the backs of unarmed highway patrolmen who were "successfully moving the crowd back," and did they do so, according to the grand jury report, "for the purpose of inciting a riot"? Variations of this allegation were made in all but one of the reports critical of the federal government—and oddly enough that one was published by the Citizens' Council.[14] One answer is that almost every account of the riot by newsmen present, Mississippians and others, stated that the marshals were justified in using tear gas and/or that they took an amazing amount of punishment before resorting to gas. To choose but one example, Scripps-Howard reporter Richard Starnes wrote that the marshals "had the choice of using their gas guns or being torn to pieces by the mob."[15] It is worth noting that the University report published six weeks later barely mentioned the initial firing of gas as a factor in the riot.

It is clear that the mob was not under control for almost thirty minutes before the gas was used, and that any group of people not bent on insurrection would disperse after being gassed. It is also clear that the mob was too close to the marshals when the gas was used, although there was little the marshals could have done about that. A curious statement in the legislative committee report is that the gas guns were fired at "point-blank range," and that some persons were hit by "projectiles."[16] If the range between the marshals and the mob was so short, it is obvious that the mob had not been moved back very far or the powder and wadding fired from the short-range guns could not have hit individuals. No one could have been hit by "projectiles" before 9:30 P.M., because the marshals had none until then. Those injured were hit by gas canisters thrown by hand. My conclusion is that the marshals were justified in using gas, but that they should have first informed the highway patrolmen that they would start arresting rioters if the patrolmen refused to make arrests.

When I asked federal officials why the marshals were not prepared to control the mob first by methods short of gas, the answer was that this would have ended what little cooperation they were receiving from the Highway Patrol and would have produced criticism for bypassing state authority. The difficulty with this explanation is that cooperation ended and criticism resulted anyway. The argument comes back to the fact that there was no worthwhile plan for preventing a riot, so it was inevitable that the situation would mushroom out of control. It is true, as reported by the legislative committee, that Nicholas Katzenbach was surprised that gas had been fired, but he was not outside with the marshals.[17] But it is ridiculous to claim, as the legislative committee did, that the mob was "less noisy and boistrous [sic] than it had been for an hour" and that the gas was used "without warning."[18] The crowd was out of control at 8 P.M., and only a small number of highway patrolmen and University police were doing anything to control it. Tear gas seemed the only way to control it, and the man who ordered its use, James McShane, was neither "trigger-happy" nor "inexperienced." Given the actions and inactions of the state officers who had primary responsibility for maintaining order, it is hypocrisy to blame the riot on those who took action to control it.

The sixth point of controversy concerns the alleged brutality of the marshals and the soldiers.[19] The easy answer is that the rioters had gone to war against federal forces. They used far more deadly weapons and inflicted more serious injuries than did the marshals or soldiers. Neither the marshals nor the troops returned the gun-fire of the rioters. Beyond this it is clear enough that the marshals and soldiers were rough—no doubt sometimes unnecessarily rough—on their prisoners. Had the operation been better planned for dealing with a riot in the initial stages, or had it been an overwhelming military action from the beginning, the prisoners could have been captured and treated more nearly in accordance with the Geneva Convention. But it was rough on everyone, and it is significant that most of the "Mississippi reports" had no word of criticism of the rioters for their "brutalities."

Finally, there is the charge that the use of regular troops and the Mississippi National Guard was "illegal." Mississippi authorities made no legal attempt to prove this because it was completely without substance. As long ago as the Pullman Strike and as recently as Little Rock, the power to use troops to enforce court orders had been clearly established. The Mississippi legislative committee criticized federal officials—justifiably in my opinion—for not taking earlier action to use the National Guard, but the same committee would no doubt have criticized such earlier action had it been taken.[20] It is regrettable that troops must occasionally be used to enforce federal law, but the federal government has no police force. If there were no cases of massive law violation, and if state and local authorities always maintained order in an effective manner, there would be no need for the use of troops.

There remain some necessary comments concerning the two reports which purported to be based upon extensive questioning of witnesses—those of the Lafayette County Grand Jury and of the Mississippi General Legislative Investigating Committee. Neither made a serious attempt to gather all of the evidence, and both are as noteworthy for what they omitted as for what they included. I offered to supply the grand jury with a long list of eyewitnesses to the start of the riot, but they were interested in only one additional person. I gave them the name of someone whose evidence was not as complete as most, assuming that they would call the major eyewitnesses. They did not. The legislative committee criticized a University professor who did not "offer" to testify, yet the committee did not announce that it welcomed testimony. The general opinion on the campus was that it was interested only in the testimony of carefully selected witnesses. The major omission of both groups was an investigation of the violation of Mississippi laws by the rioters. Except for the grand jury's mention of the deaths of Gunter and Guihard, a reader unfamiliar with the case might assume that the rioters' behavior was commendable. The legislative committee had much praise for the Highway Patrol, and it reported not a single case of improper behavior by patrolmen.[21] It concluded that "plans were carefully made to assist in maintaining order and preventing violence." It pointed out that the Patrol had maintained order on three occasions before September 30, but completely neglected to mention that on a *fourth* occasion —September 27—it had lost control so completely that James Meredith and his escort of marshals turned back only twenty miles from the campus. This is but one specific instance of the transparent bias of the report. It is perhaps unnecessary to note that none of the Mississippi reports has any words of criticism for Governor Barnett's defiance of court orders and of his other actions.

Within Mississippi the net result of the reports was again to justify insurrection and violation of court orders. When combined with other less sophisticated reports of the riot, they helped to make heroes of those who were later called "brick and bottle" veterans. The destruction of what the 128 business leaders had called "honor, dignity, and respect" now bore the stamp of approval of the Citizens' Council, the Junior Chamber of Commerce, the state legislature, a circuit judge, and a grand jury. The perversion of fact by those who should know better reached its apotheosis when the National Junior Chamber of Commerce gave an award for "community service" to the Mississippi branch for the pamphlet containing its report, of which it distributed 200,000 copies. The official presentation of evidence concerning Mississippi's resistance against national law awaits the criminal contempt trials of Ross Barnett and Paul Johnson.

The struggle which now continued at Ole Miss was related to the issues which have just been described, but it was much more personal and immediate. It was also time consuming, and those on both sides—and in the middle—on the Meredith question had little spare time. During the critical period which lasted until February, 1963, the campus was obsessed with the issue, so that it was hard to find any field of activity unrelated to it. Golf, coffee, concerts, eating, visiting lecturers, and academic pursuits were all affected to some degree. James Meredith was accused by some—including some of his supporters—of wanting to obliterate segregation in Mississippi singlehandedly. He may have been over-optimistic in his goals, but the fact remains that he never attended an athletic event, never attempted to use the swimming pool, and never even had coffee at the normally public Alumni House grill. (The Alumni House always disclaims any relation whatsoever with the University whenever the question of Negroes is mentioned.) It is not possible to describe everything which occurred by the end of January, 1963, but by that time the University had struggled through a number of seemingly impossible problems and crises.

At 5:10 P.M. on October 3 the University chapter of the A.A.U.P. held the meeting that some members thought should have been held the day after the riot. A special resolution committee (appointed before the riot) reported that it had no recommendations, but Richard S. Stewart, Assistant Professor of Ancient History, introduced a resolution to place the chapter on record on the issues. Some members wanted it made clear they did not personally know that the marshals had not precipitated the riot, and an amendment was unanimously adopted that the supporters of the resolution only had "evidence" to that effect. The main concern was that something needed to be done to demonstrate the integrity of the University and of the faculty. Along with several others I suggested that further argument over rhetoric was pointless and that we should adopt the resolution and all be willing to sign it. It was adopted by a vote of 19 to 3, and we proclaimed to whoever would listen:

> RESOLVED, that we, the members of the University of Mississippi chapter of the American Association of University Professors, deploring the tragic events centered about this campus during the past few weeks, do declare our belief that:
>
> 1. While it is obvious that errors of judgment were made by those in authority on the University campus on Sunday, September 30, we have evidence that the attempt of men in prominent positions to place all the blame for the riot on the United States marshals is not only unfair and reprehensible, but is almost completely false. We encourage an investigation by the proper authorities.
>
> 2. Some news media in Mississippi have entertained irresponsible and secondhand stories in distortion of the facts, and have thereby helped to provoke a general state of confusion, alarm, and misdirected wrath. We join with those fellow Mississippians who resolved in Jackson, on October 1, their hopes that all news media would "cooperate with sane, sensible, public utterances and . . . refrain from the publication of inflammatory statements."
>
> 3. While all citizens of Mississippi and of the United States of America have the right to disagree in every peaceable and legal way with the law of the land as interpreted by the Supreme Court, it is the duty of every patriotic citizen to obey the law and to encourage others to obey it. We believe in the use of courts and ballot-boxes to state our convictions; we oppose and deplore the useless employment of clubs and missiles against fellow citizens on behalf of any conviction whatsoever.
>
> 4. Riots, weapons, and agitators have no place at a university. This University can better carry on its important part in the march toward progress and prosperity in Mississippi without any of these. With the cooperation of the overwhelming majority of law-abiding Mississippi citizens, the University of Mississippi can return in the near future to the normally peaceful conditions essential to education, to Mississippi, to the nation, and to constructive work for the future.

My wife and I hurriedly typed and duplicated the resolution, and at 8:15 P.M. A.A.U.P. president Barton Milligan and I showed it to the chancellor at his home. Like dozens of others later, he questioned the use of the word "reprehensible," but he had no other objections. Milligan and I then took copies of the resolution to newsmen at the Ole Miss Motel, where we handed it out door to door. We finished with interviews for NBC and CBS television at about midnight, and the overall result was a deluge of favorable publicity in the outside world. When we cut off the signing of the resolution three days later, it had been signed by forty-five A.A.U.P. members and nineteen non-members. The signers included one dean, two former deans, nine department chairmen, four former department chairmen, two Rhodes scholars, twelve members of Phi Beta Kappa, and twenty-nine full professors. All were secured without any campaign for signatures and with only informal hints that signatures were welcomed. Ailing English professor Mildred Topp left a sick bed to sign it.

The response aside from publicity came in the form of many letters and telegrams. There were letters from President Kennedy, Burke Marshall, and all of the Mississippi congressional delegation except Senator Eastland and Representative John Bell Williams. The President wrote:

> May I say how pleased I was over the action that you took, which is in the best tradition of academic responsibility in a free university. The citizens of Mississippi should be heartened by your statement, the statement of the clergymen of Oxford, of the important business groups in the State and the conduct of the Mississippi National Guard during the recent difficulty.

We received letters or telegrams from fifty A.A.U.P. chapters or other faculty groups at other colleges and universities, only one of which contained anything but praise. There were countless letters from individuals—two-to-one in support of our stand—and one of the few from Mississippi said in part, "It may have taken courage, but if we are afraid to stand up and be *counted,* how much do we 'count' wherever we are, whatever we may be doing?" We answered all of these communications, and I distributed excerpts from many of them to those who had signed the statement. The unanticipated response was an important factor in making our efforts seem worthwhile.

Another type of reaction was less heartening. The Citizens' Council sent out from its Greenwood office a list of resolution signers, copied exactly from a news story even to three misspelled names. This was partly the cause of a long siege of harassing telephone calls to faculty at inconvenient hours, particularly late at night. These consisted variously of silence, argument, profanity, and occasionally threats. "Hello, nigger lover," was the usual opening remark, and the threats were to run us out of town or to come over and beat us up. One conservative signer of the statement suggested to a pre-dawn caller that if he would bring his mother along, the professor would serve her a helping of a well-known dog food. Responses to the harassment were as varied as the abuse of the callers, although my wife and children—and occasionally I—were polite to those who phoned. On one particularly difficult night, an Army Counter-Intelligence Corps investigator made several calls before convincing me that he was not a heckler—the initial trouble being that he would not identify himself but wanted to come over to see me. Federal investigators spent much time trying to track down the calls, but without success. My family soon solved the problem by covering the telephone with pillows at 10:30 each night and answering no calls even if we were awake to hear the faint buzz. Meredith received many such calls, but the marshals usually answered his phone. The overall effect of the calls—besides loss of sleep—was to make the recipients more determined in their support of Meredith's right to be at the University. University officials also got their share of calls; and sometimes segregationists were called by other segregationists who thought the former were traitors to the cause.

For several weeks after the riot I spent many hours in an attempt to secure financial reimbursement from the A.A.U.P. Academic Freedom Fund for those whose cars were burned. As it turned out, the insurance companies finally liberalized their rules in order to pay for all but two of the cars. A.A.U.P. offered to reimburse psychology professor William Crowder—one of the signers of our statement—but he refused the money on the ground that this was his "contribution to academic freedom."* Although there was no

*One of the ironies of teaching at Ole Miss came later when Crowder received a letter from an executive of a large New York corporation, in which he referred to Crowder as "an ape" instead of a man and as a "lousy stupid son-of-a-bitch." He added for good measure that the University "should be burned down to the ground and the ground kept foul for the next 1,000 years." After his signature was the identification, "White Protestant (French Evangelical Church)." We assumed that the writer was an integrationist, but his language was worse than that used by radical segregationists.

admission of legal liability, the University was later authorized by the Board of Trustees to pay for damage to faculty and staff cars beyond that covered by insurance. During a year when these officials were criticized unmercifully, this demonstrated an unnoticed regard for the individuals who suffered losses from the riot.

On October 3 the ministers of Oxford called upon the "people of our community and state to make Sunday, October 7th, 1962, a specific time for repentance for our collective and individual guilt in the formation of the atmosphere which produced strife at the University. . . ." Their statement called for "positive leadership and influence such as that provided on October 2 by certain businessmen of our state." Episcopalian Rector Duncan Gray emphasized that although church members did not riot, they were "responsible for the moral and political *climate* in our state which made such a tragedy possible." He recalled that after the Civil War, when a Negro sought Communion in an Episcopal Church and others refused to join him, General Robert E. Lee went forward and knelt beside him. In the Presbyterian Church Murphey Wilds called for "obedience where we have been disobedient, speaking where we have been silent, striving to undo the evil which has been done rather than adding to it, and living with Christian love and respect for every child of God rather than with hatred and contempt for any." Other Oxford ministers spoke similar words, but again, as before the riot, most of those who engaged in violence were not there to hear.

The military forces on the campus were gradually reduced to the number necessary to provide protection for James Meredith and the marshals. On the night of October 2, Lieutenant Henry Gallagher picked sixteen men for the "Peanut Patrol" which was to be within a hundred yards of Meredith at all times. With "Peanut" as the basic radio call signal, Gallagher worked out a system of communication based on the Army version of the "10-6-4" code, using building numbers from a campus map to indicate locations and movement. A message might say, "Peanut, 56 to 23, 10-8-3," and the student rebels who monitored the broadcasts with citizens' band receivers could not tell what was to happen. The special patrol always had four radio-equipped jeeps in a planned deployment around Meredith at any given time, and the marshals could communicate with them on walkie-talkies carried in their coat pockets. Other soldiers in jeeps also patrolled the campus and the Oxford area during this critical period, and jeeps regularly passed the homes of certain Oxford residents. If I wanted to locate Meredith for some purpose, I simply looked for the jeeps of the Peanut Patrol. During this first semester there was, in addition, a Department of Justice attorney always on the campus, who was the main point of contact with University officials and key faculty members. The principal ones were Arvid A. Sather, John Martin, Gerald Stern, and Robert Owen, and John Doar was likely to appear at any time. Frank Vandergrift, Robert Haslip, and Chester Smith were the marshals with key responsibilities. All of the marshals and soldiers had an unbelievably difficult task of dealing with unexpected problems and with people who were not happy about their presence. Yet we waited a whole year for a responsible commitment to preserve order from someone at the state or local level, and it never came.

James Meredith went through his first week with no major difficulties but with regular verbal harassment from the minority still willing to cause trouble. This came particularly from a group of about eighty which gathered outside Conner Hall when he left his 9 A.M. class. He ate his first meal at the cafeteria on the night of October 4 without difficulty, and one undergraduate student, Paul McDonald, took the step of shaking hands and talking briefly with Meredith. Trouble did come on October 8 while Meredith was eating later than most students, at about 6:30 P.M. A crowd of about sixty students gathered north of the cafeteria, and repeatedly during the meal a few of the crowd would run up and yell through the window, "Eat—eat—eat." One student threw a fist-size rock through the window, barely missing Meredith and scattering glass on the table. The marshal eating with Meredith rushed out to make certain there was sufficient protection, and Lieutenant Gallagher summoned two more soldier-laden jeeps. As the crowd grew larger, Meredith was hustled out a back door and to his room in Baxter Hall. The marshal then found that a flat tire had immobilized his car north of the cafeteria and asked Gallagher to take care of getting it moved. During the half-hour or more that it took to get the tire changed, the crowd grew larger and meaner, and its members began throwing cigarettes, rolls of toilet paper, rocks, and one or two bottles. During the confusion someone pasted a large "mickey mouse" emblem on the back of a jeep, which the soldiers didn't discover until later. The soldiers took no action, although they did ready their gas grenades and riot sticks. Gallagher and other officers were afraid the mob would really get out of hand, and a jeep-load of soldiers with a tear gas dispenser (their main riot weapon) was standing by only fifty yards away. One of the two generals in town came on the radio wanting to know where Meredith was, but he did not know the code and the soldiers had orders not to communicate in any other way. Finally he shouted, "I don't give a damn about your secret code—is Meredith back in Baxter Hall yet?" A soldier answered, "Yes, sir." After the marshal's car was moved, Chief Tatum and Dean Love managed to disperse the crowd. Lieutenant Gallagher later had considerable praise for Tatum's ability to get the students under control when he was given a chance to do so.

Gallagher later explained why this incident bothered the military guards so much, although he agreed with Dean Love that news reports of it were sensationalized.[22] He could not understand why some students were willing to throw bottles and rocks at soldiers, since they were there under orders to take whatever steps were necessary to prevent order from breaking down completely. He was also haunted by the fear that neither the soldiers nor the students could be sure when a tense situation might explode if, for example, a soldier should be seriously injured. I explained to him that this trouble was caused by a group of about two hundred who had neither respect for authority nor any interest in the University, and that they would have welcomed a repetition of September 30. The question remained *when* the University would get them under control.

A small beginning was made on October 12, when Dean Love warned in the student newspaper that there would be "immediate and drastic" disciplinary action against demonstrators. This announcement brought support from a *Mississippian* editorial, and from statements by the Presbyterian student group, the leadership organizations Omicron Delta Kappa and Mortar Board, and the student government organization. The last of these might have been more effective had it not continued to support the contention that Meredith was "an unqualified student." But there was no doubt that the great majority of students wanted an end to the demonstrations and harassment.

A major behind-the-scenes battle was now taking place over the power of the University to discipline students who had been arrested by marshals for taking part in the riot of September 30. Attorneys appointed by Governor Barnett to defend the students attempted, with others outside the University, to prevent the Student Judicial Council from trying the eight students, including the threat of a state court injunction against their trial. The University finally won the argument, and the students received sentences ranging from disciplinary probation for one semester to its equivalent for the remainder of their attendance at the University. This type of penalty meant that any subsequent violation would lead to their expulsion.[23] The evidence against the students was deficient for several reasons (among others, it was dark the night of the riot), but the fact remains that these eight students were the only persons convicted for actions during the riot. Later attempts to prosecute non-student rioters in the federal courts did not result in convictions by Mississippi juries, although impressive evidence was presented.

During most of October and until the Christmas vacation the battle over student discipline continued. It developed into more than a simple conflict between faculty and administration, and an important part of it was the changing attitudes of several administrators which produced action later. There were charges and counter-charges, which might have been prevented by adequate communication between the faculty and the administration. For all practical purposes the University continued until almost the end of October a soft policy on student discipline, even though it made noises about toughness. No action was taken against those involved in the October 8 demonstration near the cafeteria, and

Dean Love later indicated the administration attitude when he wrote in the University's "Meredith Report"—released on November 15 and called by many faculty the "grey paper" because of the color of its binding and some of its contents—that the crowd was "small"—it was at least three hundred—and gathered only because of the flat tire on the marshal's car.[24] There was apparently a fine distinction between a "small crowd" and a potentially dangerous mob.

Although some reporters and others charged that Meredith made statements in order to seek publicity and stir up trouble, he made only one statement during the three months before Christmas that might be justifiably criticized. On October 9, the day after the incident described above, he issued a handwritten statement charging that the Army had "re-segregated" the troops on campus and criticizing a reported statement by an NAACP official that he had been "picked" to integrate Ole Miss. "Integration or desegregation have never been my goal," he said. "Better educational opportunities for myself and my people have always been my major consideration."[25] The statement could hardly have produced the demonstration of the previous night, although it did reflect Meredith's over-optimistic assumption that public statements would improve the situation.

Another element in the problem of discipline resulted from the allegation that several faculty members had threatened in their classes to use grading as a penalty against those engaging in demonstrations or harassment of Meredith. This produced much more immediate action from the administration than the demonstrations. Although faculty members had not made public statements on the matter, the Academic Council (the provost and the deans) adopted and issued to the press two statements. One congratulated and commended the chancellor and stated that the council "commends to the faculty, staff, and students the rapid restoration of normal academic routine." It could be argued that the two parts of the resolution were contradictory, for the second statement clearly implied that the student activity against which faculty members complained—verbal and sometimes physical harassment—was part of "the academic freedom of students." There was not even implied criticism of the harassing activities of students. The statement did state that the "support and cooperation of the faculty in maintaining student discipline outside the classroom are to be encouraged. This . . . can best be expressed by working through established University procedures for dealing with disciplinary problems." This statement infuriated those faculty members who had expressed disapproval of the slowness of the "established University procedures" (the punishment of rioters was not announced until ten days later), and one result was the year's most bitter meeting of the A.A.U.P. There was majority agreement that grading was not a proper disciplinary device, but there was sympathy with those who made the threat as a last resort against a complete collapse of student discipline. Several of those who were among the accused faculty pointed out that the administration had issued the statement on the basis of unverified accusations from students. One suggested half-jokingly that we might put "Impeach Ross Barnett" stickers on our cars. The incident led to a further deterioration in faculty-administration relations.

A unique answer to the frustration of many of the faculty was the publication of a dittoed *Ole Miss Coloring Book,* distributed anonymously in an edition of less than one hundred copies. Copies were passed around and reproduced in a variety of ways. The captions were bitterly satirical, and even the faculty came in for criticism. Along with remarkably appropriate caricatures, some of the captions read: "This is the Governor. Color him off-white." "This is —, leader of the band. Color both sides of his mouth." "This is the Provost. Color him little." "This is the Ole Miss Faculty. Color it silent." "This is an Ole Miss student. Color his brick red." The last page carried a drawing of Meredith with the caption, "This is a new student. He is already colored." At least two administrators were able to see some humor and even appropriateness in the barbs aimed in their direction. In terms of supply and demand, no more sought-after publication came out of the whole affair. The coloring book served a real purpose in providing some humor during a period when grim was the word for almost everything.

Yet another statement of faculty opinion came on October 17

from the Phi Beta Kappa Associates, a group of about twenty-five. This moderate declaration stated in part:

> . . . Individual freedom and a respect for human dignity are the lifeblood of a university. If these principles are abandoned, the institution loses its integrity, and the degrees it confers become a mockery. . . . We commend those who have acted responsibly in the present crisis, and we call upon those who are unwilling to accept their responsibilities to reconsider their attitudes. We support "drastic disciplinary action" [the quote was from Dean Love's statement of October 12], including possible dismissal of students, for those whose behavior discredits the University, the state, and the nation.

Theodore Bieber, Paul Hahn, and I had submitted proposed statements to the Phi Beta Kappa meeting, and the result was a combination of the three. Among other things, it was intended as a partial reply to the statement of the Academic Council. The Faculty Senate was also arguing about the problem of student discipline, but at this point it failed to agree on a firm statement of any kind.

As we struggled through October, several administrators began to move in the direction of a stronger position, partly because the situation was becoming intolerable and also because the University's accreditation status was to be considered in November. On October 22 Vice Chancellor W. Alton Bryant broke the silence in a speech to the Forrest Lions Club. After reviewing the achievements made by the University through the efforts of many Mississippians, he pointed to the danger of the loss of accreditation of all of the public colleges and universities of the state and tactfully stated, "However much we may disagree with court decisions, we must school ourselves and our children to obey the law and assure that future riots and bloodshed will not occur." He called for the saving of the educational system by "taking a calm and sensible view of our problems" and by bringing "the best features of the Mississippi Way of Life into full flower: A way of life filled with respect and pride for the graciousness, the hospitality, the honesty, and the courage of our past; a way of life that looks forward to a greater tolerance, a greater justice, a greater prosperity than we have ever known." Bryant was trying to remind Mississippians that riot and lawlessness were not their real tradition. For him and for others who kept trying, it was not to be an easy task.

The next outbreak of student protest began on October 24 when Meredith for the first time stopped in the Student Union grill for refreshments. All of the students except one girl immediately left, and the usual crowd began to gather in the hall outside. The crowd cursed Meredith as two marshals cleared a way for him to leave. Someone asked the girl why she stayed, and her answer was, "I've got to study. I don't have time to mess around with this stuff."[26] Meredith never returned to the grill during his stay at Ole Miss. Some students began that night to harass a different girl by telephoned and other threats, on the mistaken assumption that she was the one who had remained in the grill.

On that same Thursday there appeared the first edition in 1962 of the *Rebel Underground,* which opposed "Brotherhood by Bayonet" and proclaimed, "We will never accept integration at this or any other institution. We propose to resist by every effective means from now on. We serve notice to the forces of integration that 'We have only begun to fight.' " The publishers explained their anonymity with the argument: "Since armed troops occupy our campus and since there are carpetbaggers and scalawags on the faculty our resistance is necessarily underground."[27] The publication was mimeographed on a pre-printed two-color letterhead, with the Confederate "stars and bars" at the top and a flaming torch at the bottom. My copy of this came in the mail in an envelope sealed with Citizens' Council stickers, and on it the sender had crudely lettered, "Remember This, Communist," and had underscored several passages. The typing was similar to that of mimeographed material which I had received from the Citizens' Council. It was the first of about a dozen issues which appeared with varied typography during the year.

The *Rebel Underground,* which was almost certainly produced off-campus by rebel students and their supporters, was matched throughout the state by other signs of support for continued resistance. The Lexington Rotary Club passed a resolution claiming that the rights of Ole Miss students were being violated by the national government, the NAACP, and "particularly the Fifth Circuit Court of Appeals." This piece of dangerous nonsense was topped by an editorial in a Lexington weekly which stated that those who rioted and demonstrated at the University "continue to display the indomitable spirit and enthusiasm of freedom loving patriots." Calling their anarchist behavior "magnificent," the editor continued, "All members of the administration and faculty who have suggested compromise, should be regarded as enemies and treated thusly. Perhaps, one day the state will be fortunate enough to rid itself of these menaces to our society."[28] On October 26 the state Junior Chamber of Commerce issued its pamphlet, "Oxford: A Warning for Americans." By the end of October there was almost as much advocacy of rebellion as before September 30—but now there were voices on the side of law.

My answer to the special copy of the *Rebel Underground* was to have coffee with Meredith in the cafeteria on Friday, October 26. Only a few other faculty had shown any public cordiality to him. Although many Ole Miss faculty members drink coffee and eat with students, it rapidly became some kind of special crime to do so with Meredith. Newspaper publicity invariably provoked harassment for such acts, so it was important to me that both the AP and UPI reporters—sitting nearby while Meredith and I had coffee—told me they would not report the occurrence. But a student reporter for the *Memphis Commercial Appeal* who was not even there did report it, and as a result I experienced a sharp increase in attacks.[29] My answer was to make a point of having coffee with Meredith each time the *Underground* was published, and there were so many issues that it became somewhat tiring. The faculty and students who ate and had coffee with Meredith received criticism from some University administrators as well as from on- and off-campus rebels. Of course we could have avoided this by stopping our activities, just as Meredith could have avoided criticism of himself by never having come to Ole Miss. It is difficult to say how much this "social mixing" provoked retaliation by our minority of student resisters, but the only alternative was Meredith's complete isolation.

On October 27 the national council of the A.A.U.P. issued a statement calculated to strengthen the position of the University and the faculty, which declared in part:

> The deplorable events which took place in Oxford, Mississippi, would not have occurred if the political authorities of the state had supported the University in adhering to the law of the land and its academic obligations. The basic issue in the University of Mississippi situation and at many other institutions of higher education, especially in the South, goes deeper, however, than the matter of institutional government. It concerns the willingness of our society and of the educational community finally to accord fundamental justice to Negro citizens.

This statement resulted partly from a special report by the vice president of our A.A.U.P. chapter, English professor Tom Truss, and the statement was later endorsed by our chapter. The national office of the A.A.U.P. of course maintained its interest in our situation throughout the year, although most of its actions were conducted through private communications.

By Monday, October 29, the University had worked out an agreement with federal officials to relax controls over students in Baxter Hall (Meredith's residence), where identification cards had been required of everyone entering the building. Dean Love was to explain the new policy to the dormitory residents at 10 P.M., but trouble began at 6 P.M. Outside groups had cooperated with student rebels to ship in a supply of firecrackers, including large "cherry bombs." As Meredith and his escort of marshals were leaving the cafeteria after their evening meal, about a hundred students who had gathered outside began throwing cherry bombs. Marshals and military police who tried to chase offenders had their way blocked by other students, who began throwing eggs and bottles. The crowd dispersed soon after Chief Tatum arrived, and he arrested one student.

Just as Dean Love was speaking to Baxter Hall residents, students began a barrage of firecrackers, which was directed particularly at Baxter Hall. Students working in two-man teams were using slingshots to propel cherry bombs at the soldiers who surrounded Meredith's dormitory. One would hold the slingshot while the other lighted the fuse and fired the explosive ball. It was difficult to track down the rebel "patriots," because they were shooting from dormitory windows and from behind one dormitory. Several University officials and student leaders broke up the crowd, and the attack finally subsided to an occasional explosion.

The following day was another busy one. Deputy Attorney General Katzenbach flew in during the afternoon to confer with University officials on the problem of discipline. In the evening a bottle was thrown through the window of a car in which Meredith was riding, and it slightly injured a marshal. During the night students threw leaflets from a window in Powers Hall, but the residents denied any knowledge of them. Directed at "Soldiers of America," the sheets referred to President Kennedy as a "sick, sick, Communist" and asked the soldiers not to obey "Red Jack Kennedy."

Our A.A.U.P. chapter met at 5 P.M. on October 30, and we could hear cherry bombs exploding in the dormitory area as we talked. It was reported that a "committee of nine" had been organized, with equal representation from the Faculty Senate, the A.A.U.P., and the general faculty, and that its purpose would be to provide communication between the administration and the faculty. The committee had been spearheaded by Provost Charles F. Haywood, and indications were that it would press for stronger disciplinary measures. The chapter approved formation of the committee and delayed proposals for a strong public statement on integration. There was discussion of the possibility of the faculty patrolling the campus, and several faculty agreed to meet that night to begin such action.

So it was that about eight of us took flashlights and overcoats on a cold night and joined several members of Dean Love's staff at the Union Building. We did little other than walk around the dormitory area, occasionally stopping to talk to students, but the effect was to keep them reasonably quiet. There were a few firecrackers, but the situation was almost normal when we left the area at 1:30 A.M. We returned the next night, after another A.A.U.P. meeting at which the provost explained the situation. He pointed out that University officials believed that the recent violence had been instigated by outsiders who wanted to force the closing of the University, an action advocated in a recent pamphlet distributed by the Citizens' Council. Haywood announced that Lester Hall was being searched as we met, and that the finding of any fireworks or weapons in any student's belongings would mean expulsion. He also said that there was now better coordination between federal and University agencies, and that the chancellor would make a strong statement to the students on November 1. He expressed approval of the faculty patrols and added that we could identify demonstrators but had no authority to arrest them. The meeting set a record for communication with the administration, and we were at a high point of cooperation and understanding.

The search of Lester Hall did not turn up dynamite as expected, and the haul included only two dismantled guns, a souvenir gas grenade from the night of the riot, a few fireworks, and, in one student's trunk, about fifty unauthorized student identification cards. One soldier was injured when a cherry bomb exploded close to his eye. Our faculty patrol increased to forty that night, but there was only an occasional firecracker explosion after 10 P.M. Sidna Brower had editorialized in the *Mississippian* that morning that the "get tough" policy needed to be enforced: "It is disgusting to see such demonstrations permitted, especially when the rules are supposedly enforced."[30] Long after midnight a soldier fired a rifle shot into one dormitory after allegedly seeing someone in a window with a Molotov cocktail. This added to the turmoil, although it was true that the soldiers had to take unbelievable insults from the students.

Chancellor Williams made a speech to a combined meeting of civic clubs in Greenville on October 31, in which he stated that the University's troubles had been caused by a minority of students and implied that there would be policies to control them. He thanked those who had worked to keep the University open, and in emphasizing the importance of a "free university" warned against "mental stagnation and dry rot."

On November 1 all male students were summoned by the chancellor to meetings in Fulton Chapel. At these meetings he combined reasoning with threat in calling for an end to "jeering and shouted obscenities, shattering of glass, and cherry bomb barrages." He reasoned that their time would be wasted "if we cannot maintain peaceful and orderly conditions on the campus." He added that further demonstrations might cause the University to lose its accreditation, and that "the very survival of the University" was at stake. His threat left no doubts:

> Let me be as explicit as possible about our present situation. The shooting of fireworks, the possession of firearms and ammunition, the use of obscene and profane language, the committing of any act of violence or any act tending to disorder will be regarded as *serious* violations of University regulations. Swift and drastic disciplinary action, including expulsion from the University, can be expected. . . . If there are any who cannot support the establishment of peaceful and orderly conditions, be advised that I am prepared to see us part company.

The chancellor stated pointedly that the cases against students who took part in the violations of October 29 and 31 would be processed rapidly. They were—and five students were expelled. There was a pep rally the night of November 1, but the demonstration was all football. The policy which should have been adopted six weeks earlier was now in effect, and it appeared that we were finally on the road to solving the peculiar problems of Ole Miss and James Meredith. There now seemed to be less fear of outside pressure against a tough policy. Disciplinary action had been taken against those arrested during the riot of September 30, and later violations would soon produce even greater penalties. We were unified and optimistic—no one would have predicted the difficulties that were yet to come.

7 A DEGREE OF CHANGE

The strict disciplinary policy announced by the chancellor reduced group demonstrations against James Meredith, but November brought a new kind of pressure which annoyed him more than personal harassment. He had not been particularly bothered by the noise of the demonstrations, and only once had he lost his temper because of verbal attack. The demonstrators bothered other white students, but Meredith slept through most of the nighttime demonstrations. The few people with whom he had a chance to talk candidly had difficulty in understanding his viewpoint. What he said was: "I don't blame these young students, because they are not really doing and saying these things. They are doing what the system makes them do—what older people have taught them to do—and it is the system that has to be changed." There was no doubt that the demonstrations were hurting the University and that they had to be stopped—but as anti-Meredith activity they were not effective.

The type of pressure which was effective was not easily understood by those who had a legal responsibility and educational interest in Meredith's successful and continued attendance at the University. The problem was complicated by Meredith's reluctance to seek help from anyone. Events during the two weeks after November 1 began to point up the new difficulty, and on that date the second issue of the *Rebel Underground* appeared. It called for the organization of R.U. "teams" on every floor of all student residence halls, and stated the primary goal: "To encourage James Meredith to transfer to some college where he would be welcome." The publication noted that I had "socially mixed" with Meredith by having coffee with him, referred to the marshals and troops as "Kennedy's Koon Keepers," and congratulated Professors Farley (law), Harley Garrett (education), Silver (history), and Barrett (political science) for having been appointed "honorary niggers." It suggested that we "and a few other racial perverts" on the faculty should move to Tuskegee Institute or Tougaloo College (in Jackson). The *Underground* and the first "honorary nigger" cards were mailed within a day of each other, the latter by Citizens' Council members. My reaction to the cards was neither professorial nor particularly wise, but I did get out my World War II campaign ribbons and wear them to class on my lapel alongside the card. I also wrote a polite reply to one card-sender, in which I asked whether he was aware of the damage he was doing to the University.

The next disruptive move came in the form of a printed circular, *Rebel Resistance,* which was distributed widely on the campus on November 7. The message was that Meredith was an "NAACP leper" who should be kept "in a state of constant isolation," and so: "Let no student speak to him, and let his attempt to 'make friends' fall upon cold, unfriendly faces . . . the students should banish from their midst ANY white student who tries" to provide "social acceptance" for Meredith. The circular suggested that "pledge cards" might be printed to encourage ostracism, and concluded, "LET US STRIKE WHILE THE IRON IS HOT!" The importance of this type of harassment was not in the distribution of materials like the *Rebel Underground,* but that it proved the existence of a coordinated resistance group with members both on the campus and elsewhere in the state.

The first University administrator to warn publicly of the danger was Vice Chancellor Alton Bryant, who spoke in Jackson on November 8. After giving due credit to the great majority of students, he charged that the disruptive minority was receiving material support and instructions from "adult agitators" who preferred to remain "faceless and nameless." He stated that these "moral and physical cowards" were using students as "pawns" in order to force the closing of the University and the ruin of other public colleges. Bryant concluded that the time had come for "responsible citizens" to take steps "to insure a continuation of order and sanity in our educational system." These were strong and courageous words—particularly under the circumstances—yet the vice chancellor knew it would take more than a speech to save the situation.

Although there were no demonstrations during the first week of November, it was a rough time for Meredith. He did not know of the "underground" propaganda, but he noticed that students who had been saying "hello" had stopped. "Even the small number of professors and students who had occasionally eaten or had coffee with me weren't around," he told me about a week later. What happened was that the whole University had become so preoccupied with the battle over student discipline that almost everyone—including his friends—forgot about Meredith. We were busy and intent on saving the University, so that James Meredith sometimes seemed to be incidental. I did not see the dangers of this unconscious attitude until we had two long talks at the end of the second week in November. Like Hamilton Holmes at the University of Georgia, Meredith never cared whether he was accepted by the whole University community.[1] He did care that the minority who wanted to be friendly were either afraid or unwilling to do so. As he summed up the situation, "Sympathy doesn't mean much unless it is demonstrated where it can be seen."

There were also several practical problems which bothered Meredith in ways not appreciated by others. Newsmen hounded him, and when he did make statements it was charged that he was a "publicity seeker and troublemaker." A reporter told me that one newsman would get a remark out of him, after which another would say that he had to have a statement too or it would show that Meredith was unfair. Hindsight shows that reporters—of whom the least accurate was a student "stringer" who reported each of Meredith's absences while missing more classes than Meredith during the first semester—should have been asked to leave the campus or sharply curtailed in their activities. Although this was later done at other Deep South schools and at Ole Miss, such action at this time would no doubt have brought charges of "whitewash" and "censorship." The constant presence of the marshals and soldiers bothered Meredith, too, because normalcy could not come while they remained and because they kept him from having much real privacy. With a few exceptions, Meredith's guards were not outwardly friendly toward their charge, since they were there to do a job, and a tedious job at that. He had been unable to study in his room, because of noise from students and from a sort of communications center for the marshals and troops which operated in the room next door. He did not feel able to study in the library during the first six weeks. It also irked him that he had to go to Memphis rather than Jackson to see his wife, since federal officials believed that guarding him would be more difficult in Jackson. It all added up to a heavy load of frustration for a man who had entered Ole Miss almost two weeks late and who was taking courses chosen for him by others.

Human being James Meredith reacted to the pressure by leaving the campus a day early on November 8 for a weekend in Memphis. He missed examinations in algebra and English literature, and a student news correspondent reported, in a typically inaccurate dispatch, "Most agree the Negro's chances of passing either course, unless the tests are made up, would be slim." Many students at Ole Miss manage to pass courses even though they have missed exams, and policy on such matters rests solely with the professor. In Memphis Meredith held a news conference in the office of attorney A. W. Willis, Jr., who handles NAACP cases and had advised Meredith earlier.[2] He began by discounting rumors that he might withdraw from school, but said that the "abnormal campus situation" was such a burden that "I can't continue to meet my responsibilities" both as a "symbol" and as a student. He properly refused to discuss grades, and then made a statement that brought a torrent of criticism: "What we're involved with is the right to get an education. The right to fail is just as important as the right to succeed." The second sentence of that comment was usually quoted without the first, so that the word "right" took on a special meaning to some people. His meaning was clear for those who wanted to understand, but as with most other arguments over Meredith's statements, this was used as an excuse for criticizing him. Although he pointed out that his guards bothered him, Meredith emphasized that something needed to be done about the cause of their being on the campus—the disruptive leadership of the "faceless and nameless."

After Meredith returned to the campus for the week of November 12, a few individuals began to show concern over his academic situation. Although the faculty "committee of nine" was holding meetings almost daily and was working diligently under the leadership of William H. Willis, chairman of the Department of Classics, it bothered me that the group had shown little concern with Meredith's academic and personal situation. On my initiative Meredith and I had two discussions of more than an hour each, in which we candidly considered grades, absences, ostracism, and several other problems. One thing I learned was that he needed a friend to talk with about something other than race—someone who was not a reporter, a civil rights worker, or a guard. These conversations pointed up what really bothered Meredith most—his non-acceptance as a human being, and they prompted me to write a memorandum to the committee of nine. In this I went through a lengthy discussion of Meredith's attitudes concerning his problems and concluded, "Up to the present, the faculty, the administration, and the students remain in contempt of court, because they have not made it possible for Mr. Meredith to attend the University on the same basis as other students. We have gone perhaps one-tenth of the way in doing this, but it is not even a minimum good faith compliance." I argued that to prevent the catastrophe of his leaving the University we needed a plan which would introduce some semblance of normality in his class attendance, studying, attendance at public concerts and lectures, and contact with other students. My other recommendations included the elimination of news reporting of his every move, an intensified search for the "underground" group, and the issuance of a public statement by the University that Meredith was "to attend the University *on the same basis* as other students." The result of the memorandum was to make some committee members angry with me, apparently because they were already tackling impossible problems and thought my suggestions went too far. Because the committee depended on unanimity for the rather limited influence it had been able to gain, I withdrew the memorandum.

The University's accreditation was of course affected by most of what happened during October and November, but relations with the Southern Association of Schools and Colleges were a matter of reports, visits, and conversations which it was never polite to discuss. On October 18 the Board of Trustees informed the accreditation association that improper actions taken during September had been rescinded and that the board would be "assiduous" in avoiding political interference. Governor Barnett on October 25 assured the association that all authority for operating the institutions of higher learning was again in the hands of the board: "It is not my wish or purpose to accept or assume any of these prerogatives." Even so, he did not go so far as to request the legislature to repeal the law which gave him authority to close any school.

The association's action of November 28 was a relief for the University community. It placed *all* state colleges and universities in Mississippi "under continued and careful observation" and placed them on "extraordinary status" which could be reconsidered "at any time." The accrediting body warned specifically against weakening the constitutional board, encroachment by pressure groups or investigating committees, manipulation of appropriation bills as punitive measures, and "failure of the administration and faculty to maintain through normal student discipline a climate conducive to intellectual pursuits." This provided an important protective screen against those who were still trying to close the University, and the closure threat was a major reason for placing all state schools on "extraordinary status." The accrediting agency tried to make it clear that its action was against the Board of Trustees and especially the state political leadership, but much of the national news reporting made the action look like nothing more than the censuring of Ole Miss. On the campus there was relative joy that accreditation had not been lost, but state segregationist leaders continued their attack on the whole concept of accreditation.

The state legislature was back in special session again in November, because the voters had rejected a legislative apportionment proposal adopted by the legislature six weeks before. The legislators also found time to follow up their earlier challenges to the federal government, first with a joint resolution which called for the removal of troops from University property but carefully avoided any implication that the state was responsible for maintaining order at the University.[3] Next came a Senate resolution which expressed the Senate's "entire and utter contempt for the Kennedy administration and its puppet courts" and called the administration "despotic, ruthless, and corrupted."[4] This followed by less than a week an order from the U.S. Court of Appeals that the Department of Justice bring criminal contempt charges against Governor Barnett and Lieutenant Governor Johnson. Circuit Judge M. M. McGowan, one of the leading Citizens' Council activists in the state judiciary, summed up the attack on accreditation in an article in the *Jackson Daily News*.[5] He accused the accreditation association of "arrogance" and of wanting Mississippians to take up the "hammer and sickle" in defense of "the veritable hordes of socialist-minded professors who have wormed their way into the very heart of our society—our schools." His remedy was that "this self-anointed accreditation organization should be abolished by law" so the states could organize one which would "more nearly meet the needs of the people and the students." The judge neglected to mention that the accreditation agencies are composed of college presidents under the authority of their managing boards, and that Mississippi would have no allies among other states in his proposal for secession from the recognized agencies.

On November 15 seven Ole Miss students ate supper at the cafeteria with James Meredith; retribution from the "underground" was swift and drastic for two of them. A group of students broke into their room and wrecked it, scattering books, phonograph records, and clothing in such a manner as to ruin some of the belongings. Next to their door in black shoe polish was crudely lettered, NIGGER LOVERS. This incident eventually led to the collapse of the committee of nine, and with it much of the faculty-administration cooperation. Some University officials took the position that the students had "asked for it" by eating with Meredith, and partially rationalized their position by saying that the room was not badly damaged. The student body president, who frequently expressed his dislike for Meredith, was quoted as saying that the students' action in eating with Meredith was "ill advised."[6] As days passed and no action was taken against the vandals, faculty members began to question whether the investigators were really looking very hard. This angered University officials, who never made substantial progress on the case, and there was a period of bitter argument. At least two of the students were advised by University officials that it would be better if they did not eat with Meredith. Only two of the seven students completed their academic programs at Ole Miss; the others were hounded off the campus at various times during 1963. The names of the two who succeeded had not been included in news reports, a fair indication that some reporters were unwitting allies of the "underground."

Another cause of continuing unrest was the threat and then legal action against Ole Miss officials to force back into the University a student, Leroy Taylor Robertson, who had been expelled as a result of the dormitory search on October 31. After an attorney had failed to get the student readmitted by threatening to go to court, he obtained an admission order from Hinds County Chancery Judge J. C. Stennett. Robertson was readmitted to the University on November 30, but what his defenders did not realize was that he had already missed too many classes to have a chance of making passing grades. Yet another disruptive factor was a move in the student Senate in which student leaders who in effect supported the "underground" pressed for "censure" of *Mississippian* editor Sidna Brower. The Senate finally passed an odd resolution which praised her for deploring violence, disavowed interference with her editorial freedom, and yet "reprimanded" her for failing to uphold the students' "national image." Those who secured the passage of the compromise patted themselves on the back, but the impression outside of Mississippi was uniform—that student representatives were condemning one of the few positive voices on the campus.

The faculty response to both of the preceding developments came on December 6. In actions which again reflected a strong spirit of faculty-administration unity, the faculty commended Sidna Brower as well as University officials. The first resolution was moved by Paul Hahn and seconded by the provost:

The faculty of the University of Mississippi commends Miss

> Sidna Brower, editor of the *Mississippian,* for her unwavering determination to follow a constructive editorial policy of her own choosing during the extended crisis at the University. By holding to the American ideal of a responsible free press, she has significantly contributed to the preservation of the University's integrity.

Having thus answered the student condemnation of the editor, the faculty then voted to commend the Student Judicial Council and University officials for initially expelling Leroy Robertson and asked that "the chancellor be requested to make to the Board of Trustees the strongest possible representations urging that prompt and appropriate action be taken to secure the setting aside of the order of the Chancery Court of Hinds County." As on several previous occasions there was great optimism, but it was not to last long.

By the time of the Christmas vacation it was clear that there would be no effective challenge of the court order which had returned Robertson to Ole Miss. December brought a sharp increase in the harassment of students and faculty who had befriended Meredith. Senator Eastland had chosen November 30 to charge that professors were "intimidating" students who merely wanted to "protest" against integration.[7] He released some highly imaginative accounts by student spies of what professors had allegedly told their classes. The worst of these was from an "affidavit" regarding purported statements by me which a student had taken to a reporter for the *Jackson Clarion-Ledger;* after telephoning me, the reporter had the decency to prevent its getting into print. Some of my attempts at humor the student recorded as serious statements and others he simply fabricated—for example, that students "should have been machine-gunned along with other rioters." What I did say was that students should consider it fortunate that none of them had been shot the night of the riot. I was correctly reported as saying that students should turn in the names of demonstrators to the chancellor. Obviously Senator Eastland believed that this would interfere with the students' "constitutional right of protest."

Other examples of faculty harassment included a letter to English professor Mildred S. Topp, who at sixty-five years of age was in poor health and who died in 1963. A man who signed himself as state finance chairman of the Citizens' Council wrote to her from the Greenwood headquarters:

> You should be helping to get the negro *out* of the University, not interfering with students who are trying to do just that. At least 80% of the people of the State will support the students. Why not take your stand with them? The Citizens' Councils are busy taking names too, and when this thing is over, some Southern renegades are going to lose their jobs.

Another man from Brandon accused her in a January 11 letter of trying to "brainwash" and "threaten" students and threatened to "hang an injunction around your neck." He added that "a lady of your type should stay in her place and not make threats of this type." (Mrs. Topp was a native Mississippian and former member of the state legislature.) An anonymous "Mississippi Taxpayer" from Clarksdale wrote me a letter on November 28 with the salutation "Dear Nigger Lover" and the message, "What a pity one of the marshals [sic] stray bullets didn't glaze [sic] your scalp and knock a little sense in your head." Another example of the flood of such harassment was a card printed in large quantities and addressed to the Board of Trustees and the chancellor:

> As a taxpayer supporting state schools and as a loyal Mississippian promoting Americanism, I respectfully demand that Dean Farley, Jim Silver, Alton Bryant, Barrett and all other integrationists be removed immediately from the pay roll of Ole Miss.
>
> Also, please have University officials cease coddling Katzenbach and cease allowing him to attempt to brainwash our fine pro-American students.
>
> Further, the intimidation of our students must be halted.

Harassment of students was much more serious—and physical—and the "underground" group, which seemed to be known to everyone but University officials, followed Meredith's friends around and showered them with profanity and an occasional cherry bomb. What always amazed me about this harassment was its bitterly personal character. I asked one of the group much later about this, and he replied simply, "You have to be personal."

An important and disheartening December development was the resignation of two officials who had become valuable promoters of stability, Provost Charles Haywood and John B. Morris, Director of Institutional Research. Neither stated that he was resigning because of the disciplinary situation, but such was the common belief. Various faculty members had already begun casting around for other jobs, and it took the administration a long time to discover what was happening to the teaching staff. The replacement for the provost was Charles E. Noyes, an English professor and former president of the A.A.U.P. chapter. Noyes later found that he had moved into a job in which he would be lucky to satisfy anyone.

After classes resumed in January, the first *Rebel Underground* appeared, and six other issues were to follow in the next two months. While previous issues had limited themselves to the organization of "protest," this one was a call to violence. It adopted a slogan not used before, "Disobedience to tyranny is obedience to God," and stated, "Welcome back, students, to this occupied farce that was once a free school in a free land." The *Underground* advocated "force and/or violence . . . when correctly employed" and praised a "national organization" called "The Brick and Bottle Minute Men" and its Ole Miss local affiliate, the "Brick and Bottle Greys." It called for the "execution" of President Kennedy—no mention of a trial—and quoted "Brick and Bottle Leader Omega 1" as saying, "If the Coon should fall tomorrow, as well he may, this will not delay or stop us from our unflagging effort to destroy the Marxist Monster in Washington who now holds the free people of the U.S. in subjection and terror."[8] This reads almost like a parody composed by someone with a vicious sense of humor, but to anyone who has received abusive letters from the pathological individuals who write them, its words have a familiar ring.

On January 7 James Meredith, unaware of how well organized was the movement against him, issued a prepared statement which stunned most of his friends and delighted his enemies:

> For some time I have considered my course of action for the future. There are many factors, many issues, many aspects, and equally as many consequences.
>
> I have decided not to register for classes during the second semester at the University of Mississippi unless very definite and positive changes are made to make my situation more conducive to learning. This decision was based on a consideration of all the elements pertinent to the "Mississippi Crisis" at its

> deepest meaning of all the aspects of my personal relationship in it, with it, and to it.
>
> It should be noted that I have not made a decision to discontinue my efforts to receive educational training at the University of Mississippi. Rather my decision is not to attend the University next semester under the present circumstances.
>
> We are engaged in a war, a bitter war for the "equality of opportunity" for our citizens. The enemy is determined, resourceful, and unprincipled. There are no rules of war for which he has respect. Some standard must be set. Some pattern must be established so that those who are fighting for equality of opportunity and those who are fighting for the right to oppress can clash in the struggle without disaster falling upon either group. Presently, there is too much doubt and uncertainty regarding the procedure to be followed in settling our problems. No major issues have been decided legally or officially, illegally or unofficially.
>
> When I combine the political and educational reality with my personal possibilities and probabilities, the results lead me to the foregoing decision.
>
> As to what I will do, I am not prepared to say at this time, since I am still studying two or three alternatives. However, I plan to remain in Mississippi.
>
> I think that I should also add that I will have nothing further to say about this matter until after the end of this semester at which time I will be free to answer any questions and acknowledge any request.

My reaction to Meredith's statement was less explosive than that of some of my colleagues. At the time I did not think it was either a very wise or risky act on his part. Two things were very clear to me: his departure would hurt everything he and others had worked for, and it would be disastrous for the University. Some middle-ranking University officials greeted the statement with ill-concealed glee, but those capable of real consideration for the University's welfare were troubled. James Silver and I discussed the statement with a seemingly untroubled Meredith, and we concluded that we could only wait to see what would happen.

After Meredith read his statement to newsmen at Baxter Hall, there were taunts from the several hundred students who had assembled. For the rest of the week there was increased harassment of Meredith and those who had supported him, and faculty patrols were resumed. Firecrackers, bottles, and profanity were hurled on the nights of January 8 and 9 at the door of the same two students whose room had been ransacked in November. On the second night a bottle was thrown through the transom, but the only effective action by University officials was to ask the students to move to Baxter Hall (soldiers were still on guard there). There was a rash of table-banging in the cafeteria—the assumption being that this was a form of protest against Meredith—and on January 10 there was a demonstration against Meredith outside of the cafeteria, again including the throwing of at least one bottle. One student was arrested by Chief Tatum during the course of these events and was suspended from school, although he was not one of the main instigators of the trouble.

On January 9 Attorney General Kennedy issued a statement in which he praised "many members of the faculty" but alleged that "a number of officials charged with the administration of the University have not met their responsibilities." He added that University officials and state law enforcement officials should make it possible for Meredith "to continue his education without interruption." He concluded that Meredith was free to leave the University, but pointed out that in doing so he would be letting down those who supported his desire to attend, and that leaving would also be a reflection on the University, the state, and the United States. Chancellor Williams replied that the administration and faculty "have done all that was reasonable and proper to insure the best possible education for all students," and that the University "has fully complied with the orders of the courts at all times."[9] He also stated that the University was "getting along quietly and normally" until Meredith issued his statement. Some University official who could not possibly have known the facts was reported as stating that Meredith did nothing in his classes except "sit around and chew on a pencil." And presumably the same official also violated academic ethics by giving information on Meredith's grades to a favored reporter—information which he could not have known at that. Several faculty members who had Meredith in their classes told me that this reporter claimed to have authorization from the administration to talk to them about Meredith's academic performance. They also said that they refused to tell him anything. Whatever cooperation might have remained between the administration and the faculty was obliterated by this sequence of events.

No one except Meredith's teachers really knew of his academic standing, although the almost meaningless "progress report" grades (based on the first six weeks of classes) demonstrated that he was not likely to make the honor roll. Meredith was studying a good deal, and certainly more than a "little," as the reporter had stated. To claim that the University was getting along "quietly and normally" when two major administrators had resigned, the *Rebel Underground* was coming out regularly, the committee of nine had ceased to function, and when there had been a regular campaign of harassment of students and faculty before and after Christmas—all this is to make a sad commentary on what is "normal and quiet" at Ole Miss. There is no doubt that Meredith's statement added to the furor, yet the chancellor had nothing to say about the *Rebel Underground* or the group of students connected with it who continued their campaign to ruin the University and who had already driven from the University one of Meredith's student friends.

I sat down at my typewriter on January 11 and wrote another letter, this time to the chancellor. I pointed out that the University "has not been able to maintain an atmosphere in which James Meredith could be a student in a manner even remotely close to normal" and made some of the points explained above. I warned that unless the situation changed the results would be a major loss of faculty, a drop in enrollment, a continued lack of faculty-administration unity, the possible withdrawal of Meredith from the University, and an increasing possibility of loss of accreditation. My final suggestion was that the committee of nine be reactivated.

On January 12 one of the most vicious issues of the *Rebel Underground* appeared, calling the chancellor a "liar," a "quisling," and an operator of a "Soviet type of government at its worst." It also referred to Sidna Brower as a "vicious wench" and called for physical reprisals against her. Its new slogan for getting rid of Meredith was to "separate the coon from the curriculum."[10]

Also on January 12 I took to the chancellor a candid and somewhat caustic letter which had been adopted unanimously by the A.A.U.P. In it we praised him for the attempts to control discipline, but detailed several violations during the preceding two months which had not resulted in disciplinary action. His reaction was positive and reflected an almost desperate desire to get something done. It also demonstrated that we could still communicate with each other, even though neither of us was very optimistic. The reaction of A.A.U.P. members continued to be that disciplinary action was still not effective enough, and the virtual collapse of the committee of nine left no possibility of faculty-administration coordination.

After James Meredith finished his last final examination on January 22, he appeared for a promised conversation with Professors James Silver, William Willis, and me. He was well pleased with his efforts on final examinations, although he had decided some days earlier to settle for failure in algebra without bothering to take the exam. He seemed as cheerful as though he had just made the honor roll, and we ended up with the impression that he was not even thinking of withdrawing from school. In retrospect I wonder if he was not almost amused by the energy with which we put a series of arguments that he simply could not leave. We pointed out that he had already accomplished a great deal, that he would hurt his "cause" if he left, and that the situation was bound to improve during the second semester. We even pointed out the effect on the U.S. image in international affairs, which would have been very real. I stressed that the Department of Political Science would probably resume its meetings of departmental majors, which had lapsed because everyone was so busy. One major aspect of campus life that Meredith had been missing was the opportunity to talk with small groups of students and without the presence of newsmen. All James Meredith would say was that he was feeling fine and that he would consider all aspects of the problem when he made his decision. We knew we had not told him much, if anything, of which he was not fully aware.

Professor Silver wrote a second letter to presidential assistant Arthur Schlesinger, Jr., in which he suggested an appeal to Meredith from President Kennedy as a last resort.[11] I decided to write a letter to the editor which might serve more than one purpose, and my letter of January 26—of which I sent a copy to Meredith—was published in the *Jackson Clarion-Ledger* on February 1:

Those who are interested in education might want to consider the following:

1. James Meredith has been a properly enrolled student at the University of Mississippi. His behavior has been restrained and dignified, particularly when compared with that of the minority of students who have violated both the law and University regulations in protesting his presence at the University.

2. The members of this minority of students have shown their willingness to damage and even to destroy the University. They have done all in their power to ruin the national reputation of the University and to make it impossible for the University to attract good students or good faculty. In this they have been supported by adults outside of the University who seem to be equally willing to damage the University and the state.

3. The University administration, the faculty, and most of the students have attempted with varying degrees of success to keep the University in operation as an educational institution. They have had some encouraging and courageous support for their efforts by responsible leaders throughout the state. They need much more support if the University is to survive and grow as a respected place of learning.

4. What is needed in this situation is clear. People need only to accept their responsibilities as rational and law abiding Americans. South Carolina understands this, and South Carolina will grow and prosper. Cannot Mississippi do the same?

Many individuals and some faculty groups from all parts of the country wrote to Meredith, requesting that he stay at Ole Miss. Meredith learned that his grades were moderately above the average required to stay in school, and he had talked with Chancellor Williams in a mutually friendly fashion during the week before final examinations. If this is a surprise to anyone, I note that in many conversations I never heard Meredith criticize the University administration. Rightly or wrongly, he blamed others for his difficulties.

On January 30 James Meredith held a brief news conference in Jackson. He began by stating, "It is a great tragedy for America that whether a student will attend a University has become a big news item." In a statement that was as misunderstood as some of his earlier ones, he announced, "I have concluded that the 'Negro' should not return to the University of Mississippi. The prospects for him are too unpromising. However, I have decided that I, J. H. Meredith, will register for the second semester." Meredith said that

Ole Miss students were "basically good people" and that he saw signs in recent months that he could attend the University "under adequate, if not ideal, conditions."

I commented to a reporter at the time that it was good to see Meredith emphasizing his status as a student rather than as a symbol, and that Mississippians now had a chance to demonstrate that they could follow a path of "decency and compliance with the law." James Silver stated that Meredith's decision was a "crushing" defeat for the Citizens' Council and gave Mississippi a chance to "turn to the kind of responsible leadership recently demonstrated in South Carolina."[12]

At the University, administrative officials had prepared for Meredith's announcement by readying a new set of policies, which—as usual—did not please everybody. What almost everyone—critics and otherwise—failed to notice was the contrast between the advance announcement by the chancellor of the policies to be followed in the second semester, and the absence of such statements *by the University* during September, 1962. In a stern policy announcement of January 30, Chancellor Williams stated that Meredith would receive "the same treatment" given to other students, and that students or outsiders who opposed this would not be welcome on the campus. He warned, "No demonstrations, harassment of persons, distribution of unauthorized publications, or other actions disruptive of orderly academic life will be tolerated. Should incidents occur, administrative personnel, campus police, selected members of the faculty, and responsible students will work in concert to identify the troublemakers, who will receive swift and severe disciplinary action."

In a follow-up statement on January 31, the chancellor reaffirmed his responsibility for the maintenance of conditions "conducive to teaching, study, and research," and stated:

> Under existing conditions public statements and press, radio, and television interviews which appear likely to create disorder or impair the effectiveness of the educational program at the University of Mississippi must be regarded as unacceptable behavior on the part of all those associated with the University.

He added that disregard of the "request" might subject any individual to "appropriate action" and that the policy does not "limit the fundamental rights of all American citizens." In an attempt to soften the impact of what appeared to be a severe restriction of freedom, Williams noted that although freedom of speech "is an ideal of our society," it does not include "the right to shout 'Fire!' in a crowded theater." Along with these statements there was yet another announcement that during the two days of registration, reporters would not be permitted in the campus area west of the Lyceum Building. That included the cafeteria, Union Building, men's dormitories, and Gymnasium (registration building).

Under the restrictions of the new policy, registration on January 31 and February 1 ran smoothly, and James Meredith went through the line with the rest of the students. There was little visible guarding, and no obvious troops except for one soldier on the roof of the library. Meredith conferred first with his major advisers in political science, and within the limits of degree requirements enrolled in courses which he chose.[13] Another Negro, Dewey Roosevelt Greene, was denied admission to Ole Miss because of low grades at Mississippi Vocational College (Negro), from which he attempted to transfer.

At least registration brought no interposition by the governor, and the normal noisy talk of some Mississippi politicians and newspapers seemed almost irrelevant. The *Jackson Clarion-Ledger* headed its story, "James Registers," avoiding the use of Meredith's last name.[14] Jackson newspaper columnist Tom Ethridge relieved his frustration by an apparent attempt to establish that Alabama and Mississippi were not part of the United States.[15]

On the same day the Army announced it had dropped plans to build permanent housing for the three hundred troops still at the University. Numerous Mississippi political leaders had repeatedly asked for the withdrawal of troops—and of Meredith—but not a single one of them had even implied that the state would accept its obligation to assume responsibility for enforcing the law at Ole Miss.

While Meredith's campus situation went along in a way that had at least become tolerable, the faculty and the administration became embroiled in an argument over the chancellor's tough memorandum of January 31 regarding public statements. The Department of Journalism on February 6 sent to the chancellor and the Faculty Senate a statement that the chancellor's policy "seems to give credence to extremist views concerning the limited status of freedom at Ole Miss." Professors Willis, Truss, and I were delegated by the A.A.U.P. to seek clarification from the chancellor, and he explained that his memorandum applied only to those statements which caused major difficulty. To pin this down, I asked whether it would apply to the type of statements made by Silver and me during the preceding semester, and the answer was "no." After some debate in the Faculty Senate and some candid conversations with the national office of the A.A.U.P. —and nearly a month of almost normal campus life—the chancellor issued a new memorandum on February 25 which tactfully and honorably buried the previous policy. Although there had been justified criticism of the chancellor's January 31 statement, it had helped to maintain a reasonably successful policy of student discipline.

The *Rebel Underground* continued to come out during the first five weeks of the semester, and it descended to lower and lower depths in its vilifications of Meredith, his faculty and student sympathizers, and the University administration. In the issue which appeared on February 10 it reported with its usual disregard for facts that the NAACP would name Meredith "Nigger of the Year," that Meredith had violated the chancellor's policy by holding a "press conference" at the Episcopal Church, that the Department of Political Science had sponsored a "social" for Meredith, and that the chancellor, the FBI, and the Army were trying to suppress "free speech" in their attempts to identify the publishers of the *Underground*. It also noted that Meredith had recently played golf with Jim Silver and Reverend Wofford Smith—although the latter does not play golf.[16]

The "press conference" was a routine interview between Meredith and a visiting Japanese newsman, and its content was not reported in American papers. The political science "social" was the first of two meetings of departmental majors, at which coffee was served and professors talked about political party organization and legislative apportionment. Few of the students talked with Meredith during the informal part of the meeting, and he made no effort to initiate conversation. There were *Underground* supporters at the meeting, and students were afraid to get on their blacklist by even speaking to Meredith. The *Underground* publishers were hardly in a position to talk about free speech, since they were unwilling to accept any responsibility for their statements. (During the year many signed letters in support of segregation were printed in the *Mississippian.*) On the matter of golf Meredith played on many Thursday afternoons with faculty members and others. His fellow golfers included professors Silver, William E. Strickland, and me, and occasionally Presbyterian minister Clifford McKay and Colonel Frederick Harris, one of the commanding officers of the troops stationed at Ole Miss. On the first several rounds of golf there were imposing escorts of marshals, soldiers, and even a helicopter, but this was rapidly de-emphasized. The golf was important to Meredith, because he could relax completely. Thursday afternoons were the time scheduled for ROTC drill. It bothered Meredith that there were no ROTC programs in any of the Negro colleges in Mississippi, and he had entered Ole Miss too late to enter the military training program.

The remaining efforts of the *Rebel Underground* degenerated into increasingly personal attacks against University administrators, professors, Meredith, the Kennedy administration, and student friends of Meredith. It published phone numbers and addresses to promote harassment and can claim credit for driving political science major Judith Gardner from the campus and her parents from the state. She committed the crime of sitting next to Meredith in one of my classes, and nothing was ever done to reduce the vicious harassment inflicted upon her. The *Underground* argued the self-contradiction that Meredith had been "given" high grades by his instructors, but that the University administration had refused to dismiss him from school because he received failing grades.[17] The final issue criticized one professor for having a collection of "cosmopolitan pornography" and suggested that English professor Mildred Topp might have posed for some of the pictures.[18] Mrs. Topp replied in a letter to the *Mississippian,* in the course of comments on a future Mississippi legislator who had defended the *Underground,* "This is the only funny thing I have been able to find in the *Underground.* Since I am a grandmother and look every day of it, and since 94 pounds of my 95-pound weight consist of bones, such a picture would mean the end of the pornographic industry in the United States." Mildred Topp, who taught creative writing until her death in 1963, included in that letter a parody of a nightmare, and concluded with a comment on the nightmare:

> I walked through the shadows to the center of the grove, where, in my nightmare I had seen the brick and bottle statue. I put out my hand in the darkness and touched the flagpole. And I knew in the morning sunlight that flag, the flag of my country, the United States of America, would be floating over this campus, for the forces of evil, the powers of darkness that are now trying to destroy this University will not prevail. Though maimed, stabbed, and crucified by her own sons, this University will survive—and that flag will fly forever.[19]

The *Rebel Underground* of 1962-1963 died with a cheapness that matched its life, by a decision of its own segregationist supporters that it was hurting not only the University but also the cause of segregation.

For James Meredith the spring semester was definitely an improvement, yet he could still write accurately in April, "Most of the time, I am perhaps the most segregated Negro in the world."[20] Although I argued with Meredith that he was accomplishing more than he realized, he was correct in writing, "The basic problem is that none of us knows how to make the transition from one way of life and one status to another. People are afraid of change." He might have added that some people are afraid of other people who are especially afraid of change. Meredith did say just that when he appeared on *Meet the Press* on May 26: "The students are still not free to associate with me or to take a position that they would want to, if they wanted to take one different from what is the normally accepted position." The harassment of Meredith took place in those little ways which insult more painfully than demonstrations. Students liked to let the air out of the tires on his

Volkswagen, and another favorite trick was to take a call for him on the dormitory telephone and promise that he would make a speech before some group. In yet another case a student stole his glasses while he was studying in the library. It all added up to a considerable load of petty annoyances.

Meredith was invited to dinner at the homes of three faculty members, and for the two who lived off-campus the results were immediate. The difficulty was that two marshals' cars always accompanied Meredith on these visits, and they parked in front of the house of Meredith's host. With two hefty marshals in each car equipped with two-way radio antennas, the result was as though they carried a large banner proclaiming, "Meredith is here." There were torrents of telephone calls, and in one case the son of the offending professor was beaten up at school and drummed out of the Boy Scouts. I told a marshal that when Meredith was free to come to our house without a procession of guards, he would be welcome. As far as harassment goes, it made no difference, because Oxford segregationists always believed he visited our house frequently. For several weeks the telephone poles in front of the three faculty houses on our street bore the chalked inscription, NIGGER LOVERS. On the other hand, Meredith ate at the faculty apartment of art professor Ray Kerciu, and almost no one knew of it.

Professor Kerciu came to the attention of the segregationists soon after he opened a one-man art show on the campus on Sunday, April 7. Most of his paintings were non-controversial, but in a side gallery he displayed about a dozen pieces of poster art. Most of the paintings had as a background an extremely free rendition of a Confederate battle flag. One had printed on it the words SOVEREIGN STATE OF MISSISSIPPI (with the s's backwards), while another larger one contained epithets and slogans from the *Underground,* bumper stickers, and actual comments from the rioters. They included "Impeach JFK," "Back Ross," "Kennedy's Koon Keepers," "Never," "Would you want your daughter to marry one?" and some of the words from a poem scribbled on the wall of the men's room in the Lafayette County Courthouse. This collection of trash did not of course represent Kerciu's ideas, but was intended to be a graphic representation of what the insurrectionists did to their own Confederate flag. On the opening day of the show the reaction of those who attended, including University administrators, was that the regular paintings were good and that the "riot paintings" were interesting and in some cases humorous. But early the next week some Oxford Citizens' Council members—not regular patrons of art—came out and took pictures of several paintings.

The poster paintings were eventually removed from the gallery, and law student Charles Blackwell initiated a criminal charge against Kerciu on the ground that the paintings were "obscene and indecent" and a "desecration of the Confederate flag." Pickets protesting the removal of the paintings appeared on the steps of the Fine Arts Center. The pickets included art instructor Aline Cantrell and art student Paul McDonald, and their signs read, "We Protest Censorship" and "Ours Is a Visual Language." Editor Sidna Brower asked rhetorically, "Will the University of Mississippi suppress this freedom of expression because it does not adhere to the principles of certain groups?"[21] Our A.A.U.P. chapter on April 9 adopted a resolution defending Kerciu and calling on the University to provide legal defense for him. The administration finally requested authorization from the Board of Trustees to defend him, but Kerciu had already hired a private attorney. The charges against him were dropped eventually, at least partly because the legal case against him was shaky.

The end of the second semester looked almost normal, but there were discouraging signs that enrollment would be down for the coming year and that a substantial number of faculty would be resigning. I watched for a statement from some official which might indicate an interest in holding down the number of resignations, but there was none. The best anyone would say was that *only* 10 percent had resigned by May 17, but the faculty already knew that at least twice that proportion would leave. Meanwhile, there was a Negro applicant for admission to the School of Law, and Meredith had applied for an apartment during summer session in the University-operated "veterans' village." Meredith's grades were up considerably from those of the first semester, and it appeared for the first time that he might actually graduate by the end of the summer.

On June 4 Judge Mize ordered the admission to the School of Law of Cleve McDowell, a graduate of Jackson State College. The School of Law had already approved his qualifications, and the court order was little more than a formality. On the same day Mize rejected Meredith's appeal from a University decision against providing an apartment for Meredith and his family. Mize accepted the argument that there were other applications ahead of his. Governor Barnett had submitted an affidavit that the housing of Meredith's wife and young son on the campus could produce "riots and bloodshed."[22] The chancellor on May 16 had stated in a letter to the Board of Trustees an argument that was no great compliment to the Ole Miss student body: "The other students cannot be compelled to accept this or any other student as a member of the University community, nor can they be forced to accept his family. The presence of the family on the campus could readily occasion the aggravation of existing tensions." The result was that McDowell joined Meredith as his roommate.

Registration for the summer session took place with no difficulty, although Governor Barnett again made it clear that the state would accept no responsibility for protecting the Negro students. The guard activities of the remaining 250 troops had been sharply reduced during the last weeks of the spring semester, and on June 11 they moved from their campus quarters to a camp south of Oxford. Soon after midnight on June 11 there occurred in Jackson an event that had major repercussions on the campus, the murder of Medgar Evers, Mississippi field secretary for the NAACP. He was shot in the back as he was entering his home after a long day's work. There were many expressions of sorrow from leading Mississippians, but the usual result of such cases eventually came—there was no conviction of the murderer. Evers had been a close friend of James Meredith, who promptly issued a statement in which he blamed "the governors of the Southern states and their defiant actions, the blind courts and prejudiced juries." Remembering the cases of Emmett Till and Mack Parker, Meredith charged that "a white man can do anything he wishes regarding a Negro and go unhampered."[23] James Silver and I agreed that one part of his original statement might cause difficulties for Meredith, and Meredith agreed to delete it. Even so, the Board of Trustees later used against Meredith, in a continuation of his housing suit, the deleted part of his statement.[24] Only three months before Evers' murder, the State Representative of Coahoma County, Tom L. Gibson, had written in a letter to the Chicago Chamber of Commerce: "Enclosed you will find newspaper clippings regarding some gangsters who killed a Negro up in Chicago who was offensive. Will you put me in contact with them? We might be able to get them a job down here. Yours very truly."[25]

During the summer Meredith played a good deal of early morning golf and on at least one occasion he was visited by his family, who toured the campus with him and ate at the cafeteria. On July 5, in Chicago, Meredith directed some candid comments at the leadership of young Negroes and found them no more receptive than Mississippi segregationists. About three hundred members of the NAACP Youth Freedom Fund heard Meredith criticize "the childish nature" of youth activities, and it was clear that he referred to sit-ins not backed up by any attempt to establish legal rights. Meredith and I had discussed the problem several times, and there was no doubt he felt strongly that Negro groups should be emphasizing educational preparation for economic and political improvement, rather than activities which resulted in nothing more than mass arrests. He was particularly critical of well-heeled middle class Negroes who might participate in one-day demonstrations, but who would not take on the steady grind of attending the still-segregated educational institutions of Mississippi and other Deep South states. But the young Negroes greeted his remarks with stony silence, and cheered wildly later on when another speaker rebuked Meredith.[26] The disturbing fact was that during a year when the NAACP spent nearly $300,000 on fines and bail resulting from sit-ins, very little was being accomplished with the integration of Mississippi schools.

Cleve McDowell met with some friendship in the law school, but it ended abruptly when he and other law students left the building. I was told by several law students that he never really "joined the club" in the law school, that he was never part of any of the groups of students who cooperate with each other on briefs and assignments. Even so, McDowell seemed to be reasonably satisfied with his academic work, and he studied energetically. By July 25, after almost ten months, the last of the troops were removed from the Oxford area, and a small contingent of marshals were the only remaining guards.

As the end of summer neared, the Sovereignty Commission and —of all things—the Building Commission teamed up with Governor Barnett in an attempt to dismiss or expel James Meredith on the ground that his public statements violated the chancellor's order of January 31. After a subcommittee of the Board of Trustees investigated and determined that the statements did not violate the order, the board voted six to five that there was no basis for denying Meredith his degree. The chancellor had warned that denial of Meredith's degree would cause all state schools to lose their accreditation, and all negative votes were cast by appointees of Governor Barnett. University officials did an effective job in this attempt at political interference, and the chancellor pointed out that Meredith spoke as a "citizen" and criticized both federal and state governments in his statement after the murder of Medgar Evers.[27] James Meredith marked his last day of taking final examinations by wearing a "Never" button on his lapel—upside down.

Commencement at the University of Mississippi on Sunday, August 18, was remarkable from many points of view. A carefully planned ceremony went off with deceptive simplicity. There were marshals on the outskirts of the large crowd, but those who watched the audience for any signs of difficulty were University police and about thirty faculty and staff members. They wore armbands imprinted tactfully with the word "Host." Approximately fifty Negroes attended, and although most sat in a group, others seated themselves at random—this was no segregated audience. One visitor who called himself a preacher was found with two knives hidden in a Bible, but this was the only important cause for alarm and it was dealt with efficiently. The final element of planning was the ending of the ceremony with a recessional, usually dispensed with because it lengthens a program which is already too long. In this case it provided an ideal method for getting Meredith out of the large crowd of milling people which commencement audiences turn into.

Present to see James Meredith graduate in addition to his parents, wife, and son were Mrs. Medgar Evers, state NAACP president Aaron Henry, and R. Jess Brown, who had been the first attorney to work on his case. The audience seemed quieter than usual when Dean A. B. Lewis reached the name "James Howard Meredith," but the handshake from Chancellor Williams looked no different than that extended to thousands of other Ole Miss seniors. The University had not looked better on any day since September 30 than it did on August 18. There were many who had said that neither the University nor Meredith would ever see this day. Many had worked both for and against it. The main thought that occurred to me was how easy it all could be.

When Cleve McDowell returned to Ole Miss in September, 1963, he encountered no physical resistance, although all white students moved off the floor of the dormitory where his room was located, and there was a resumption of the low-key verbal harassment which had gone on all summer in front of the Student Union Building. He was somewhat surprised to find that the marshals were no longer present and that there was no evidence of guarding by the University. All summer he had driven alone to and from his home in Drew, Mississippi, with only occasional difficulty, apparently because the main attention was still focused on Meredith. But on a few occasions other drivers had tried to force him off the highway or had driven in such a way as to throw gravel onto his windshield. This situation had grown worse since Meredith's graduation, partly because McDowell had bought Meredith's car—including its well-known license plate. Because he was afraid of more dangerous action from his tormentors, McDowell bought a pistol to carry in the car. For many months possession of guns on campus had been prohibited by University regulations, and all students had been required to sign cards stating that they would abide by the rule. McDowell's action pointed up a difference between him and Meredith —his lack of a tendency toward tactical strategy. Meredith's action in such circumstances would have been to call a press conference. McDowell, who had made no statements to the press and never seemed to complain to anyone about anything, tried to solve his own problem—and he failed.

Apparently some Citizens' Council headquarters in Jackson learned of the fact within thirty minutes after McDowell bought the pistol.[28] He had told Episcopal Chaplain Wofford Smith of buying it, and Smith advised him to get rid of it. On Monday morning, September 23, McDowell drove to the U.S. attorney's office in Oxford to leave a letter in which he asked for a resumption of protection. This caused him to be late for a 10 A.M. class, so he parked in an illegal zone in order to get to class as soon as possible. Because he feared that his car might be searched when it was ticketed by University police, he put the gun in his pocket. As he hurried up the steps of the Law Building, he dropped his sunglasses. When he stooped to retrieve them, the pistol fell from his pocket. Two law students saw him and they promptly telephoned Lafayette County Sheriff Joe Ford. McDowell hurried to his class, and Sheriff Ford was waiting to arrest him when it ended.

The disciplinary machinery of Ole Miss moved with remarkable speed. The University suspended McDowell on Monday, and on Tuesday the Student Judicial Council voted unanimously for expulsion. Although he could have had no knowledge of how other expulsion cases were handled, Charles Evers (who had assumed the duties of his murdered brother) stated that the University had treated McDowell fairly.[29] Some University officials were sorry to see McDowell go, because he had indeed been a model of behavior and because they knew his departure in some ways put the University back where it had been a year before. A few officials seemed to be pleased at the development. The *Jackson Daily News* rejoiced in a headline, MCDOWELL EXPULSION ERASES ONLY MIXING BLOT IN STATE.[30]

I later stated my reaction to the development in a speech in Chicago: "McDowell's departure from the University resulted from a monumental piece of bad luck and personal indiscretion, plus an unconscious conspiracy among the Citizens' Council, the NAACP, the Department of Justice, the University, and law enforcement officers."[31] My immediate reaction I stated in a letter to Burke Marshall:

> You may or may not regard this as fair criticism, but I believe the Department of Justice erred in not continuing the use of marshals at the University. I recall saying to a friend when I learned that there were no marshals here, "I hope they know what they are doing." I think you could have expected that certain University administrators would have been looking for some ground for getting rid of McDowell. Furthermore, a University guarantee of protection would be worthless unless you were prepared to check on compliance with the guarantee.
>
> Finally, I would emphasize that we at this University are a long way from the time when an unguarded and unadvised Negro can hope to attend the University successfully. Many of the sympathetic faculty members have resigned, and the student body is still almost completely hostile. Even if there were no physical danger to the student, there is still the nagging isolation from regular human contacts and the presence of an administration which is at best neutral. The purposeful "man with a mission" such as Meredith may make it, but the young man such as McDowell who "only wants an education" will not make it.

Burke Marshall's answer to my somewhat testy complaint came in a later letter (and in his book, *Federalism and Civil Rights*):

> The point about protection is the most difficult and frustrating we have to live with under the federal system. I say over and over again—hundreds of times a year—that we do not have a national police force, and *cannot* provide protection in a physical sense for everyone who is disliked because of the exercise of his constitutional rights. . . .
>
> There is no substitute under the federal system for the failure of local law enforcement responsibility. There is simply a vacuum, which can be filled only rarely, with extraordinary difficulty, at monumental expense, and in a totally unsatisfactory fashion.

I had no real answer to this argument, and the tragedy of November 22, 1963, demonstrated the fundamental correctness of Marshall's position that complete protection is impossible.

On February 20, 1964, ABC news commentator Howard K. Smith came to the campus for a speech in the Omicron Delta Kappa–Mortar Board Forum Series. Novelist Allen Drury had appeared earlier to present the conservative position, and Howard K.

Smith was expected to—and did—deliver a strong defense of liberalism. With some collaboration from Ole Miss students, five Negro students from Rust College in Holly Springs (Mississippi) appeared to attend the Forum. The University administration and police did an effective job of protecting the Negroes, and they attended in spite of the presence of a small mob. Chief Tatum arrested one student who took a swing at one of the Negroes—Lafayette County officials did not prosecute. At the end of the Forum the Negroes were asked to remain in the building until the audience left, and they were then conducted through a bad-tempered mob—almost all non-student adults—by University police and officials and were escorted safely out of Oxford. About two weeks later the first of that year's editions of the *Rebel Underground* appeared, intimating that a "brazen clique" of "integrationist leftists" had engineered the "sit-in." An interesting allegation was that the clique was composed of Professors Barrett, Silver, and Fortenberry, plus Episcopal Chaplain Smith, and was "aided and abetted by Chancellor J. D. Williams and his assistants"—Dean Love, Chief Tatum, and housing director Binford F. Nash. Several of these men found it humorous—or worse—to be included in this group.

Although the University had done what was required to prevent violence, some results of the episode were less satisfactory. One was the adoption of a new policy which stated that those not connected with the University could attend "public" events only as invited guests of University personnel or students. The other result was that one student charged by the *Underground* with aiding the sit-in was threatened and harassed so much that he was forced to move out of his dormitory. A small group of students broke into his room and damaged and dirtied his belongings, using human feces among other things. The University did reimburse him for the damage, but his tormentors were never found and punished. After living at the home of a professor for two weeks, he moved to a private room in Oxford.

The remainder of the 1963-1964 academic year was only marginally related to integration. The University made important progress in improving its tenure system for professors, which had been authorized by the Board of Trustees on November 15, 1962. There were thirty-nine resignations of faculty members of professorial rank who had been at the University during the previous year, not as many as reported in the press but a tremendous loss to the University. A major concession to political pressure—or the fear of it—was the resignation of Dean Robert J. Farley of the School of Law. Probably he could have gained reappointment as a professor (deans must relinquish their positions at the age of sixty-five), but he feared that a battle would further harm the University. The University did remarkably well in filling faculty vacancies so that those with Ph.D. degrees equalled the number in the preceding year, but there were major weaknesses in several departments. Enrollment on the Oxford campus dropped by more than four hundred, slightly under 10 percent, and this hurt Ole Miss financially as well as academically. In spite of this the University on November 1, 1963, adopted a modest tightening up of admission standards by specifying a minimum cut-off score on entrance examinations.

Although many good faculty left, there was a solid group who remained, and it included two-thirds of those who had signed the A.A.U.P. statement of October 3, 1962. James Meredith had received his degree in the minimum time possible, and even Cleve McDowell's short stay on the campus demonstrated that a Negro could attend the School of Law if the problem of outside harassment could be solved. The failure of Governor Barnett to "stand in the schoolhouse door" when McDowell entered was an indication that some change had taken place. Those of us who stayed at Ole Miss—both faculty and administration—knew that the problem was not to be solved by running away from it. We waited to see what would happen in 1964—and some did more than wait.

8 BLUEPRINT FOR SUCCESS

In Mississippi during the long, hot summer of 1964, two very different events provided a striking contrast. One of these was the "Freedom Summer," and it was characterized by publicity, conflict, and, for three human beings, death. Its most important effect was to force many white Mississippians—and Negroes—to realize that the myriad problems tied neatly in a package called "civil rights" could not be solved by the simple negativism of the Citizens' Council. The other happening involved only one Negro at the University of Mississippi—and for him it was a kind of private freedom summer. It was characterized by a minimum of publicity, almost no conflict, and a remarkable amount of cooperation among those who had not cooperated much before. In some ways it was surprising that the hot freedom summer did not cause more difficulty for the cooler one on the campus. It later became clear that the former absorbed most of the energies of those Mississippians who felt impelled to resist, so that a more rational and peaceful process of change could take place at Ole Miss.

One ominous background note had been the election as governor in 1963 of the candidate who had purportedly "stood tall" with Ross Barnett in the disastrous attempt to keep James Meredith out of Ole Miss—Paul Johnson. Yet those who had watched the primary and general elections knew that all of the major candidates had attempted to outdo each other in yelling "nigger," and it would be difficult to award first prize in the contest. Those who were optimistic remembered that Paul B. Johnson, Jr., had not always talked like a racial extremist and expected that he would show some desire to live up to the constructive record his father compiled as governor from 1940 to 1943. They also knew that behind the scenes Johnson had been an influence for moderation during some phases of the Meredith debacle. Those who were pessimistic remembered that on October 25, 1963, he had promised at a meeting of the Citizens' Councils of America, *"We can and will maintain a system of segregated schools!* . . . Interposition of your governor's body between the forces of federal tyranny and his people, including our children, is a price not too great to pay for racial integrity. I pledge you here tonight that I am prepared to pay such a price!"[1] But this was the only meeting during the campaign for the governorship at which Johnson made such a statement, and even on that occasion he said he would not close the schools. By the time of his inauguration in January, 1964, Governor Johnson was able to say that "hate, prejudice, or ignorance" would not lead Mississippi during his term, and that he would not fight a "rear-guard defense of yesterday" but would make "an all-out assault for our share of tomorrow."[2] This speech won more favorable national comment than any event in Mississippi during the preceding four years.

It was in this atmosphere that Cleveland Donald, Jr., a Jackson Negro, mailed an application for admission to Ole Miss on February 27, 1964. Although the details were not revealed publicly until his court action in June, in an accompanying letter he requested issuance of a "provisional certificate of admission," as provided for in the application instructions. He received the acknowledgment of receipt of his registered letter of application, but after a delay of two months he still had no word from the University. On April 15 he wrote a letter of inquiry to Acting Registrar G. F. Gober, explaining that he needed a decision on his application so that he could make plans for the summer. (Gober, a retired Marine Corps general, had replaced Registrar Robert Ellis while the latter was away on sabbatical leave at Florida State University.) On May 5 Gober sent a standard form letter stating that Donald had been provisionally admitted. An item checked on the letter pointed out that he would receive a regular certificate of admission upon receipt of a supplementary transcript from Tougaloo College indicating eligibility for readmission to that college and a grade-point average of at least "C," the required average for admission to the University for transfer sophomores. The Tougaloo College registrar mailed the supplementary transcript (indicating considerably above a "B" average) on June 2, and two days later he mailed the certificate establishing eligibility for readmission. All of this was remarkable, because up to this point Donald's application had been handled as an ordinary application—the two-month delay was not much more than average. The bare facts understate one element of key importance—the acting registrar was under pressure from forces outside the University to find a reason for denying admission, but he was also an honest man.

It was a potentially disturbing sign that the first public announcement of Donald's application came from Governor Johnson. On May 22 he announced that a Negro had been "temporarily admitted" to the University and that the Board of Trustees wanted "to look at his credentials carefully."[3] Some of us at the University remembered what the accreditation association had said in 1962 about the governor's role and about intervention by the Board of Trustees in specific cases of application for admission. Moreover, the board was in an odd position because the governor had not appointed replacements for five board members whose terms would normally have ended on May 7. A widespread speculation was that Johnson was delaying filling appointive jobs until the legislature adjourned, since he knew there were not enough appointments to make all of his supporters happy. In any case the members of the board, including those not yet replaced, were not likely to risk contempt action again, and the choice of new members by the governor was thus crucial to Donald's application.

The next step was a letter from Chancellor Williams to the board, and it turned out to be more significant than he imagined, mainly because it was received by the "old board" and acted upon a week later by the "new board." The letter, which could have been taken as a request for more University police or as a basis for court action against Donald's admission, read as follows:

> The purpose of this letter is to bring to your attention for

> whatever consideration and action you believe appropriate the serious situation the University of Mississippi may face in the possible enrollment for attendance at the summer session of Cleveland Donald, Jr., on June 9, 1964.
>
> The applicant has revealed that on two occasions he has been charged with the violation of a municipal ordinance of the City of Jackson, Mississippi, through his participation in mass demonstrations. It is possible that this information may give some insight into the applicant's background and character.
>
> The press has indicated that college students and others from all over the nation are scheduled to come to Mississippi this summer to participate in various civil rights activities. The tension resulting from their presence in the area at the same time as the possible enrollment of this applicant could cause the campus to become again a battleground for outside groups over which the University could have little or no control and for which it could assume no responsibility.
>
> The University administration is aware that its personnel and facilities are inadequate to provide for the safety of the applicant under the extreme conditions envisioned above. At this time it is not aware of any provisions made to provide protection from any other source.
>
> The primary responsibility of the University is to maintain the best possible conditions for the accomplishment of the learning and research expected of such an institution. Unwarranted strife and turmoil in the past have made impossible the maintenance of these conditions, and it is hoped that such difficulties will not be permitted to impair once more the performance of our responsibility.

Although this letter was on the surface a reversal of the University's position, University officials had already undercut the possibility of *successful* action by the Board of Trustees to prohibit Donald's enrollment. They had already admitted him provisionally, subject only to the qualification that his second-semester transcript from Tougaloo College show a continuation of his previous academic record. They also continued to make plans for Donald's enrollment during the week after the chancellor's letter was sent to the incumbent board. At this point, the significance of the letter was that the chancellor was protecting the University's position—he was "playing both ends against the middle," a not uncommon practice of university administrators. The letter soon became important in a different way.

Amid speculation that the incumbent members of the Board of

Trustees would permit Donald to enroll by their "inability" to assemble a quorum, Governor Johnson took action. On June 3 he appointed four new members of the board (and reappointed one special member who serves only a four-year term), and they were hastily confirmed by the State Senate. On June 4 the new board voted to seek a court order to delay Donald's admission and sent the following directive to Chancellor Williams and Registrar Gober:

> In response to the letter of Chancellor Williams dated May 27, 1964, the Board of Trustees of State Institutions of Higher Learning hereby directs the Acting Registrar of the University of Mississippi to defer the issuance of a certificate of admission to the above named applicant until such time as this Board can present the entire matter of this application to the United States District Court for the Southern District of Mississippi and obtain from that Court a proper ruling on the legality of the Board's proposed action at this time.
>
> The matter will be promptly presented to the Court and as soon as we have been advised by the Court of its ruling, we will in turn advise you. A copy of our pleadings on this application is being served on the applicant forthwith.

This action occurred while the legislature was struggling with other matters, including proposals for combatting "freedom summer" visitors, for frustrating the court-ordered desegregation of public schools in three counties, and for a teachers' salary increase. One bill which became effective on June 6 was directed specifically at the college which Donald had attended, and in effect it could have withdrawn Tougaloo College's Mississippi accreditation by eliminating the provision in existing statutes which automatically gave state accreditation to schools approved by the regional association.[4] Another bill aimed specifically at Donald authorized the Board of Trustees to examine the previously confidential records of juvenile courts. Donald had stated on his Ole Miss application that he had two such convictions (for civil rights demonstrations during the previous summer).[5] For reasons which were never explained publicly, this bill did not receive the governor's approval until June 11.

During the last week in May another faculty member told me that Cleveland Donald was interested in talking with someone at the University, partly because he wanted some advance academic advice, and because he was uneasy about his reception at the University. Since I had already planned to attend a meeting of the Mississippi Council on Human Relations at Tougaloo College on June 5, it was arranged that several faculty members would see him there. There was nothing particularly unusual about this procedure except the locale; I have often given informal advice to white students prior to their enrollment at the University. In fact, the possibility of personal assistance from faculty members to students is one of the worthwhile features of the University. The fact that James Meredith had no such advice before his enrollment was one factor which complicated his problems at Ole Miss.

Early in the week of June 5 Assistant Attorney General Burke Marshall telephoned me to inquire about the adequacy of the University's security arrangements. I told him that the University was in favor of admitting this student and therefore had a positive attitude which I thought would produce adequate security plans. (The chancellor's letter of May 27 was not revealed until later.) I suggested that Marshall contact University officials directly, but that he might wish to have observers here for insurance even if the University's plans were adequate. He later talked with several officials, and one of them told me that Marshall seemed to be pleased with the arrangements that had been made.

In the course of making some inquiries about the University's plans, I told one official of my intention to see Donald. It developed that the University was interested in finding some means of unofficial communication with the student. I was asked to tell Donald of the University's plans and to assure him that they were adequate, partly so that Donald would not ask for protection from the Department of Justice and partly to make him feel better. The University was not eager to see federal marshals return. I was also asked to tell Donald when and where the University preferred that he arrive and to find out whether this would fit into his plans. The main features of the plan were that Donald would be housed on the third floor of LaBauve Hall, in which the Student Housing Office is on the first floor. This dormitory is located at the center of the campus, across the street from the Union Building and also convenient to the cafeteria, library, and classroom buildings. The dormitory has no back entrance and can be watched easily from the Union Building. Donald was to be protected by University police and by staff members of the Division of Student Personnel, who would be particularly watchful during the first days of his attendance. Surveillance would be relaxed progressively as conditions seemed to justify a more normal situation. The dormitory manager (a graduate student) had been carefully selected so that he would be reliable and not subject to pressure. Newsmen were to be excluded from that part of the campus where Donald would normally be, although the University would arrange a press conference on his first day at the University if he wished. There was also to be an issue of the *Mississippian* which would call for proper behavior from the students (it never appeared, however). County and city law enforcement officers had committed themselves to maintain order off the campus, and part of the plan was to avoid any necessity or excuse for intervention from either the Department of Justice or the Highway Patrol.

The University was also interested in an assessment of Cleveland Donald as an individual, particularly with reference to his personality and his attitude. All of this seemed very satisfactory to me, so I agreed to serve as an informal channel of communication as requested. Before June 5 I was informed that the Board of Trustees was probably going to take some kind of legal action regarding Donald's admission, but also that the University was assuming that this would not interfere with plans to have Donald arrive on the day before registration, Tuesday, June 9. The University assumed that this was just a legal gesture, and I was told the board attorney had remarked that the board could not win in its attempt to deny admission to Donald.

Before going to Jackson on June 5 I read in the newspaper that the hearing on the board's case would not be held until June 15, and my immediate reaction was that this would cause Donald to miss the equivalent of about two weeks of school and would hurt him academically. I phoned the University official with whom I had talked before, and he was surprised that the date was so late and agreed this would cause Donald to miss too many classes. He said we should still operate on the assumption that Donald would come according to the original plan.

On arriving at Tougaloo I talked with Donald's adviser there, a professor of physics, who told me that NAACP attorney Derrick Bell was already planning to ask Judge Cox on Saturday morning for an immediate admission order, pending the later hearing. He showed me the letter from the Board of Trustees which ordered the chancellor and the acting registrar not to issue an admission certificate to Donald before the June 15 hearing. We phoned Bell to emphasize the handicap of missing this many classes and emphasized the accelerated nature of summer school. Donald also phoned the registrar to ask whether he could be provisionally enrolled on the basis of the provisional certificate of admission which he had received from the University. The registrar, who had demonstrated considerable courage in issuing the certificate, said he did not know. The fact was that many students register in summer school on the basis of provisional certificates, but Gober did not know whether the board knew that.

On returning to the University I reported to University officials that Donald was willing to cooperate with the University in every way to facilitate his attendance. He was satisfied with the plans and was willing to arrive at the time designated by the University. During all of our conversations throughout the day I had never seen Donald react emotionally to anything. He impressed me as being intelligent, serious, reserved, and extremely able in verbal expression. I think these officials were reasonably confident that if Donald's attendance produced difficulties, they would not be caused or made worse by his statements or actions.

Attorney Bell filed two petitions for hearings, one to be held before Judge Cox on Saturday, June 6, for a temporary admission order, and the other to be held on June 12 for a permanent order. After hearing the arguments on Saturday, Judge Cox ruled that he would receive affidavits on Monday and then decide on the temporary order. Donald submitted an affidavit detailing the University's requirement that students "attend each and every class," the number of classes he would miss,* his intention to attend the University

*There is one odd fact about the University's rules on the deadline for late registration which neither Donald nor I thought of including in the

for educational rather than publicity purposes, and the fact that he had been advised that the University had worked out adequate plans for his safe attendance. I was asked to file an affidavit supporting his claim that a delay in admission would cause "irreparable damage" to him academically, and I spent all day Sunday on a trip to Jackson to sign it. I might not have signed the affidavit, but I had just learned of the chancellor's letter of May 27 implying that Donald was only a troublemaker and arguing that the University could not guarantee to preserve order—yet I had been asked by the University to assure both Donald and the Department of Justice that those plans were adequate.

On the following day the dean of the School of Liberal Arts filed an affidavit not directly disputing mine but stating that late enrollment would not prevent Donald from completing his academic work. Donald had pointed out in his affidavit that he not only wanted to pass but to keep up his rather good grade-point average. Lieutenant Governor Carroll Gartin also filed an affidavit arguing that the "invasion" of Mississippi by Freedom School "agitators" might produce violence that the University could not control, and that Donald's arrests showed that he was a troublemaker. Governor Johnson was out of the state attending the governors' conference in Colorado. When my affidavit became public on Monday, the *Jackson Clarion-Ledger* headlined a typically distorted front-page story, UM PROF SUPPORTS NEGRO IN COURT PLEA, and identified me as a "controversial professor."[6] (The chancellor later defended both the contents of my affidavit and my right to submit it to the court.)

At 11 A.M. on Wednesday, June 10, Judge Cox ordered the University to admit Donald "with all of the rights and privileges at the institution accorded a white student"; ordered Donald not to participate in any civil rights activities or publicity; ordered "all other persons and corporations" not to interfere with him as a student; and canceled the hearings set for June 12 and 15. He

affidavits. Under the rules a student who registers on the last date permitted in a regular semester would miss only one week of classes, but a student registering on the deadline date for the accelerated summer session would miss the equivalent of two weeks of classes. Each session lasts only six weeks.

specifically ruled that delayed enrollment would cause Donald "irreparable hardship" and thus upheld Donald's and my affidavits. I was glad to see the June 12 hearing cancelled, since I had been subpoenaed to testify on my conversations with University officials regarding the adequacy of security arrangements. In a sense their conversations with me had put them in a position of being unable to testify in any way other than to support Donald's claim, particularly since I was to be put on the stand first. In any case they had already told me that they could hardly lie about the University's plans. One of them remarked, "Are we going to get up there and testify that we consciously made *inadequate* plans?" They were also aware that Burke Marshall was in a position to testify that the University had assured him the plans were adequate, a somewhat touchy point because neither the University nor the Department of Justice had provided adequate protection in September, 1963, for Cleve McDowell.

My phone calls and correspondence had already become entirely too active as a result of the news of my affidavit. One person named Christian from Friar's Point, Mississippi (both names are genuine), wrote that I was "worse than a traitor" and asked the rhetorical question, "What kind of low bread [sic] scum are you?" I sent him a polite answer which said in part, "I realize that the race problem is difficult, but I am convinced that the welfare of Mississippi as well as of the United States requires that it be approached in a peaceful and lawful manner."

There was a change in plans for Donald's arrival on campus, mainly because Judge Cox delayed his decision until 11 A.M. on June 10, the day of registration. Those who were bringing Donald to the campus decided not to risk driving through the numerous small towns between Jackson and Oxford and instead to fly in on Southern Airways. This would have meant arrival after 4 P.M., too late to register him easily and disturbingly similar to the time of James Meredith's arrival twenty-one months before. In addition, the Department of Justice wanted time to bring some observers into the area, and this could not be done within a few hours. No one had expected Judge Cox to rule favorably or so rapidly. The upshot was a decision to delay another day.

On June 11 Cleveland Donald and NAACP attorney Derrick Bell were met on the 9:22 A.M. flight by University Police Chief Tatum, the Lafayette County sheriff, and an Oxford taxi driver. After pictures by a small group of newsmen, they drove to the campus and parked behind LaBauve dormitory, and as Donald walked into his dormitory even the few casual passersby did not seem to know he had arrived. He registered rapidly for the courses he had planned to take and attended his first class at 11 A.M. At a brief news conference he said, "Since I am here for an education, I will not be holding any press conferences. I would appreciate it if the reporters will leave me alone for at least the first two or three years." During his first day on campus he ate lunch and dinner at the cafeteria with attorney Bell, while campus police, University Student Personnel staff members, and a Department of Justice observer looked on unobtrusively. At lunch Donald ate at one end of the cafeteria while at the other end was Mississippi Attorney General Joe Patterson, who earlier had made the sensible comment, "He will be registered, and that will be the end of it."

Throughout the whole series of developments, Mississippi officials had made no defiant public comments and had limited themselves to a perfunctory court challenge of Donald's admission. University officials had made careful plans and had done an effective job of executing them. Neither the newspapers nor the Citizens' Council had made inflammatory statements. Judge Cox had accelerated the normal plodding procedure of the courts. Almost everyone in contact with him seemed to regard Cleveland Donald as an ideal student who was easy to cooperate with, but it must be remembered that James Meredith was amazingly good-natured and cooperative considering the tumult which accompanied his admission. In almost all respects this was a different story from that of 1962.

On June 27 the Board of Trustees issued an order apparently intended to prevent University officials or faculty members from engaging in the type of conversations which preceded—and facilitated—Cleveland Donald's enrollment:

> It is hereby ordered by the Board of Trustees of Institutions of Higher Learning that all communications between the Justice

> Department or other federal law officials or any attorney or attorneys representing actual or potential litigants against the Board of Trustees shall only be conducted by a designated attorney for the Board and the aforesaid officers or attorneys. Any attempt by such persons to communicate with the officials of the Board of Trustees should be referred to the Executive Secretary of the Board. All employees of the several institutions are expected to comply with this order.

The confused wording of the order produced varied reactions. One University official commented that the order "told Department of Justice lawyers they could not talk to each other." One of those lawyers read it and shook his head in amazement. I remarked that it could not apply to me, since I had never attempted to speak for the board. One faculty member remarked that he "wasn't high enough to be an official or low enough to be an employee," so it didn't apply to him. An NAACP attorney stated that this was the "worst" action taken by the board since the Meredith case.

Cleveland Donald's first days at Ole Miss were days of quiet tension, except for that small group of students who liked to loaf in front of the Student Union Building and make harassing remarks. His reply was a smile and an invitation to them to come around and talk with him. His nights were made easier by a television set, obtained with the cooperation of several faculty members.

Students in classes with him were increasingly impressed by his quiet ability, and some students occasionally talked with him outside of class. He once inquired into the possibility of attending meetings of the Baptist Student Union, but Oxford adults vetoed the idea by moving the student meetings off the campus. Several of the students later came around and apologized. This paralleled Cleve McDowell's experience a year earlier. Cleveland Donald had been warned that he would encounter this kind of behavior, and he accepted it without any show of bitterness. He used the cafeteria, the library, and occasionally the Student Union from the first day on, and the obvious security measures were rapidly decreased. One security measure which did not last long was a red light on the roof of his dormitory, which he was supposed to use as a signal in case of difficulty. University officials were subjected to so much ribbing about the red light that it was taken down after a few days.

On one weekend during the summer Donald's parents visited him, and the family ate Sunday dinner in the cafeteria. On several occasions when small groups associated with the "freedom summer" visited the campus, they were informed that Judge Cox's order made it unwise for them to talk with him. The only difficulty came on August 19 when Donald had lunch at the cafeteria with Derrick Bell and several others with whom the attorney was associated in an integration case being tried before the federal District Court in Oxford. They were met by the jeers of a small crowd when they left the cafeteria; this extra integration of the already integrated cafeteria excited some segregationists. What few people realized was that several of the state's radical segregationist leaders had come to town for the trial, and with some local assistance they were responsible for the demonstration of hostility at the University. The episode took place on the first day of final examinations, but it did not seem to upset Donald seriously. His grades for the summer session were of honor student caliber. The University received little credit in national news media for a remarkably successful summer, but a policy of discouraging news coverage had been at least partly responsible for the success. Dismal events at Philadelphia and elsewhere in Mississippi had helped to distract reporters as well as radical segregationists.

The Board of Trustees, apparently reacting to both the integration of the Ole Miss cafeteria and a few visits to the campus by individuals with some interest in the "freedom summer," adopted a long resolution on August 20. After referring to Mississippi as "a law abiding state," criticizing the national trend against "states rights and conservative government," and attacking the "invasion" of the state during the summer "Mississippi Project," the board concluded:

> NOW, THEREFORE, be it resolved that the heads of each state institution of higher learning in Mississippi shall do everything reasonably possible to maintain good atmosphere for educational pursuits of students on any college or university campus in the State of Mississippi, under the jurisdiction of this Board, and that authority be vested in the heads of these institutions to pro-

> tect student life from undue pressure by those engaged in activities contrary to the laws of the State of Mississippi and to the image of the citizenship of the state; and that all things be had and done which may be considered proper to eliminate development of socialistic and communistic trends among the college or university youth where violence is done to constitutional government, to local and state governments and to education, and they will use all reasonable means to prohibit as far as possible invasion of state institutions of higher learning by outside influence contrary to the established and well-known policies of the State of Mississippi relating to good government; and it is the desire of this Board that the heads of the several institutions be free to carry out the expressed policies herein contained in such manner as may appear appropriate and with desire on behalf of the Board that there be kept and maintained a proper balance in the ongoing of institutional life in order that peace and tranquility may prevail without disruption by pressure from without. Previous instructions to college and university heads identified with clearances of all speakers from the outside who enter the institution are not affected hereby and will continue in full force.

This declaration apparently was intended mainly for public consumption, since it was released to the press but not distributed to faculty members. It had no discernible effect at the University of Mississippi, except to prove what was already known—that the Board of Trustees could not be accused of excessive "liberalism."

The University of Mississippi had gone through a summer which contrasted sharply with the events of less than two years before. There had been no governor's stand at the gates, no marshals, no soldiers, no highway patrolmen, no demonstrations, and no riot. The acting registrar had looked at an application for admission from an honor student and had decided that he should be admitted. University officials had prepared adequate plans for the attendance of the student. Several faculty members had taken a lead in facilitating the process of admission. The students of Ole Miss had, except for a handful, acted in a manner which did credit rather than injury to the University. News reporting had been restrained and factual. It all added up to a very different blueprint from that of 1962—and it worked.

At the opening faculty meeting on September 9 Chancellor Williams made a statement which received a record amount of applause and favorable comment. These words were a heartening beginning for the year.

> Columbia University's bicentennial theme was "Man's Right to Knowledge and the Free Use Thereof." To many people this is "academic freedom." However, to others "academic freedom" means an attempt by professional conspiracy to protect teachers whose purpose is to poison the minds of our youth with un-American ideas or foreign philosophies, and to bring only contempt for our way of life. . . .
>
> Who should decide what is worth knowing? Should it be the legislature, the Board of Trustees, the faculty, the Congress, or others? One of the greatest privileges Americans have is the right of each of us to decide what is worth knowing. Should college students be deprived that privilege because they are in college and the college is supported by funds from some source that decrees that the source shall determine what students shall know? . . .
>
> That men may be free, let us not only defend but promote and support with dedication the students' right to know. The survival of our nation and of our society depends upon it. No other freedom means more to human development.
>
> The State of Mississippi and the University have many problems. I have confidence in the members of this faculty, in their dedication, in their ability, and in their judgment. This is a group of professional and responsible men and women. I know that the people of Mississippi, the parents of our students, and students themselves believe that we take our respective responsibilities seriously. We shall do these things that will contribute most to the primary purpose of the University, namely, to bring thought and knowledge into the world.

Another encouraging sign was the state of the faculty. With a few exceptions departmental teaching staffs were back to the pre-crisis level or better. For two-thirds of the vacancies young Ph.D.'s had been hired as assistant professors at salaries which are good by Mississippi standards and about average by national standards. The legislature had approved a budget 25 percent under that requested by the Board of Trustees, although the funds approved increased 25 percent over the previous budget period. The board and the various state schools had argued that Mississippi could regain some of its loss in national prestige by voting a 50 percent increase in college and university funds, but the economy-minded legislature did not agree. One major result of the drop in Ole Miss enrollment in 1963-1964 was that it cost faculty members an average of nearly

$500 a year in salary (because of the board policy of distributing money among the various schools on the basis of enrollment). Enrollment for 1964-1965 increased to more than that before the crisis, and we were hopeful that the worst damage was over.

Registration for the fall semester of 1964 brought a second Negro student, Irvin Walker, who was admitted as a freshman without a court order. Walker even wore a freshman "beanie" and stood in line for the standard freshman haircut. Mrs. Robert Moses, wife of the Negro who had directed the freedom summer campaign, apparently saw her application approved by the School of Law but not by the Board of Trustees. Cleve McDowell failed in his attempt to get Judge Mize to order his readmission, but his possibilities of appeal are not yet exhausted.

Negro students Donald and Walker registered without difficulty, although a disheartening note was that because of a policy of the Board of Trustees their parents were not allowed to eat in the cafeteria. Another result of this policy has been the exclusion of all members of the general public—except alumni—from the concert and lecture programs at the University. The effect of this is to exclude hundreds of white members of the general public from these events in order to keep out a few Negroes. At least this policy is technically non-discriminatory, whereas the policy of excluding the parents of the Negro students from the cafeteria is clearly discriminatory—since any white members of the general public can eat at the cafeteria. The policy has been relaxed somewhat for athletic events to permit Negro students from the schools of visiting teams to attend. This reflects the standard Mississippi—and American—policy of placing greater emphasis on the athletic than on the cultural aspect of college and university life. Except for this controversy—which has implications for federal aid programs because of Title VI of the 1964 Civil Rights Act—Negro students Donald and Walker have had only minor difficulties. Walker did get into a scuffle with a white student who made insulting remarks to him—not surprisingly, the same student who had caused trouble at the Howard K. Smith forum eight months before. The Student Judicial Council meted out appropriate punishment to both. One indication of normality was the fact that the incident was reported in the

Mississippian with no special emphasis.[7] There was even a riotous "pantie raid"—with no racial overtones—on October 29, which resulted in strong disciplinary action by the University and in successful prosecution in a local court. Except for the fact that the football team was in a losing slump, it was almost like old times.

At the close of 1964 the University of Mississippi was finally on the way back. It had been through political interference, riot, military occupation, threatened loss of accreditation, loss of students and faculty, verbal combat between administration and faculty, and almost total loss of national prestige. Ole Miss had seen the other still-segregated institutions of Mississippi emerge from the crisis with what amounted to rewards for their lack of integration, including what appeared to be preferential treatment in some federally assisted programs. Yet James Meredith had attended Ole Miss and had received his degree in less time than that taken by most white transfer students. An impressive number of administrators, faculty members, and students had engaged in what sometimes seemed to be a hopeless struggle to save the University. Even the Board of Trustees, particularly those of its members appointed by former governors White and Coleman, had taken strong action at certain key points when the existence of Ole Miss was at stake. They too were criticized and harassed by radical segregationists, even though they defended segregation by every legal method available to them. Through it all, there were unrelenting pressures which tested the honesty, morality, legality, and even the physical stamina of the participants. I have no difficulty in appreciating the statement made by one perceptive Ole Miss administrator, "You never know whether you're going to be hurt more by your friends or your enemies." James Meredith could have made the same statement.

One facet of our "Meredith year" which bothered me almost as much as the mistakes made in Mississippi was the tendency of some commentators to see the cause of all the difficulties in the internal weaknesses of the University. Clearly Ole Miss is not "great" by national standards—it is an average Southern university. Its faculty in 1962 included an impressive number of Ph.D.'s; it had won a moderate number of Fulbright and other fellowships; it had published an average number of books and articles; and it included an average number of Phi Beta Kappa faculty members. Statistics show we are even above average in some areas, but the point is that we are not much better or worse than average. We had endured somewhat more political interference than the average state institution, yet I wonder how much better a transplanted faculty from another state school—North or South—would have performed when the crisis came—or in averting the crisis.

The problem is that many faculty members in America have come to shirk their moral responsibilities—they have joined "the establishment." As American universities have developed more and more into trade schools of varied quality, teachers have changed accordingly. They do their teaching and research so they will be "successful" and not get into trouble. They see less and less of students outside the formal confines of the classroom. They apply for research and travel grants regularly, and the results are happily reported to the boards and legislatures which approve their schools' budgets. When the work day is over, they drive to their suburban homes, turn on the TV, and have a drink. The important policies of their universities are determined by an impersonal entity known as "the administration" or "the board," which also handles any crises which develop. Of course it is the duty of the administration to prevent problems, and all usually goes smoothly because each cog performs its function. When crisis does come it may or may not be handled adequately by the administration—certainly the faculty is the last group likely to tackle it. When the establishment falters, the result may be loss of accreditation, a reduction in appropriations, or censure by the American Association of University Professors. The system does not encourage a responsible faculty role in dealing with difficult problems—and the faculty does not demand it. This was the central internal problem at Ole Miss.

The system encourages much the same lack of responsibility among students, and university administrations find it troublesome to give students too much responsibility—because responsibility means nothing without power. The Ole Miss student body is similar in most respects to those of most state and private schools. We no doubt admit too many who should not be in a university. Yet our students have done well in winning Rhodes scholarships, although not so well on Fulbright and Woodrow Wilson awards. Their college entrance exam scores are slightly above average, and they have little difficulty in gaining admission and financial assistance for graduate study elsewhere. But quality was not the problem with our students' reaction to James Meredith—it was their incitement by adults, both in 1962 and for the eight years before, while they were growing up. Even during the worst events at Ole Miss the students who participated actively constituted much less than a majority of the student body. The problem was for the responsible to check the irresponsible, and too many adults opposed that course.

Finally, there is the question of our administration, which made major mistakes in pretending that it was not segregated before 1962, in waiting too long before adopting a strict policy of student discipline, and in failing to protect the rights of the minority of students who were willing to befriend James Meredith. Yet this same administration was capable of taking strong action on other matters. It is worth noting that the accrediting agency criticized the Board of Trustees and the political leadership, but not the University administration. None of this excuses the administration, any more than the"system" excuses the faculty and students. The University only began to meet its challenge effectively when it discovered that no one else was going to solve its problems. Plenty of others were willing to complicate the problems.

My conclusion is from a speech which I gave on November 18, 1963, four days before the assassination of President John F. Kennedy, who had carried out his oath of office with reference to the University of Mississippi.

> Where does all this leave us as part of a University in a state where it is not easy to maintain a university in the full meaning of that term? It leaves us in a weak position, in a position that has been made still weaker by criticism from outside the state which should have been directed at others. It leaves us in the inescapable role of either fighting to regain a position of academic honor or of leaving the University to be defended or ruined by others. . . .
>
> We therefore need good faculty members who will not leave. We need good faculty members who will join us, and most of them will find the situation less difficult than they imagine. We

> need good students from other states, both graduate and undergraduate, partly because they produce a student body with broader and more varied interests and viewpoints. . . . After all of the pluses and minuses are considered, the fact is that education can be and must be carried on at the University of Mississippi. There is certainly no more challenging place for the teacher; and if teachers are unwilling to face challenges, they are in the wrong field.

The problems which confronted the University of Mississippi in 1962 could have been solved less painfully if more individuals had accepted their responsibilities sooner and more willingly. But neither the system nor the logic of events forced that, and the problems were solved only when the very existence of the University was at stake.

Those with educational responsibilities both at the University and on the Board of Trustees should have challenged the "closed society" sooner and more effectively. But an important qualification is that they might also have lost sooner and more completely than they did. The formidable custodians of the closed society were the political leadership, the Citizens' Council activists, the dominant newspapers, and their allies in the fields of business, religion, and education. The successful challenging of these groups would have required the active cooperation of moderate leaders from some of the same groups. This combination of moderate forces had succeeded in North Carolina and Georgia, and to some degree in Louisiana. It had not yet succeeded by 1962 in Alabama and South Carolina, although the Mississippi tragedy of that year showed those states what they should not do.

The Mississippi failure demonstrated that neither Mississippi nor the United States as a whole yet knew how the problem should be settled when tackled in its most resistant form. The elements of inevitability in the situation do not excuse the failure of individual courage and responsibility, but they do help explain the failure. And as the moderately successful integration of both the University and of some Mississippi public schools in 1964 demonstrates, failure need not be permanent. Mississippians as well as other Americans can learn from adversity. Although they may not like the road they must follow, in increasing numbers they know what the road is.

APPENDICES

APPENDIX A. Legal chronology of the case of *James Howard Meredith v. Charles Dickson Fair, et al.*

1961

May 31—Meredith files complaint and motion for preliminary injunction; hearing set for June 12.

June 5—Motion for order requiring registrar to appear for deposition; hearing set for June 9. Show cause order issued for registrar's deposition; hearing set for June 6.

June 6—Notice by Board of Trustees of intention to take Meredith's deposition June 8.

June 8—Mize denies motion for registrar's deposition, grants motion for Meredith's deposition.

June 8—Meredith's deposition taken over objections on many points.

June 12—Mize begins hearing on motion for preliminary injunction; adjourns hearing until July 10.

June 20—Meredith requests inspection of student admission records July 1-7; hearing set for June 28. Notice of intent to take registrar's deposition on June 30.

June 23—Mize advises by letter that motion on records cannot be heard before July 6.

June 27—Board of Trustees presents *and is heard* on motions for additional time because of poor health of Assistant Attorney General Shands; requests postponement of deposition and extension of time for answering complaint (due June 28) by 15 days. Both motions granted.

June 29—Meredith renews motion for preliminary injunction; hearing sought for July 11 based on July 17 opening of second summer session.

July 10—Board granted postponement of answer to complaint until July 19 because of illness of Shands. Trial reset for August 10. Meredith withdraws second motion for injunction.

July 15—Amended motions on inspection of records and taking of depositions filed; hearing set for July 25.

July 18—Mize sets hearing on all motions for July 25.

July 19—Registrar's answer to complaint filed as answer for all defendants. Board moves to vacate notice of taking registrar's deposition on July 27.

July 25—Notice of intent to take registrar's deposition July 28.

July 27—Hearing on motions taken under advisement for ruling August 1. Registrar moves to vacate notice of taking deposition July 28. Board files affidavit against inspection of records.

July 31—Meredith requests orders Nunc Pro Tunc to begin trial on merits immediately. Notice by Meredith of taking depositions August 4.

August 1—Mize denies Meredith motion to take depositions and limits inspection of records to transfer students who applied for 1961 summer terms; records to be examined August 7-9. Mize refuses to sign Nunc Pro Tunc orders.

August 10—Mize resumes hearing on preliminary injunction.

August 11—Mize continues (delays) hearing until August 15.

August 15—Hearing resumed.

August 16—Hearing concluded. Board allowed until September 5 to file brief, and Meredith until September 15.

September 5—Proposed findings of fact filed by both sides.

December 12—Mize decides against preliminary injunction.

December 14—Mize denies injunction. Trial on merits set for January 15. Meredith files notice of appeal.

December 16—Motion by Meredith for advancing argument on appeal and for hearing on original papers (rather than waiting for printed record to be transmitted).

December 21—Judge Tuttle orders hearing before Court of Appeals on January 9 on original papers.

1962

January 12—Court of Appeals for Fifth Circuit denies preliminary injunction.

January 16—Hearing started on trial on merits for permanent injunction.

January 17—Board moves postponement because of Shands's illness. Mize grants postponement until January 24.

January 18—Meredith moves to recall mandate of Court of Appeals (of January 12) and petitions for rehearing.

January 24—Hearing resumed.

January 27—Hearing concluded.

February 3—Mize decides against Meredith. Meredith files notice of appeal.

February 5—Mize issues order dismissing complaint and denying relief. Meredith files motion in Court of Appeals for injunction pending appeal.

February 12—Court of Appeals hears and denies motion for injunction pending appeal.

June 7—Meredith jailed in Jackson on charge of false voter registration.

June 12—Court of Appeals issues injunction against Hinds County Attorney to prevent prosecution of Meredith on voter registration charge.

June 25—Court of Appeals reverses Mize and orders issuance of injunction as requested in Meredith complaint.

July 8—Meredith's request for immediate issuance of mandate of Court of Appeals denied (preventing enrollment in summer session). Judge DeVane files dissent to June 25 decision.

July 18—Mize receives mandate from Court of Appeals. First stay issued by Circuit Judge Cameron.

July 27—Court of Appeals vacates stay and reissues mandate.

July 28—Court of Appeals amends mandate of July 27 and issues its own order for admission of Meredith, immediate evaluation of his credits, and prohibition of prosecution. Second stay issued by Cameron.

July 31—Cameron issues third stay.

August 4—Court of Appeals vacates all stays by Cameron.

August 6—Cameron issues fourth stay.

August 12—Meredith applies to Supreme Court Justice Hugo Black for order vacating stays by Cameron.

August 31—United States filed Amicus Curiae brief with Black supporting Meredith.

September 10—Justice Black vacates all stays and enjoins Board of Trustees from taking action to prevent enforcement of judgment by Court of Appeals.

September 13—Mize issues permanent injunction for admission of Meredith.

September 18—Court of Appeals designates United States as Amicus Curiae.

September 20—District Court enjoins prosecution of Meredith on state charge. *Meadors, et al, v. Meredith, et al,* removed to U.S. District Court on petition of U.S. (individual civil action against Meredith's enrollment). District Court sets hearing for September 24 on Meredith and U.S. request for injunction against enforcement of state moral turpitude law. District Court sets hearing for September 24 on Meredith motion for injunction against *Meadors, et al.* Court of Appeals enjoins against proceedings against Meredith under moral turpitude law and against action by *Meadors, et al.* District Court issues show cause order on contempt against registrar, Dean Lewis and Chancellor Williams.

September 21—Mize hears contempt charges against University officials. Court of Appeals issues show cause order on contempt of board.

September 22—Court of Appeals issues show cause order on contempt of all original defendants (board and University officials). Mize clears University officials of contempt.

September 24—Court of Appeals hears contempt charges against board and University officials. District Court postpones scheduled hearing.

September 25—On petition of U.S., Court of Appeals issues temporary restraining order against Mississippi, Governor Barnett, and other officials, and on petition of Meredith issues temporary restraining order against governor and Hinds County sheriff. Also issues show cause order against governor on contempt, on application of U.S.

September 26—Court of Appeals issues show cause order against governor on contempt on application by Meredith, and against lieutenant governor on application of U.S.

September 28—Court of Appeals finds governor in contempt of orders of September 28 and imposes fine of $10,000 per day.

September 29—Court of Appeals finds lieutenant governor in contempt of orders of September 25 and imposes fine of $5,000 per day.

October 2—Counsel for governor and lieutenant governor appears to oppose contempt finding. Court of Appeals clears board and University officials of contempt and hears argument on Mississippi motion to dismiss orders of September 25.

October 8—U.S. Supreme Court denies certiorari request by board (for reversal of lower court decisions).

October 12—Governor, through attorney, tells Court of Appeals he will comply with such orders as he can legally and physically obey.

October 16—Department of Justice requests $100,000 fine for Barnett for October 2-12 period, and $10,000 per day thereafter.

October 19—Court of Appeals issues injunction against Mississippi officials.

October 25—Department of Justice offers to prove in Court of Appeals that governor had made agreement to protect Meredith's arrival at University.

November 6—Department of Justice requests Court of Appeals to appoint special master to take evidence on contempt of governor and lieutenant governor.

November 15—Court of Appeals directs Department of Justice to start criminal contempt proceedings against governor.

December 21—Court of Appeals issues show cause order for criminal contempt against Barnett and Johnson.

1963

February 8—Court of Appeals holds hearing on criminal contempt charges against Barnett and Johnson.

February 18—Supreme Court rejects appeal of civil contempt convictions of Barnett and Johnson.

April 9—Court of Appeals deadlocks by 4-4 vote on question of whether Barnett and Johnson are entitled to jury trial; certifies question to U.S. Supreme Court for ruling.

May 16—Meredith petitions Mize to order University to provide student apartment.

June 4—Mize denies Meredith request for student apartment.

1964

April 6—Supreme Court rules against jury trial for Barnett and Johnson unless major penalty to be requested.

APPENDIX B. Excerpt from the Annual Report of the Chancellor of the University of Mississippi to the Board of Trustees of the Institutions of Higher Learning for the Period July 1, 1962—June 30, 1963 (Section on Academic Division by Provost Charles E. Noyes).

A sober and objective reappraisal of the year can only conclude that the University, because of the Meredith crisis, paid a price academically in terms of students, faculty, financial support, and reputation in the academic community. That it did not suffer more grievous and even irreparable damage is a testament to the efforts of devoted members of the University administration, faculty, and staff, the courage and faith of the University's friends in high places, and the loyal support of University alumni throughout the trying year. The paragraphs immediately following attempt to give a clear picture both of what the University has lost and of what has been done to restore that loss.

During the first two weeks of uncertainty and legal maneuvering, and immediately following the period of disorder, there was inevitable distraction from class work; but despite the continuing tension on the campus both students and faculty quickly settled into routine work and made up for lost time. The student body's academic average for the year was not significantly different from that of previous years; indeed, the grades for the first semester indicated a slight increase in achievement over those for the same period last year.

Student enrollment was a more serious problem. A number of students withdrew from the University immediately following the disorder, and the Oxford enrollment dropped from 4,770 in September, 1962, to 4,280 for the spring semester. Summer School enrollment was slightly under the enrollment for the 1962 summer term. An active recruiting campaign, it is hoped, will restore the loss; but there seems no hope that a previously anticipated fall increase can be realized.

More dangerous in implications for the long-term welfare of the University was the number of faculty departures. Of approximately 230 faculty members in the professorial ranks, some 50 will not return to the campus in September. Those leaving include 33 who have resigned for various reasons, 5 who have retired, and a dozen others going on leave or terminating one-year contracts.

Through active recruiting by deans and department chairmen, these faculty losses are being replaced, and there will apparently be little if any overall loss in faculty quality in terms of degrees and teaching experience. Yet the University has, in terms of individuals, lost some able men who have made great contributions to it in the past, and some departments have been definitely weakened through losses which have not been restored.

Balancing these debit items are two factors: first, there have been many highly able faculty replacements; and, second, for the 1963-1964 year there is the prospect of a greater degree of faculty unity. Those faculty members remaining and those newly accepting positions on the staff are, by and large, those who have made a conscious decision to make their future at the University of Mississippi.

The financial loss occasioned by the decline in the number of students, whose fees make up approximately 40 per cent of University income, comes at a particularly unfortunate time when faculty salaries are rising steadily elsewhere in the United States. Since the sum of money allocated by the Board of Trustees is keyed each year to the previous year's enrollment, this financial strain may be greater in the coming year even than in the present. The difficulties under which the University has labored, especially the unusually large faculty turnover, will probably also occasion some loss in grants and contracts with Federal agencies. Because of this loss of revenue, needed increases in faculty salaries cannot be made for the coming year, and it will be necessary to reduce budgets for badly needed supplies and equipment, especially in the science areas.

A most particular danger faced by the University was possible loss of accreditation by the Southern Association of Colleges and Schools, the regional accrediting agency of which the University was one of the founding members. A close investigation was made to determine whether standards of the Southern Association had been violated during this academic year because of actions by officials of the University administration, the Board of Trustees, or the State and Federal government. Results of this investigation were presented to the Executive Council of the Commission on Colleges of the Southern Association at its annual meeting at Dallas, Texas, in November, 1962. The determination made was not to withdraw the University's accreditation, but to place the University and the other institutions controlled by the Board of Trustees of Institutions of Higher Learning in an "extraordinary status." This action is to be reviewed at the next meeting of the Association in Memphis, Tennessee, in December, 1963. Such evidence as exists gives every reason to hope that the institutions will be restored to their original status at that time.

There can be little doubt that the University has lost prestige in some parts of the academic community. Much has been done to restore that prestige through attendance and the presentation of scholarly papers at professional meetings, publications, visits to the campus by outstanding educators, and the vigorous prosecution of educational and research activities. Given time and good fortune, the University can recoup its losses.

APPENDIX C. The following faculty members of the University of Mississippi signed the statement adopted by the local chapter of the American Association of University Professors on October 3, 1962, which defended the federal marshals and called for law and order on the campus. They are listed in the order in which they signed the statement.

MEMBERS OF THE A.A.U.P.:

Barton Milligan, Associate Professor of Chemistry
Russell H. Barrett, Professor of Political Science
Richard S. Stewart, Assistant Professor of Ancient History
James W. Silver, Professor of History
Samuel F. Clark, Professor of Chemistry
William H. Willis, Chairman, Department of Classics
Evans Harrington, Assistant Professor of English
Tom J. Truss, Jr., Associate Professor of English
Carl Alette, Associate Professor of Music
William E. Strickland, Chairman, Department of Modern Languages
Theodore I. Bieber, Professor of Chemistry
William C. Herndon, Assistant Professor of Chemistry
Dwight Van de Vate, Jr., Associate Professor of Philosophy
Lucy C. Turnbull, Assistant Professor of Classical Archaeology
Russell W. Maatman, Associate Professor of Chemistry

Karl Morrison, Professor of Economics and Marketing
Robert L. Rands, Professor of Anthropology
Harley F. Garrett, Professor of Education
J. H. Bruening, Assistant Professor of Sociology
L. E. Noble, Jr., Associate Professor of Political Science
P. A. D. deMaine, Professor of Chemistry
William J. Wallace, Assistant Professor of Chemistry
George Vaughan, Professor of Chemistry
Edward H. Hobbs, Chairman, Department of Research in Business and Government and Professor of Political Science
Donald S. Vaughan, Acting Associate Professor of Political Science and Assistant Director of Bureau of Governmental Research
Paul G. Hahn, Associate Professor of Anthropology
Richard W. Joslin, Assistant Professor of Art
George R. Kerciu, Assistant Professor of Art
Parks Grant, Professor of Music
Hal L. Ballew, Associate Professor of Modern Languages
Julien R. Tatum, Professor of Sociology and Anthropology
John Kozy, Jr., Assistant Professor of Philosophy
James E. Savage, Professor of English
Hector Currie, Professor of Law
C. N. Fortenberry, Professor of Political Science
Donald G. Rhodes, Instructor of Political Science
R. J. Farley, Professor of Law
Evelyn Lee Way, Professor of Latin
Richard Edwards, Associate Professor of Music
William F. Crowder, Associate Professor of Psychology
Thora H. Crowder, Associate Professor of Psychology
Gerald Walton, Assistant Professor of English
William A. Wilbanks, Associate Professor of Psychology
Lutz Leopold, Associate Professor of Physics
Joseph Baylen, Professor of History

NON-MEMBERS OF THE A.A.U.P. WHO EXPRESSED A DESIRE TO SIGN THE STATEMENT:

Mrs. Mildred S. Topp, Assistant Professor of English
Mrs. Mildred M. Harrison, Acting Assistant Professor of Psychology
Roscoe Cross, Professor of Law
Tom W. Stallworth, Professor of Civil Engineering
Benjamin I. Harrison, Professor of Modern Languages
Robert K. Rushing, Associate Professor of Law
John B. Wolfe, Professor of Psychology
John H. Fox, Jr., Professor of Law
H. B. Howerton, Professor Emeritus of Political Science
Joyce M. Cronk, Assistant Professor of Health, Physical Education and Recreation
A. Peter Foulkes, Assistant Professor of Modern Languages
Anita C. Hutcherson, Preceptor for the Scholars

Joe M. Richardson, Acting Assistant Professor of History
William I. Gardner, Assistant Professor of Psychology
John H. Moore, Professor of History
Margaret D. Moore, Associate Professor of History
Lillian S. Wolfe, Associate Professor of Psychology
Hubert D. Abadie, Acting Assistant Professor of History
Ronald F. Wagner, Associate Professor of Art (on leave, Arizona State College)

APPENDIX D. Excerpt from a speech delivered by Russell H. Barrett at the University of South Carolina, November 30, 1962.

It may seem unnecessary to begin with a defense of the University of Mississippi as an educational institution, yet the large number of incredibly misleading news reports requires such a beginning. Perhaps this should emphasize the worst of these, which would include *Time* magazine, that journal of opinion which calls itself "*The* Weekly *News*magazine." I limit myself to but one example of *Time's* inaccuracies, the statement on page 22 of its October 12 issue that there were virtually no faculty members on the campus during the rioting. Many faculty were there, but the riot of September 30 rapidly developed into one which could only be controlled by individuals with effective methods of controlling mobs.

It is probably more instructive to examine a case of misleading reporting in one reputable publication and its further distortion in another, namely the *New York Times* and the *St. Louis Post-Dispatch*. The *Times* carried a story on October 21 which reported that Ole Miss students live in "profound isolation," that the range of political and social opinion among students is "from Y to Z," that literature is not taught "in translation," that few undergraduates "have seen a foreign film with English subtitles, a play or listened to a symphony," that the student newspaper "compares unfavorably with those of other colleges of similar size," and finally that "the similarity of outlook among the students is reinforced by the fact that virtually all are from the Scotch-Irish or Celtic stock." None of these statements was supported by references to citations of fact, because they are not facts, as could easily be demonstrated.

This story did contain some important factual criticisms of University students and of other aspects of the University which deserve criticism, but it found nothing at all to commend. When this story and another one of October 8 were compressed into an editorial in the *St. Louis Post-Dispatch,* the picture became even worse. The University is "not a seat of enlightenment but a last-ditch refuge of bigotry, cut off from the streams of thought and action in the rest of the nation and the world." It stated that the legislature "lays an oppressive hand on the selection of texts, on the content of teaching, and on the expressions of opinion by student editors of the university newspaper . . ." During certain years our legislatures might have wanted to do all of these, but the facts are that the legislature has had no effect whatsoever on the selection of texts, has had no effect on the content of teaching, and has not silenced the expressions of opinion by a notable succession of student editors.

The author of the *Times* stories had not said that the University failed to demand scholarship and had in fact pointed out that 90 percent of the lowest quarter of entering freshmen flunk out or leave school. Yet the *Post-Dispatch* concluded that the University does not demand scholarship. I do not know how to explain these distortions of fact by publications which are usually responsible, but I would like to state a few facts very briefly.

The three local theaters show an impressive number of foreign films each year and they are well attended by students. The University Artist Series is an excellent one. Symphonies, ballets, and plays on tour usually fill our 1,300-seat auditorium, although the turnout for chamber groups and the less well-known soloists is about 600 to 800. This year the nine presentations in the series include Hal Holbrook in *Mark Twain Tonight,* the Goldovsky production of *La Traviata,* the San Francisco Ballet, the New York Pro Musica, Judith Anderson in *Medea,* and the violinist Erica Morini. Our Forum Series this year is presenting Vance Packard and Santha Rama Rau, among others, and in the past it has presented, in spite of the screening of speakers, Lord Attlee, J. K. Galbraith, Edward Weeks, Ralph Lapp, Eric Sevareid, and many others of similar caliber. Our very active University Players have presented *The Crucible, Waiting for Godot, Tiger at the Gates,* and *The Chalk Garden,* to name but a few. I do not pretend that we have no major weaknesses in our academic program, but the criticisms to which I have just referred did not even refer to the major one, the shortage of library funds for major library acquisitions and for new staff. We are better off than some state universities in certain fields, for example, travel to professional meetings and legislative interference with the curriculum. Adequate consideration of all this would mean another speech, but I do suggest that you read some of the news stories about the University with considerable skepticism.

NOTES

My emphasis in documentation has been to use material provided by eyewitnesses or others with direct knowledge of the events. There is almost no use of secondary sources. Where possible, documentary information is from the original. Much valuable citation of newspaper reporting has been omitted because it duplicates material already used. News commentary has been used sparingly; greater use would necessitate another book.

CHAPTER 1 | BUILDING THE WALL

1. *Jackson Clarion-Ledger,* December 2, 1962.
2. *Memphis Commercial Appeal,* June 1, 1955.
3. Mississippi Constitution, Section 213-A.
4. Mississippi Constitution, Section 213-B.
5. Mississippi Code, 6232-21-32.
6. *Tupelo Daily Journal,* December 3, 1954.
7. *Memphis Commercial Appeal,* August 12, 1955.
8. *The Citizens' Council,* November, 1956. Official monthly publication of Citizens' Councils of America; now replaced by *The Citizen.*
9. *Memphis Commercial Appeal,* August 21, 1955.
10. *Memphis Commercial Appeal,* May 22, 1955.
11. *The Citizens' Council,* July, 1959.
12. Mississippi Code, 9028-35-41.
13. Mississippi Code, 4065-3.
14. *Jackson State Times,* December 30, 1957.
15. *Memphis Commercial Appeal,* November 11, 1955.
16. *Memphis Commercial Appeal,* September 29, 1957.
17. *Bulletin of the University of Mississippi, General Catalog Issue, 1953-1954,* p. 38. Hereinafter referred to as University of Mississippi Catalog. The statement that requirements are not uniformly applied assumes that the schools state all of their admission requirements in their catalogs. See the following 1964-1965 catalogs: Mississippi State University, pp. 5, 19; University of Southern Mississippi, pp. 7, 19-21; Mississippi State College for Women, p. 40.
18. University of Mississippi Catalog, 1954-1955, pp. 51-52.
19. University of Mississippi Catalog, 1960, pp. 82-83, 121-123.

CHAPTER 2 | IN THE EERIE ATMOSPHERE OF NEVER-NEVER LAND

1. *James Howard Meredith v. Charles Dickson Fair, et al.* Hearing on Motion for Temporary Restraining Order and Preliminary Injunction. Printed as Vols. I and II, Plaintiff's Exhibit 16. Hereinafter referred to as Hearing.
2. Hearing, pp. 13-55.
3. Based upon correspondence.
4. Minutes of the Meeting of the Board of Trustees of the Institutions of Higher Learning of the State of Mississippi, May 15, 1961. Hereinafter referred to as Board Minutes.
5. *James Howard Meredith v. Charles Dickson Fair, et al.* Transcript of Record of Trial on Motion for Permanent Injunction, pp. 490-491. Printed as Vols. I to V. Hereinafter referred to as Record.
6. Deposition of James Howard Meredith, pp. 24-25. Printed as Defendant's Exhibit 7.
7. Hearing, p. 2. See also pp. 106-110.
8. Mississippi Code 6220.5.
9. Mississippi Code 6694, 6703, 6711, and 6714.
10. Mississippi Code 4065.3.
11. Hearing, p. 402.
12. Hearing, pp. 280, 397.
13. Hearing, p. 398.
14. Hearing, p. 404.
15. Hearing, pp. 422-423.
16. Hearing, pp. 420, 426.
17. *Hunt v. Arnold,* 172 F. Supp. 847 (1959), and *Ludley v. Board of Supervisors of Louisiana State University,* 150 F. Supp. 900 (1957) and 358 U. S. 819, denying certoriari.
18. Hearing, p. 265.
19. Hearing, pp. 299-305.
20. Hearing, pp. 129-132.
21. Hearing, pp. 199-203.
22. Hearing, pp. 226-257.
23. Hearing, pp. 452-453.
24. *Jackson Daily News,* February 7, 1961; *Jackson State Times,* February 7 and 8, 1961.
25. Hearing, pp. 454-474.
26. Hearing, p. 473.
27. Hearing, p. 166.
28. Hearing, p. 217.
29. Hearing, pp. 91-93.
30. Hearing, pp. 115-118.
31. Hearing, p. 84.
32. Hearing, p. 353.
33. Hearing, p. 86.
34. Hearing, p. 393.
35. Hearing, pp. 368-375.
36. Hearing, p. 198.
37. Hearing, p. 202.
38. Hearing, p. 489.
39. 199 F. Supp. 754 (1961).

40. *The Citizen,* January, 1962.
41. 298 F. 2d 696 (1962).
42. Hearing, p. 379.

CHAPTER 3 | NONE SO BLIND

1. Record, pp. 278-304.
2. Record, pp. 309-352.
3. Record, p. 497.
4. Record, pp. 558-559.
5. Record, pp. 524-527.
6. Record, pp. 380-381.
7. Record, pp. 417-421.
8. Record, pp. 514-515.
9. Record, p. 718.
10. Record, pp. 389-409.
11. Record, pp. 656-669, 706-715.
12. Record, p. 684.
13. Record, pp. 599-601.
14. Record, pp. 485-488.
15. Record, pp. 621-642.
16. Record, p. 653.
17. Record, pp. 671-682.
18. 202 F. Supp. 224 (1962).
19. *Mississippian,* March 30, 1962. Student newspaper of the University of Mississippi.
20. *Mississippian,* March 2, 1962.
21. University of Mississippi Catalog, 1962, pp. 81-85.
22. Mississippi Code, 1962 Cumulative Supplement, 6800-11.
23. University of Mississippi Catalog, 1962, pp. 120-122.
24. Edward H. Hobbs, ed., *Yesterday's Constitution Today,* Bureau of Public Administration, University, Mississippi, 1960, pp. 95-109.
25. 305 F. 2d 353 (1962).

CHAPTER 4 | BLUEPRINT FOR RIOT

1. *Memphis Commercial Appeal,* June 8, 1962.
2. 305 F. 2d 21-343 (1962).
3. *Memphis Commercial Appeal,* July 18, 1962.
4. *Memphis Commercial Appeal,* July 28, 1962.
5. *Memphis Commercial Appeal,* August 5, 1962.
6. *Memphis Commercial Appeal,* August 7, 1962.
7. *Jackson Daily News,* September 2, 1962.
8. *The University of Mississippi and the Meredith Case,* University of Mississippi, November 15, 1962, pp. 17-23.
9. *Jackson Daily News,* September 14, 1962.
10. *New York Times,* September 14, 1962; *Bush v. Orleans Parish School Board,* 188 F. Supp. 916 (1960).
11. *Memphis Commercial Appeal,* September 14, 1962.
12. *Jackson State Times,* December 15, 1960.
13. *Memphis Commercial Appeal,* September 15, 1962.

14. *Memphis Commercial Appeal,* September 17, 1962.
15. *Jackson Daily News,* September 18, 1962.
16. *Memphis Commercial Appeal,* September 18, 1962.
17. Laws of the State of Mississippi Passed at the First Extraordinary Session of the Mississippi Legislature Held in the City of Jackson, 1962, pp. 17-18.
18. *Memphis Commercial Appeal,* September 19, 1962.
19. *Memphis Commercial Appeal,* September 19, 1962.
20. *The University of Mississippi and the Meredith Case,* pp. 5-6; *Memphis Commercial Appeal,* October 25, 1962.
21. *Memphis Commercial Appeal,* September 19, 1962.
22. *New York Times,* September 23, 1962.
23. *New York Times,* September 22, 1962.
24. Hearing on Order to Show Cause Why the Board of Governors and Certain University Officials Should Not Be Cited for Civil Contempt, Fifth Circuit Court of Appeals, September 24, 1962, p. 53. Hereinafter cited as Hearing of September 24, 1962.
25. Hearing of September 24, 1962, p. 56.
26. Hearing of September 24, 1962, p. 66.
27. Hearing of September 24, 1962, p. 83.
28. Hearing of September 24, 1962, p. 84.
29. Hearing of September 24, 1962, p. 88.
30. Hearing of September 24, 1962, p. 73.
31. Hearing of September 24, 1962, p. 75.
32. Hearing of September 24, 1962, pp. 77-78.
33. Hearing of September 24, 1962, p. 107.
34. Hearing of September 24, 1962, pp. 107-116.
35. *Memphis Commercial Appeal,* September 26, 1962.
36. *Memphis Commercial Appeal,* September 25, 1962.
37. *Mississippian,* September 25, 1962.
38. *Memphis Commercial Appeal,* September 26, 1962.
39. *Mississippian,* September 27, 1962.
40. *Memphis Commercial Appeal,* May 12, 1963; *Columbus Commercial Dispatch,* October 21, 1963.
41. *Memphis Commercial Appeal,* September 28, 1962.
42. *Meridian Star,* September 28, 1962.
43. *Meridian Star,* September 28, 1962.
44. Hearing on Motion for Civil Contempt Against Ross Barnett, Fifth Circuit Court of Appeals, September 28, 1962. Hereinafter referred to as Hearing of September 28, 1962.
45. *Memphis Commercial Appeal,* September 29, 1962.
46. Frank E. Smith, *Congressman from Mississippi,* New York, 1964, p. 305.

CHAPTER 5 | A NIGHT OF VIOLENCE

1. *Memphis Commercial Appeal,* October 2, 1962.
2. *Memphis Commercial Appeal,* December 16, 1962; *Look,* December 31, 1962, pp. 18-36. See also *Newsweek,* October 15, 1962, pp. 23-29, and *Time,* October 5, 1962, pp. 15-17, and October 12, 1962, pp. 19-22.
3. *Topeka Daily Capital,* October 1, 1962.
4. *Look,* December 31, 1962, p. 23.
5. *Time,* October 12, 1962, p. 20.

6. "Report on Mississippi," National Broadcasting Company, October 1, 1962. Based also on interviews with federal officials.
7. Based on interviews with federal officials.
8. *Memphis Commercial Appeal,* September 30, 1962.
9. *Vicksburg Evening Post,* September 29, 1962.
10. *Topeka Daily Capital,* October 1, 1962.
11. *Memphis Commercial Appeal,* October 12, 1962.
12. *Manchester Guardian Weekly,* October 4, 1962.
13. *The University of Mississippi and the Meredith Case,* p. 18.
14. Statement by Prof. W. Parks Grant.
15. Sermon of the Reverend Duncan M. Gray, Jr., rector, in St. Peter's Episcopal Church, Oxford, Mississippi, September 30, 1962. His emphasis.
16. NBC "Report on Mississippi," October 1, 1962.
17. U.S. Code, Title 28, Chapter 33.
18. *Look,* December 31, 1962, p. 24.
19. *Look,* December 31, 1962, p. 24.
20. Statement by Prof. and Mrs. Richard S. Stewart.
21. *Christian Science Monitor,* October 1, 1962.
22. *Charlottesville Daily Progress,* October 24, 1962.
23. *Rocky Mountain News* (Denver), October 9, 1962.
24. *The University of Mississippi and the Meredith Case,* p. 20.
25. Statement by Prof. Donald S. Vaughan.
26. Based on notes taken at trial.
27. Statement by Prof. William E. Strickland.
28. Statement by University staff member.
29. Statement by University staff member.
30. Statement by Prof. and Mrs. Richard S. Stewart.
31. Statement by University staff member.
32. *Memphis Commercial Appeal,* October 1, 1962.
33. *Look,* December 31, 1962, p. 29.
34. *Look,* December 31, 1962, p. 24.
35. *Saturday Evening Post,* November 10, 1962, p. 18.
36. *Greensboro Daily News,* October 7, 1962.
37. Statement by Prof. and Mrs. Richard S. Stewart.
38. Statement by University staff member.
39. Statement by Prof. William C. Herndon.
40. *Christian Science Monitor,* October 1, 1962.
41. *Emporia Gazette,* October 1, 1962, copyright 1962, King Features, Inc.
42. *Rocky Mountain News,* October 9, 1962.
43. *Greensboro Daily News,* October 7, 1962; *Chicago Tribune,* October 9, 1962; statements by University staff member, Prof. and Mrs. Richard S. Stewart, Prof. James W. Silver, Mrs. Eileen Joslin, and Prof. William E. Strickland.
44. Statement by Prof. and Mrs. Richard S. Stewart.
45. *Charlottesville Daily Progress,* October 24, 1962.
46. Statements by Prof. and Mrs. Richard S. Stewart and Mrs. Eileen Joslin.
47. Statement by Prof. James W. Silver.
48. *U.S. News & World Report,* October 15, 1962, p. 44.
49. Statement by University staff member.
50. Statements by Mrs. Eileen Joslin and Prof. and Mrs. Richard S. Stewart.
51. *U.S. News & World Report,* October 15, 1962, p. 44.

52. *Charlottesville Daily Progress,* October 24, 1962.
53. *Look,* December 31, 1962, p. 30.
54. *Time,* October 12, 1962, p. 20.
55. Statement by University staff member.
56. *Look,* December 31, 1962, pp. 32-36.
57. *Look,* December 31, 1962, p. 32; interview with Duncan M. Gray; Van Savell in *Topeka State Journal,* October 3, 1962.
58. *Look,* December 31, 1962, pp. 33-34; interview with Wofford K. Smith.
59. Notes of interviews with two students.
60. *San Diego Union,* October 7, 1962.
61. *Chicago Tribune,* October 9, 1962.
62. Interview with University staff member.
63. *National Guardsman,* November, 1962, pp. 4-9, 48.
64. Interview with University staff member.
65. Interview with Henry T. Gallagher.
66. *Emporia Gazette,* October 1, 1962.
67. *Memphis Commercial Appeal,* October 5, 1962.

CHAPTER 6 | INTEGRATION VERSUS DISINTEGRATION

1. *Memphis Commercial Appeal,* October 2, 1962.
2. *Operation Ole Miss,* Citizens' Council, Jackson, Mississippi.
3. Hearing on the Entry of Further Orders as to Civil Contempt, Fifth Circuit Court of Appeals, October 12, 1962. Hereinafter referred to as Hearing of October 12, 1962.
4. *Memphis Commercial Appeal,* October 2, 1962.
5. A Report by the General Legislative Investigating Committee to the Mississippi State Legislature Concerning the Occupation of the Campus of the University of Mississippi, September 30, 1962, by the Department of Justice of the United States (undated, released 1963), pp. 11-12. Hereinafter referred to as Legislative Committee Report. *Operation Ole Miss,* pp. 2-3. *Oxford: A Warning for Americans,* Mississippi State Junior Chamber of Commerce, Jackson, Mississippi, pp. 3-4. David Lawrence column of October 3, 1962, *Chicago Tribune,* reprinting University statement. Hereinafter referred to as University Statement.
6. Hearing of September 28, 1962, pp. 78, 82, 90, 93, 98.
7. Hearing of October 12, 1962, p. 112.
8. James W. Silver, *Mississippi: The Closed Society,* New York, 1964, pp. 134-140.
9. Karl Wiesenburg, "The Oxford Disaster: The Price of Defiance," *Pascagoula Chronicle,* 1962, pp. 3-6.
10. *Look,* December 31, 1962.
11. Legislative Committee Report, p. 22.
12. *Rocky Mountain News,* October 3, 1962.
13. *Meridian Star,* October 1, 1962.
14. University Statement. Legislative Committee Report, pp. 24-27. *Oxford: A Warning for Americans,* pp. 9-10. *Operation Ole Miss,* p. 3. County Grand Jury Report, *New York Times,* November 17, 1962.
15. *Rocky Mountain News,* October 2, 1962.
16. Legislative Committee Report, pp. 25-26.
17. Legislative Committee Report, p. 11.
18. Legislative Committee Report, pp. 25-26.

19. Legislative Committee Report, pp. 15-21. *Oxford: A Warning for Americans,* pp. 10-12. *Operation Ole Miss,* pp. 3-4.
20. Legislative Committee Report, pp. 32-33.
21. Legislative Committee Report, pp. 41-47.
22. *Memphis Press-Scimitar,* October 9, 1962.
23. *The University of Mississippi and the Meredith Case,* pp. 20-21.
24. *The University of Mississippi and the Meredith Case,* pp. 21-22.
25. *Memphis Press-Scimitar,* October 9, 1962.
26. *Memphis Commercial Appeal,* October 25, 1962.
27. *Rebel Underground,* Vol. 1, No. 1, October, 1962.
28. *Holmes County Herald* (Lexington), Vol. 4, No. 39.
29. *Memphis Commercial Appeal,* October 27, 1962.
30. *Mississippian,* October 31, 1962.

CHAPTER 7 | A DEGREE OF CHANGE

1. See Calvin Trillin, "An Education in Georgia," *The New Yorker,* July 13, 20, and 27, 1963. A major human factor lacking at Ole Miss was an equivalent of Georgia's Dean of Men, William Tate.
2. *Memphis Commercial Appeal,* November 10 and 11, 1962.
3. *Memphis Commercial Appeal,* November 15 and 16, 1962.
4. *Memphis Commercial Appeal,* November 22, 1962.
5. *Jackson Daily News,* November 27, 1962.
6. *Memphis Commercial Appeal,* November 16, 1962.
7. *Memphis Commercial Appeal,* December 1, 1962.
8. *Rebel Underground,* Vol. 1, No. 4, January, 1963.
9. *U.S. News & World Report,* January 21, 1963, p. 45.
10. *Rebel Underground,* Vol. 1, No. 5, February, 1963.
11. James W. Silver, *Mississippi: The Closed Society,* pp. 200-201.
12. *Jackson Daily News,* January 31, 1962.
13. *Memphis Commercial Appeal,* February 1, 1963.
14. *Jackson Clarion-Ledger,* February 1, 1963.
15. *Jackson Clarion-Ledger,* February 2, 1963.
16. *Rebel Underground,* Vol. 1, No. 5, February, 1963.
17. *Rebel Underground,* Vol. 3, No. 4, March, 1963.
18. *Rebel Underground,* Vol. 3, No. 4, March, 1963.
19. *Mississippian,* April 30, 1963.
20. *Look,* April 9, 1963, pp. 70-78.
21. *Mississippian,* April 9, 1962.
22. *Jackson Clarion-Ledger,* June 5, 1962.
23. *Memphis Commercial Appeal,* June 25, 1963.
24. Amendment of June 29 to May 16, 1963, petition of Board of Trustees.
25. *Jackson Clarion-Ledger,* March 4, 1963.
26. *Memphis Commercial Appeal,* July 6, 1963.
27. *Memphis Commercial Appeal,* June 25, August 13 and 16, 1963.
28. *Time,* October 4, 1963, p. 38.
29. *Jackson Clarion-Ledger,* September 26, 1963.
30. *Jackson Daily News,* September 25, 1963.
31. November 18, 1963, University of Illinois, Navy Pier, Chicago; *Congressional Record,* 1963, pp. A7489-7490.

CHAPTER 8 | BLUEPRINT FOR SUCCESS

1. *The Citizen,* December, 1963, p. 10.
2. *Memphis Commercial Appeal,* January 22, 1964.
3. *Memphis Commercial Appeal,* May 23, 1964.
4. Senate Bill No. 2043, 1964.
5. Senate Bill No. 2016, 1964.
6. *Jackson Clarion-Ledger,* June 9, 1964.
7. *Mississippian,* September 23, 1964.

INDEX

146, 148, 170, 175, 184, 202, 223-